Inventions on the Brink

Inventions on the Brink

ESSAYS

J. T. Barbarese

Louisiana State University Press
Baton Rouge

Published by Louisiana State University Press
lsupress.org

LSU Press Paperback Original

DESIGNER: Michelle A. Neustrom
TYPEFACE: Garamond Premier Pro

COVER ILLUSTRATION: Adobe Stock/derplan13/dmitryabaza

LIBRARY OF CONGRESS CATALOGING-IN-PUBLICATION DATA
Names: Barbarese, J. T., author
Title: Inventions on the brink : essays / J. T. Barbarese.
Description: Baton Rouge : Louisiana State University Press, 2025. | Includes bibliographical
    references and index.
Identifiers: LCCN 2025018659 (print) | LCCN 2025018660 (ebook) | ISBN 978-0-8071-8508-7
    (paperback) | ISBN 978-0-8071-8564-3 (epub) | ISBN 978-0-8071-8565-0 (pdf)
Subjects: LCSH: American poetry—History and criticism | Translating and interpreting—
    United States—History | LCGFT: Literary criticism | Essays
Classification: LCC PS305 .B37 2025 (print) | LCC PS305 (ebook) | DDC 811.009—dc23/
    eng/20250625
LC record available at https://lccn.loc.gov/2025018659
LC ebook record available at https://lccn.loc.gov/2025018660

for Cate,
who was always there

There is no critic like the memory.

—JOHN YEATS

Contents

Preface

Freelance journalists survive by their wits and through the magnanimity of editors of vision and goodwill. These essays were written over the course of three decades, on spec or assigned by editors who were generous with space and in every sense without an ideological axe to grind. One of the few advantages of working, as I did for more than decade, without a university affiliation—and there are few—is that what's published comes to you without a reputation, as it were, unwound of the mummy wrappings of classroom prejudices, academic reputations, or institutional public relations.

In retrospect, I was lucky. The generation of editors I worked with is passing quickly, and gone, will most likely be gone for good. Meanwhile, university-affiliated quarterlies and journals (along with college libraries) are being starved by cost-conscious administrations who look only at the bottom line and believe that the university's job is primarily to make a profit. Meanwhile mainstream publishers are owned by multinationals and the independents are barely self-sustaining. When respected journals themselves are not killed because they're viewed as budget drains, they may be forced to survive on whatever trickles down from the new corporate overlord, or from VPs of finance to provosts then to deans and finally to mostly helpless department chairs. This is the real information economy.

If money isn't the issue, it's politics. The editor with a single-minded vision is being replaced by cabals that, often with the best will in the world, are reshaping editorial policies to meet a narrower aesthetic, often born in writing programs and driven by social policy, an approach more befitting social workers than writers. The replacements have to be careful and may consult blacklists of the shunned (usually for ideological reasons) that are routinely circulated among the like-minded through social media, like notes passed in high school. So it is that the old rule holds: whenever we attempt to eliminate discrimination, the first thing to go is the ability to discriminate.

The interests I served were those my passion and curiosity guided me to, which will account for the more overt, impolitic, and largely circumstantial absence of women and the underrepresented. Most, such as the omission of essays on Dickinson and the seventeenth-century Spanish-American poet Sor Juana Inés de la Cruz, are the result of either deadlines or, in the latter case, my decision to include only essays on American poets and translators. Any others owe to my ignorance, the shaggy range of my interests, or the simple luck of what came my way as an essayist and reviewer. Several of these essays were written while teaching at a secondary school, where I learned more than I can say about how readers actually *read* a text, what they expect, and what questions they instinctively raise. I have gone light on the bibliographic apparatus in the interest of preserving the character of what is or should be, after all, informed gossip about the writers and the books we love. Wherever the reader hits a quoted passage not herein identified, I ask forgiveness for assuming that he or she, if really stuck, will do what we all do—Google it—though my sense is that there are few such quagmires. To be safe I include a healthy list of works cited at the end.

I owe a debt of thanks to several people who helped me put this book together. My deepest debt, though, is owed to the late George Core, who edited the *Sewanee Review* for decades and who died in October 2023. Sometime in the very early 1980s I sent George, on spec and on what whim I cannot now imagine, a review of Heinz Pagels's *The Cosmic Code:* among my dearest enthusiasms, which I imagined was shared by every literate soul on the planet, is well-written science writing. Within days George responded, firmly but not harshly, by reminding me that *Sewanee Review* was a *literary* magazine. I thought I had queered my chances for good. But weeks later I got a letter from him inviting me to review something different, and I did; I continued contributing briefs and essay-reviews off and on over the next two decades. George could be fussy: set your margins at an inch and a half (these were the days of typewriters); never use the word "authored" when you mean "wrote"; never used "penned." I could guess at George's politics; I knew they probably weren't mine but also that it didn't matter. At one point I told him, sheepishly, that I did not have a university affiliation but was teaching high school; I thought this might put him off. It did the exact opposite, probably because to George ideological credentials didn't matter as much as style and the ability to hit a deadline. Soon after, knowing something about the salaries of prep school teachers—his wife had a similar job—he began including ten- and twenty-dollar bills with his letters, pinned to which were handwritten notes: "Take your children for ice cream." It's hard to know how to repay or even acknowledge such generosity; it covers so much more than a writer expects. It's also impossible to regret enough his loss to the culture of the literary journal. He was an old-fashioned man of letters, tough-minded but never inflexible, and totally disinterested in your politics, preferences, or choice of pronoun. I miss him immensely.

Grateful acknowledgment is made to the editors of the following publications, in which the essays listed first appeared, sometimes under different titles or in different forms:

Boundary 2: "Translation Is/As Play" (vol. 37, no. 3 [Fall 2010]: 57–68) and "Owning Wallace Stevens" (vol. 42, no. 2 [May 2015]: 211–29)

Georgia Review: "Taking Poe Seriously" originally appeared in *Georgia Review* 58, no. 4 (Winter 2004): 802–15, © 2004 by The University of Georgia / © 2004 by J. T. Barbarese. Reprinted by permission of J. T. Barbarese and the *Georgia Review.*

Hopkins Review: "Prévert Now" (vol. 11, no. 4 [Fall 2018]: 514–25) and "Brinkmanship: Hart Crane" (vol. 12, no. 2 [Summer 2019]: 373–89)

Journal of Modern Literature: "Ammons: Theology for Atheists" (vol. 26, no. 3/4 [Summer 2003]: 73–83)

Sewanee Review: "Rousseau and Romanticism a Century Later" (vol. 101, no. 3 [Summer 1993]: 404–14), "The Contemporaneity of Homer's *Odyssey*" (vol. 107, no. 2 [Spring 1999]: 275–83), and "Four Translations of Dante's *Inferno*" (vol. 117, no. 4 [Fall 2009]: 647–55)

Threepenny Review: "The Poetry of John Prine" (no. 165 [Spring 2021]: 3–4)

"John Finlay's *Hermetic Light:* Religion and Poetry" appeared in *In Light Apart: The Achievement of John Finlay,* ed. David Middleton (Glenside, PA: Aldine Press, 1999).

"The Reckless Nostalgia of Gerald Stern" appeared in *Insane Devotion: On the Writing of Gerald Stern* (San Antonio, TX: Trinity University Press, 2016).

"Euripides's *The Children of Herakles:* A Preface" appeared as the introduction to *Children of Heracles, Euripides: 4,* in *The Complete Works of Euripides in Literary Translation,* Penn Greek Drama Series (Philadelphia: University of Pennsylvania Press, 1999).

"The Measure of the Eye: Pound and Imagism" appeared in *The Columbia History of American Poetry* (New York: Columbia University Press, 1993).

"Prévert Now" also appeared as the introduction to *After Prévert: Poems from Paroles* (Cheshire, MA: MadHat, 2022).

Taking Poe Seriously

Faire tous les matins ma priere à Dieu, reservoir de toute force
et de toute justice, à mon pere, à Mariette et à Poe, comme
intercesseurs . . .

—BAUDELAIRE, "Hygiene"

Many years ago I was teaching a survey of nineteenth-century American literature and spending considerable time on Poe's short fiction, especially "The Fall
of the House of Usher." One of my students noticed that we were avoiding Poe's
poetry—notably, "The Raven"—as aggressively as we were going at the prose. I
made some excuse about "coverage," or something, and in any case I sidestepped
the issue. In fact, I was lying; the problem was not coverage. It was me. Revis-
iting Poe's poetry means reading "The Raven," and to me reading "The Raven"
is and was like carrying out a painful family obligation. The same student later
took me aside and asked me if I ever noticed certain symmetries between "The
Raven" and "Bartleby the Scrivener." Symmetry is the right word—there's an
apparently innocuous bird who, like Bartleby, shows up and never leaves, an ir-
ritatingly self-conscious narrator whose self-possession is ultimately scarred by
the experience, and the confusingly ironic framings of both narrative hosts. Not
long after, in the midst of a reading of "Out of the Cradle Endlessly Rocking," I
caught myself about to launch as established fact my hunch that Whitman had
been influenced by "The Raven." "Demon or bird," the phrase that occurs past
midway, sounds, I said, like a phrase "right out of Poe."

"The Raven" was among the most anthologized American poems of the
nineteenth century. Nobody would be surprised to have found Melville or
Whitman reading it, perhaps enjoying it for its subliminal pleasures since the
story it tells is more impressive than its language, something that is true of much
of Poe. Plus, it remains and settles in your ear for the same reason that you can't
get the Armour Hot Dog jingle or "Twinkle, Twinkle" out of your head. Its

memorability owes partly to those "symmetries" but principally to the ear's easy seduction by rhyme and meter.

Still, that couldn't be the whole story. Literature is filled with hidden forces, friendly or unfriendly, that dispatch some natural agent to spy out and break through human reserve in order to remind us that Nature often does the work that humanity (or deity) can or won't do. When society refuses to recognize the Cinderellas in its midst, Nature steps in, and the result is a crisis of recognition. With "The Raven," the crisis surrounds what comes to stay and refuses to leave in part because, apparently, *it's always been there.* That the visitor is a bird has struck me at times as Poe's deliberate attempt to make fun of the hopelessly earnest narrator, who is not alone among Poe's often muddleheaded male protagonists in looking ridiculous while seeking obvious answers—take the narrator of "Usher," for instance. While Romantic art in America was essentially optimistic—none more so than that other great American hack, Alcott—and optimists don't usually write satire, Poe was unique among that group mainly because he was not only no optimist but was a victim of literary historical circumstance. He struggled with Romantic ideals and he had a sense of humor; he was far more a Classicist and historically a prisoner of his immediate moment; his opinion of what we now call Romanticism was probably closer to the skeptical Goethe's or the openly hostile Twain's. So his poem also sticks because it expresses something dark, a crisis in Poe's understanding of himself, and of his own influences. What was it that came and never left?

"The Raven," to begin at the point where it is least Romantic, reverses the nature-human polarity ordinarily found in Romantic poetry, and nearly always in Wordsworth. Wordsworth is too complex to render into philosophical generalities, but on the other hand, whether he believed them or not, he made claims for nature's restorative power that unsettled his contemporaries and still unsettle us. "One impulse from the vernal wood"

> Can teach you more of man
> Of moral evil and of good
> Than all the sages can,

riled Blake (whose "There Is No Natural Religion" is a response) and drove Shelley to write those subtly mocking lines in "Mont Blanc" about the wilderness and its

... mysterious tongue
Which teaches awful doubt, or faith so mild,
So solemn, so serene, that man may be,
But for such faith, with nature reconciled.

Nearly a century later the young Yeats was still complaining about poets who lacked what he called "the vision of evil," and specifically unruly Americans like Whitman who bought Wordsworth's optimistic claim that nature was both benign and maternal. It's unthinkable that Poe never struggled, and with stubborn humor, against Wordsworth's humorless influence—a great writer as barren of irony as a Church Father, especially when writing about himself. Because no matter how you read it, there is an element of absurdity in Poe's poem that is routinely (I almost said dogmatically) ignored. Was the raven *sent* by nature—was it on a mission—or did it just happen to wander on by, and into that study? If sent, the sender is never revealed. And it certainly does not seem benign or Wordsworthian—not a "guide and soul" of our moral being but menacing, persistent, repetitive, and aggressively unforgiving.

Playing against and at work behind the poem's darkness is its agitated, even jumpy versification and substrate of moralistic implications. Its truest thematic relative is frankly the fairy tale, though in fact it is nearly an anti–fairy tale, written against the idealism that produced that explosion of children's literature in the nineteenth century that begins in the eighteenth and culminates in the work of the Brothers Grimm, already available to English readers by 1820. This winged black herald leads no questing child to a secret garden—it is no helpful assistant—but instead is driving the narrator crazy. It is the stark opposite not only of the swallows that helped Cinderella sort the lentils but also of Coleridge's and Keats's more grown-up nightingales and Shelley's skylark. Its only motive is to violate the narrator's painful isolation and make it more so.

This too is somewhat odd, because isolation is usually a positive value in Romantic poetry. Rousseau titled his short meditative monograph *Les Rêveries du promeneur solitaire;* Wordsworth calls his "vacant" and "pensive" moods, when he can zone out and quietly recollect the day, enjoy the "bliss of solitude"; and it is also the subtitle of Shelley's *Alastor* is *The Spirit of Solitude.* Then there's the stunning conclusion to *Mont Blanc—*

And what were thou, and earth, and stars, and sea,
If to the human mind's imaginings
Silence and solitude were vacancy?

But Nature rewards Poe's poor narrator by turning isolation into a form of torture. Isolation becomes incarceration with a talking bird, but one that says only one word, the mechanically iterated, darkly trisyllabic, and somehow even more frankly ridiculous *Nevermore*. Worse, Nevermore turns out to be the Raven's *name*. The narrator seems doubly doomed. Not only is he stuck in his room with a talking bird that won't leave him alone, but he will forever represent a version of Poe himself, the American *poète maudit*, aggressively miserable, hopelessly self-absorbed, and responsible for a poem we often wish we had never heard.

Poe makes a subtle difference in, and greater contribution to, the way American literature carried on its conversation with British Romanticism; and hard as it is to admit, the specific contribution of "The Raven" is antagonistic and indispensable. Early in his career Poe sounded typically Romantic enough, writing poems filled with the usual Romantic props and stays. In "Sonnet—To Science," he complains that the spirit of analysis has driven the dryad from the wood and dispelled his dreams. The note in the *Norton Anthology of American Literature* will tell you that this early sonnet is "built on the Romantic commonplace that the scientific spirit destroys beauty, a notion well exemplified by Wordsworth's 'The Tables Turned'"; and on the surface both versions of the poem (it was revised in 1845) bear this out. But it seems directed less at "The Tables Turned" than against "The World Is Too Much with Us." It's an American sonnet arguing back at a British sonnet. Poe's first line makes the routine equation of analysis with plodding duration ("Science! meet daughter of old Time"), though he adds the interesting touch that the spirit of analysis is female. The first quatrain aligns Science with a vulture and poetry with Prometheus—again, nothing surprising.

But what is surprising is the poem's emotional violence. The spirit of analysis enters Arcadia and *drags* "Diana from her car," *drives* the dryads from the woods, and in the original 1829 version, *tears* the naiad from the fountain. Wordsworth's complaint in "The World Is Too Much with Us" is that we see little in nature that is ours, not because something is wrong with nature, and certainly not because we were in the process of poisoning the environment—

Wordsworth was no environmentalist—but because we can no longer imagine alternatives like those wild heathen gods rising out of the past, Proteus and Titan, which he smuggles into the sestet. Wordsworth's work is always about power, never "innocence," and is ultimately positive. Yet Poe's sonnet reverses Wordsworth. Poe emphasizes all the negatives—the loss of vision, the displaced faith, the surrender of Arcadia—that Wordsworth turns inside out. While Triton rises to blow his wreathed horn of prophecy, Poe is left trying to dream under a tamarind tree. From Wordsworth's point of view, poets like Poe, who have lost their ability to dream backward, are the problem.

Poe's pursuit of Wordsworth was as inconstant as his confidence in nature, whether human or "natural," and evidence for his hostility to "the scientific spirit" is hard to find. The author of *Eureka,* a late prose work on cosmology that includes reflections on Newton and Euclid, and of works on cryptology and on robotics and Babbage's analytic engine, Poe's view of science is closer in spirit to Shelley's and Emerson's and certainly friendlier than the cliché. What's more, his stance toward the version of Romantic idealism he found in Wordsworth and Coleridge was deeply ambivalent. His first dissent was from Wordsworth's twin exaltations, of Nature and childhood, optimistic abstractions that Poe, if the poems are evidence, found empty. Wordsworth claimed that "Heaven lies about us in our infancy," that childhood is a microparadise we occupy and surrender when the "glory and the dream" retreat and leave us anxious adults. The very physicality of nature—or Nature (since "nature" is ultimately a psychological work-product for Wordsworth)—stimulates a longing for a distant childhood. Conversely, the closer you are to childhood the nearer you are to natural selfhood, the "better self" that Lincoln will later associate with the "better angels of our nature." So, to close the distance between adult and child is to return to nature, but nature must be understood as the species' original psychological health. All those epithets Wordsworth lavished on the child in "Intimations of Immortality from Recollections of Early Childhood" seem silly unless you remind yourself that Wordsworthian children are, again, not innocent; they are *strong.* Wordsworthian childhood means strength, power and not fragility, because there is no "sin" in Wordsworth to stain some original "innocence." The attributes he heaps on Hartley Coleridge, who was the life-model for the child in the "Intimations" ode—the "Mighty Prophet! Seer Blest!" and "Eye among the blind"—point to still-existing adult potentials and not to the attributes of cherubs. Childhood is an intrinsic property of human consciousness that stabilizes and protects it from external corruption. At the head of the class of children is Wordsworth himself. I think this is why section 6 of the "Intimations Ode" begins with "Behold the child!" To *behold* is to hold an image, a living one, in the mind's eye. It is not merely to see. Coleridge's son, the human standing before him, is not the "real" child, because the real child we can only see with that "inward eye" of enlivening imagination. Imagination cannot lie.

This romanced vision of childhood is part of the larger and largely hidden debate within Romanticism (American or British) over the origins of evil and whether human beings are naturally good; and a good deal of that debate centers on the biblical Fall. Are we "naturally good," as Rousseau claimed, or "stained" (to echo the Baltimore Catechism) by original sin? That is why Poe's setting in "Sonnet—To Science" is interesting. Though certainly pastoral, it is not set in Eden but in Arcadia, two imaginative locations that couldn't be more different. There were no naiads and dryads in Eden, which was a scene of instruction where humanity failed its first test, a failure that to some we still struggle to overcome. But Arcadia was a physical, earthly paradise we just forget how to get back to. This is not and was not a trivial distinction. Eden stands for lingering metaphysical guilt and a disastrous, dystopian outcome; Arcadia stands for perfected physical pleasure, shepherds, swains, sheep, maids named for flowers. Eden represents the subjection of the human to a superhuman agency; Arcadia exalts the human subject, surrounds it with and measures it against the "naturally supernatural," and brings heaven down to earth. It is a child's world, fully animated, gods everywhere. When Joni Mitchell sang that "We've got to get back to the garden," she may have been talking about either place—in retrospect, she was endorsing neither—but my guess is that she had in mind not Eden, that police state garrisoned by thrones and dominions, but Arcadia, an earthly paradise we simply outgrew. Nostalgia for Arcadia lingers in Romantic topical metaphors like Kubla's Xanadu, and in later by-products like the aforementioned Oz, Barrie's Neverland, and Shangri-La. (In contrast, all versions of "New Eden" are almost uniformly dangerous, illusory utopias.) Arcadia, like Frank Baum's Oz, is a place that you can get to from here, if you know how. But its origins are pagan, whereas Eden is more guiltily ours. Romantic thought tends to get confused when it invokes the Garden, or, rather, tends to enter the preexistent confusion, and at some point most of the Romantics had a bad moment like Coleridge's when he confessed, in a 1796 letter to his brother, that he was finally over his crush on Rousseau and had "embraced John Locke and Original Sin": Arcadia, reeducated by Saint Paul and policed by Saint George, becomes Eden.

Poe sensed this dissonance between the two versions of paradise the West has had to deal with for some two millennia. His personal experience as child and adult dictated it; he probably feared the possibility that the alternative to a Paradise lost to guilt was an Arcadia recovered by solipsism and cultural amnesia and perfected over time through isolation. "The woods of Arcady are dead," wrote the early Yeats, who early or late was always a Blakean, "And over is its antique joy." His counterproposal was thenceforth to find consolation in his own subjectivity because "there is no truth / Saving in thine own heart." Yeats never altered his course or changed his mind: "all revelation," he claims in his *Autobiographies,* "is from the self." For Yeats, Stevens, Hart Crane, and figures closer to us like Ammons and Ashbery, the imagination has only one countermove against guilt, and that is to replace God's fictions with its own Fiction and join Stevens in saying, "God and the Imagination are one." A highly refined aesthetic solipsism is the end of the Road to Arcadia. So the pastoral setting that Poe lays out in "Sonnet—To Science" is admittedly a cliché, but so is most if not all of what any poet and particularly the lyric poet starts with. If on the one hand the conceit merely produced a passable sonnet, on the other it again raised the central philosophical question—can there be an earthly paradise?—that Romanticism was never fully able to satisfy. At deeper levels it is the staging area for a profoundly moral anxiety.

Poe never stopped obsessing over these competing visions of Eden, one with and the other without sin, because he recognized that Eden was ultimately all in the creative mind. Even assuming, moreover, that the "bliss of solitude" is the imagination's relaxation and openness to itself, there is always the chance that something might be horribly wrong with the imagination and that the condition of isolation might be dangerous, in fact lethal. He says in "Alone":

> From childhood's hour I have not been
> As others were—I have not seen
> As others saw—I could not bring
> My passions from a common spring—

From the same source I have not taken
My sorrow—I could not awaken
My heart to joy at the same tone—
And all I lov'd I lov'd alone—
Then—in my childhood—in the dawn*
Of a most stormy life—was drawn
From ev'ry depth of good and ill
The mystery which binds me still—
From the torrent, or the fountain—
From the red cliff of the mountain
From the sun that round me roll'd
In its autumn tint of gold
From the lightning in the sky
As it pass'd me flying by
From the thunder, and the storm—
And the cloud that took the form
(When the rest of Heaven was blue)
Of a demon in my view—

It is as if Poe took up the theme of childhood just to savage it. Wordsworth looks at a natural phenomenon—a rainbow in the sky, daffodils, the Alps—feels his imaginative strength return, and declares triumphally that the Child is the father of the Man. Poe's younger self copies the Wordsworthian stance and turns to look on nature, only to discover, as the italicized "*Then*" in line 9 signals, a disquieting "mystery," the one he alludes to in line 12 and that "binds" him still. A terrifying thought: the mind is not only its own place but *bound* to be its own place, held there forcibly and (the other sense of "bind") *destined* to be there. The jaggy typography, gapped and broken with dashes that seem to be trying to prevent conflict from breaking out among the crowding prepositions, is like an EEG, tracing the motions of a mind overwhelmed and not consoled by nature. Whenever I read this poem I think of that shower of prepositions that opens "Out of the Cradle Endlessly Rocking," the archetypal po-

* Some versions of this poem reproduce this line differently. Here, I've chosen the one reprinted by the Poetry Foundation, at https://www.poetryfoundation.org/poems/46477/alone-56d2265f2667d.

etic rite of passage for American poets. Prepositions are directional elements; Whitman feels life coming from everywhere, and his poem's first dozen or so lines begin with prepositions. Poe, on the other hand, seems literally overstimulated, too sensuously flooded to know where he will go. He can never name the "mystery," only its effects, because both the mystery and its products are his own fictions, and they do not please him. It is no wonder that another guilt-intoxicated genius, Baudelaire, found so much to praise in Poe that he became his first translator.

Though the poem is minor—its authorship was originally disputed—the point is not. When you read Wordsworth or Emerson you go to real places, places you can Google—Tintern Abbey or Concord Bridge. Blake writes about London, Shelley's work references the places he occupied (and usually had to flee to avoid his creditors) or that actually exist, like Mont Blanc, and Byron's work, the product of a man who couldn't stay still, is a versified tour guide. And then of course there's Thoreau and Melville and that homebody Hawthorne. But when it comes to the topical, Poe's work is utterly without a representational core. Give me the address of the House of Usher. Outside Chicago, in southern Virginia, or up the road from New Brunswick? From what tower hung those tintinnabulating bells—London's Big Ben or New York City's St. Paul's? Poe's writing lacks external geographical referents because it's all in his head; there is no geography outside his or any other human mind. So the mystery in a poem like "Alone" is not "in" anything (as the poem makes clear in lines 5 and 6) but the speaker's consciousness; he has (to borrow a Coleridge-ism) "filled all nature with himself" and now can't seem to tell what's what. This being the case, whether in Arcadia or Eden, a rapturous Wordsworthian communion with our earlier, original, "better" selves either never existed or cannot exist in imaginations disciplined by a different childhood and a different experience of nature to different imaginings. It's worth remembering that, even though both Poe and Wordsworth lost parents as children, Poe's childhood was disruptive and troubled and nothing like Wordsworth's.

Those "others" that Poe names, I think sarcastically, in lines 3 and 4, had more "settled" minds and lives, a fact that disturbs him to the point of real irritation. His tone in fact seems impatient. Beginning with "From childhood's hour I have not been," the poem keeps saying *no*—to *being, seeing, sympathizing* ("I could not *bring* / My passions from a common spring"), and *awakening*, all clichés associated with visionary power, especially the last two. Poe denies them importance, a denial that would have gladdened a critic like Howells, who twenty years later ridiculed Wordsworth and Thoreau for their "hysterical" wilderness enthusiasms. While Poe is writing from within Romantic idealism, and not like Howells as a conservative polemicist but rather as a friendly contributor, he registers his reservations, and in "Alone" he registers a major one. Imaginative isolation, Wordsworth to the contrary, may produce the opposite of thoughts that lie too deep for tears—i.e., anxiety too profound for analysis to reach. There *is* no nature outside the mind; and other than Shelley in "Mont Blanc," Poe seems the rare poet to have noticed or to have said it so openly. It took moral courage to confess this unfashionable terror, and his honesty discloses a major dissent from High Romantic confidence in the individual human agent and the "blisses" of solitude. Poe's dissent, to call it that, is based on his sense of his own disconnection from normative experience, life's banality, its dailyness. He feels no continuum or organic kinship, no "spousal" Wordsworthian connection between himself and either the natural or the human world, and unlike Wordsworth, this internal disruption is beyond nature's power to repair. I think that this is why both his fiction and poetry condemn every one of his catastrophically unlucky protagonists—the narrator of "Usher" or "The Raven," Prince Prospero in "Masque of the Red Death"—to suffer some version of this disconnection, which many of them call "madness." "Alone," which has come down to us as a fugitive item, is just another diagnostic.

So, too, is "The Sleeper," a long descriptive swoon that reminds you that Poe is not only the global representative of American Romanticism but, alas, the quintessential American hack. The poem is intensely overwrought, with a dead girl, a tomb, and lots of the typical fuzzy topography. The girl's name is Irene, etymologically from the Greek for *peace,* and the narrator prays "that she may lie / Forever with unopened eye, / While the dim-sheeted ghosts go by." I came across this poem years ago and dismissed it as the usual drivel gussied up in greeting card prosody. Then I looked again, more closely. The ghosts, I noticed, are not "in" the room but are the motions of the curtains and the shadows: "o'er the floor and down the wall, / Like ghosts the shadows rise and fall!" The infinite evasions of *as,* or of *like!* The speaker takes metaphor for reality and replaces the contents of the room (curtains, bedclothes) with the contents of his mind, what we'd now call mental projections. Poe, in on the joke, exposes both the speaker and the ghosts in the loaded phrase "dim-sheeted"—Irene, after all, sleeps the most peaceful sleep of all. Moreover, line 19 says that the "lady bright" would, as a child, throw rocks against the family mausoleum and pretend that the echoing sounds were groans, suggesting that, as Huck Finn says of poor Emmeline Grangerford, "with her disposition she was having a better time in the graveyard." Quite a sense of imagination, or of humor! Because the odd thing is that the speaker is doing exactly what Irene did, taking metaphor for reality, but with one difference: Irene was a child. One rarely thinks of Poe and verisimilitude in the same breath, but the distinguishing detail is psychologically acute, even realistic. In fact, it's reportorial, and launched into the merely pictorial context—Poe's usual interior overdecoration—it transforms run-of-the-mill supernatural terror into what Poe is known for, psychological horror. Like every protagonist in Poe, poem or story, the speaker is never *really* capable of seeing what's actually going on in the outside world:

Soft may the worms about her creep!
Far in the forest, dim and old,
For her may some tall vault unfold—
Some vault that oft hath flung its black
And winged panels fluttering back.
Some sepulcher, remote, alone,
Against whose portal she hath thrown,
In childhood, many an idle stone
Some tomb from out whose sounding door
She ne'er shall force an echo more,
Thrilling to think, poor child of sin!
It was the dead who groaned within.

Dim, indeed. The narrator as usual doesn't seem to *actually* get it. That the same child who threw the stones against the portal ends entombed there is either ghoulish or ironic; and that she is a girl-child was incontestably titillating to a century obsessed with images of and poems to dead children, often posed, eyes closed, in familiar positions. But that she might now be among the ghosts she once imagined moving behind the very sounds she herself made is simply creepy, even cruel. It is Hamlet's question. Do we live the consequences of our pretending and occupy those consequences in death? If the mind is its own place, is it a place that goes on forever—even if the mind is sick, or as Poe says elsewhere, "darkened"?

What has happened to Irene and the speaker happens often in Poe. A natural fact (tossed stones echoing against a vault) gets peeled away from its interpretive value (ghostly groans), and the next thing you know everything you thought you knew is wrong. In the "House of Usher," it produces serial collapses, ultimately of the house itself, as the dim-witted narrator misses all the signals, fails to understand the bearing of "The Haunted Palace" on the Ushers' immediate situation, and recites aloud, to calm Roderick, the "Mad Trist" of Sire Launcelot Canning while the house seems to disintegrate in response; in "The Raven," the disparity leads the narrator to collapse the bird's arrival into his own guilt over the lost Lenore. Loveliest of all, the detail of the thrown stones is a surprising touch of the everyday in all this phantasmagoria and points to what children do all the time: they play with what's available or what they find on the ground; they exaggerate, which is especially true of the Anne Shirleys and Mary Lennoxes of children's literature. But the phrase "poor child of sin!"—a phrase alien to any good Wordsworthian, for whom human nature was sinless and talk of "innocence" is irrelevant—alters the poem's register completely. Irene's exaggerations, if not sinful, were the products of sinful origins. The mind is not only its own place; worse, it's a fallen place. It's no wonder Milton gave that unforgettable line to Satan. There is innocence, but there are no innocents in Poe. The human child, and not the natural world, is not necessarily sinful but permanently defective, and—since nature itself is finally one more by-product of imagination—so is nature. It doesn't matter whether you call the flaw human nature or original sin, genetics or the Freudian death drive. If God and the imagination are "one," then clearly they don't always get along.

This is the argument of Poe's "The Lake," which moves through a series of reversals of Wordsworth:

> In youth's spring it was my lot
> To haunt of the wide world a spot
> The which I could not love the less—
> So lovely was the loneliness
> Of a wild lake, with black rock bound,

And the tall pines that towered around.
But when the night had thrown her pall
Upon that spot, as upon all,
And the wind would pass me by
In its still melody,
My infant spirit would awake
To the terror of the lone lake.
Yet that terror was not fright,
But a tremulous delight
And a feeling undefined
Springing from a darkened mind—
Death was in that poisonous wave,
And in its gulf a fitting grave
For him who thence could solace bring
To his lone imagining
Whose solitary soul could make
An Eden of that dim lake.

Poets remember other poets' pet usages, down to the very words—Whitman, as I suggested, remembered Poe's demon bird—and sometimes spend a lifetime working up to use them without getting caught. That "spot" in lines 2 and 8, given the context and theme, bears a powerful family resemblance to all those natural haunts, bowers, crèches, hermits' cells, and isolated micro-Edens that Wordsworth is "loathe to leave" and where "Nature hems you in with friendly arms," like "the spot" in *The Excursion* where, framed in one of Wordsworth's most inspired figures,

Haply, crowned with flowerets and green herbs,
The mountain infant to the sun comes forth,
Like human life from darkness.

"Consecrated be / The spots where such abide," says Wordsworth through one of his characters. For a joyful communion of the self and the physical world, head for such a "spot," which usually (and inevitably in Wordsworth) welcomes the return of the prodigal nature-worshiper back to his forest church.

In one of his letters Pound called Wordsworth a "dull sheep"—in *Homage to Sextus Propertius* he uses "Wordsworthian" as a synonym for what's dated and inept—but I think Pound, whose dislikes tended to overdetermine his judgments, was not just rash but deeply envious. Wordsworth may not have read Burke on the sublime, but he understood something about himself that since 1798 every poet, American or British, has tried to forget, and that's our utter, exhausting isolation even in the most beautiful natural setting. His egotism was so powerful that whatever he says about nature is nearly synonymous with whatever he says about himself. (Charles Altieri somewhere remarks that Wordsworth's landscape descriptions are extended descriptions of his own body.) His trickiest emotional proposition is that the mind is self-repairing. Moreover, the repair job always starts off as a return (in memory) to a childhood "spot of time." This has to be why Wordsworth is always tacitly asking himself the same question: why don't things *feel* the same way now as they did once upon a time? Success is measured by how much the present is in continuity with the past.

It's impossible, I think, to imagine Poe asking that question. Either he didn't want to remember or didn't want to return. By 1827, when he wrote "The Lake" (and Wordsworth was in his late fifties), the "lot / spot" rhyme was a poetic sign-countersign to the reader. Here comes another poem about a youthful convert to Nature and "natural piety." But Poe reverses the emphasis to show how different such a "return" might be. "But when the night had thrown her pall / Upon that spot," the infant spirit of the poet predictably "awakes," but not to power, vision, or natural consolations but rather to "the terror of that lake alone," and there discovers his own permanent littleness. The mind's disconnection from the natural world is a fearful knowledge; it is what Emerson near the end of his life finally conceded was the basis of human perception, the choice between the "I and the Abyss," the self and nothing. Poe had to have learned this lesson very young; probably it is behind his finding nothing consoling about childhood or isolation. The "lone lake" is inhuman, uninhabited, and unsettling. The boy who "haunts" it experiences the physical isolation felt in the presence of the Sublime, but *only* that isolation—pain with the pleasure deleted. The terror seems powerfully connected with the "tremulous delight" that, the poem says, "springs" fountain-like from a "darkened mind."

Coleridge once boasted in a letter how he was "habituated to the Vast" from the time of his childhood and elated by his experience of the infinite when he looked at the night sky. Poe's response was closer to Pascal's. The magnitude of what is not us, the Not-Me, alarmed him. Nor was he an Emersonian. Emerson said that nature was a mental projection—"mind precipitated"—but Emerson was not scared off by what he found there. The boy in Poe's poem is not prepared for such truth; instead, he plays a mirror game with the lake, the fluid reflection of mental terror, and his script is the Narcissus story. If my reading of it turns "The Lake" into a cautionary tale, so be it, because it's inescapable that the poem, like "Alone," ends on a note that carries substantial moral weight and contains some sound advice. Whosoever who would calm his "dark imaginings" by drowning them in a lake is asking for trouble—death by immersion in the image of one's (sick, darkened) fancies. I would call this Poe's Second Stipulation, a version of the law of unintended consequences: not only is what you find in nature what you put there, but whatever that is, it is probably a lot more or less, and a good deal scarier, than you intended.

Is it accidental that in the later, 1845 version of this poem Poe makes significant revisions? He adds some window dressing ("the mystic wind went by / Murmuring in melody"), inserts the melodramatic dash, and retires the adjective "infant" probably to salvage the meter. But he also and without warning redirects the poem to an unnamed beloved in the triplet that breaks out in line 15 ("A feeling not the jeweled mine / Could teach or bribe me to define— / Nor Love—although the Love were *thine*") and replaces the "darkened mind" with the obfuscating and hackneyed "jeweled mine." The later version fails maybe because Poe lost his nerve and forgot or ignored Stipulation Two. He backs away from the admission of the earlier version, that the splendor in the grass and the glory in the flower may not be apprehensions available to all of us—and certainly not to a child whose mind has been dimmed by intuitions beyond its understanding. He throws himself partly back on Wordsworth's consoling idea of a "spousal intimacy" that obtains between the mind and nature. He hedges and preempts himself by calling on love as a redemptive force. Yet like Hawthorne, that other Romantic internally at war with himself and his literary inheritance, the poetry reveals the central irony of American Romanticism: if our origin is initially a unity, our destiny is endless division. Our tragedy is how each of us is self-condemned to work out the consequences.

Which brings me back to "The Raven." I am still totally fed up with it, its tinniness, its particular appeal to Goth teens ("my favorite poem!"), to those who like it for the wrong reasons, especially to those who read nothing else or all of Poe into this one poem, and with those poor anthologists whose hands seem tied by tradition or by the mercenaries in marketing. I can never remember it without also remembering Roger Corman's parodic gem *The Raven* (1963), which opens with Vincent Price asking the visiting Raven, voiced by Peter Lorre, "Shall I ever see the rare and radiant Lenore again?" and with the irritated Raven/Lorre replying, "How the hell should I know?" The poem's metric alone always makes me laugh, as if Poe planned in advance to sabotage the narrator and his "dim" questions with this effective choice of thumping formal irony. Still, I'm impressed with how much the shorter lyrics, reorganized as a critical retrospective on Romanticism, seem nearly its preamble. Nothing really prepares you for its weaponized prosody, its unresolved tone, and especially its preposterous plot, which for all its accessibility seems hard to get at in what is, lest we forget, a narrative poem. A narrative poem, by the way, in which *nothing happens.* Even stationed beside something that has the same outrageous appeal to the middle-school mind, like "O Captain! My Captain!," "The Raven" is not a poem on which critical analysis feasts or, to change the metaphor, either the editor or the bibliographer can get much traction (check out the paucity of footnotes to any edition of the poem). Its bouncy prosody is consistently self-undermining, like the *Dies irae* set to the tune of *Seventy-Six Trombones.* And as usual, other than the fact that it's a "bleak December," we know nothing about the setting, which could be anything from a room in New York to a basement in the Usher mansion. The narrator's queer self-absorption seems at first absurdly exaggerated and preposterous, until you remember that this is from the creator of Roderick Usher, Fortunato, Prince Prospero, et al.

And yet, and yet . . . isn't this a restaging of the psychological calamities recounted in "Alone," "The Lake," and "The Sleeper"? A restaging that extends the borders of the poetic dialogue of self and soul and that assigns one of nature's deputies to represent that "outside" world and to remind the narrator that it might still exist? Isn't this narrator just one more overgrown and, to be honest, rather thick narcissist? They're all over Poe, from the insipid narrator of the Usher story, whose ineptitude would appear more comical than it does were Roderick himself not so self-involved and who may in fact be the partial cause of the very calamity he records, to the narcissist Prince Prospero and Minister D—, in "The Purloined Letter." Each confuses his image with the world's and graduates from dangerous narcissism to fatal solipsism. Or perhaps, in "The Raven," that is the point: he was *about* to graduate when the bird arrives as a corrective, exposing his anal-retentive need to know everything and further complicating his fussily organized so-called life.

And as in the lyrics, where we learn absolutely nothing about that lake, or that demonic firmament, or even that sepulcher, the natural agency that gives its name to the poem tells you nothing useful about itself, except possibly that the things that enter and do not leave may have been sent by someone or something outside human control. Perched on the "pallid" bust of Athena, goddess of wisdom, art, and what nowadays would be called homeland security, the raven represents an inversion of the ancient distinction between the higher and the lower natures, with man above and the beast below. If dispatched by Nature, it belongs more to Jack London or Darwin or that sick genius of the fairy tale, Hans Christian Andersen, than to Rousseau or the Lake Poets. But this is Poe, and in Poe, the narrator, like the cuckold, is always the last one to get the message, his lead characters usually baffled males whose self-absorption not only stops them from solving the puzzle (*Where did that raven come from?*) but actually and occasionally kills them in the end. He suspects the bird has been sent as punishment, but he claims to be innocent—Poe's answer to Job, trying to justify himself before not God but nature, lower case, in the form of a raven. Of Lenore, as with the Sleeper, we learn only the outcome (she died), but no details because the narrative is stingy, or the narrator himself doesn't know, and if he did know, he still wouldn't know what to do with them. And finally, teasingly, there is that backhanded fairy-tale opening, the "Once upon" gesture that replaces *time* with "midnight dreary," a substitution that deflects serious attention from an allusive source to the prosody as much as it reflects the autobiographical war Poe carried on all his life. A war not only with Wordsworth, the most impressive of poetic autobiographers writing in English, but with the Romantic tradition of self-discovery that teaches that the child is the father of the man— the tradition Poe felt obligated to disregard inasmuch as that tradition, learned from his own childhood, had long ago betrayed him.

—2004

The Record of
Leaves of Grass

The first poem I ever memorized, as a fourth-grader in a private school, was the worst poem Whitman ever wrote, "O Captain, My Captain." Three decades later, and teaching Whitman, I remember saying to a section of high school juniors who were enthusing over *The Dead Poets Society* that if I had been Robin Williams's department chair I would have fired him simply for having forced his class to memorize the thing. The only poem I know of from his maturity that actually rhymes, it is tedious to memorize and as a rah-rah allegorizing of Lincoln, as pompous now as it must have been then. It's mannered and imitative and, most important, it is anything but representative of what we and the rest of the world see as the *echt* Whitman.

This is so because Whitman was never a traditional "formalist" in any sense; "Creeds and schools in abeyance" meant that he would follow few rules, which makes it difficult to go looking for any. The roots of his practice are still conjectural, hidden from textual criticism and common readerly experience. One of the games critics used to play with Whitman's poetry was *find the architectonic*. Critical ingenuity has looked far and wide for an Ur-source, from the Bible, which he knew as well as any nineteenth-century sensibility raised by a devout Quaker mother, to the opera that was his favorite source of entertainment. Nobody can say how Whitman came to be Whitman or, in less fussy terms, exactly where his technical practice came from.

More than some 150 years after the publication of *Song of Myself,* it is still possible to wonder how this strange book came to be and over what it became in the thirty-seven years between its initial self-publication in 1855 and Whitman's death in 1892. Who ordered it, or ordered the poet Walt Whitman? Out of the middle of the American nineteenth century, one overrun by Americans writing poems in traditional meters and stanzaic patterns (mostly tetrameter quatrains)—one that includes the first generation of fully American writers, Longfellow, Poe, Emerson, Bryant, Thoreau, and the only other American poet of Whitman's stature, Emily Dickinson—out of the mid-century comes or erupts Whitman, age twenty-five, without precedent or introduction. The book is a formal anomaly—only twelve poems, one of them the outrageous *Song of Myself* with its eternally self-consultative speaker. The usual author's picture on the frontispiece lacks, with the exception of the requisite beard, all the decorative trappings associated with poets—no laurel-crowned gent in a suit but a guy in a simple work shirt and plainsman's or worker's hat, the right arm on the left hip, the other at his side, left hand in trouser pocket—and the poet himself is, intriguingly, nowhere identified anywhere on the page or in the book. He eyes the reader sassily, the picture like the poetry, a provocation. The book breaks all of the formal conventions that not even the Romantics, with all Wordsworth's talk of "the real language of men" and emotion recollected in tranquility, were able to ignore—conventions governing meter and rhyme especially, neither of which appears anywhere in the first editions of *Leaves*.

But I was like just about every American grade-school boy: poetry was anything that rhymed, as the Sisters of Notre Dame well knew. I missed the revolutionary character of his work until I was near sixteen and began toting the fat paperback of *Leaves* everywhere. Only then did I realize—a common recognition among his readers—how unprecedented and uncanny and seductive were his prosodic discoveries and habits. Nor was that the half of it. Partly because his verse resembled most of what I was also reading at the time—a scatter: Pound's *Cantos* with its long Sapphic lines, improvisations like Williams's "The Young Housewife," the French of Prévert and Apollinaire, Ginsberg and Corso—it was easy to overlook the bare fact that he predated his imitators not only for his discovery of free verse as a lyric vehicle but for licensing all future American poets to write frankly about everyday stuff and everyday encounters, stripped of mythological props and liberated from conventional themes and especially conventional stances.

I therefore instantly misread him. He was a lyric poet, and lyricists speak from their bare barren hearts. So I thought, naively, that he must actually have *seen* those twenty-nine bathers he writes about in section 11, had really been welcomed into those "big doors of the country barn" standing "open and ready" in section 9, had witnessed the marriage of the trapper and the Indian Maiden in section 10, and had really been to the Alamo as he claims in section 34. I had no idea then what a spectacular liar Walt Whitman would turn out to be, or that much of what he catalogues came as directly from his imagination as it was recovered from memory and that it had as little "reality" as Aeneas, Eleanor Rigby, Long Tall Sally, or Mariana of the Moated Grange.

My first encounter with *Leaves* left me believing wholeheartedly that this great sloppy "Father of free verse" for the twentieth century (as Pound called him) had, moreover, merely recorded all the things he had done and seen. His poetry to me was the honest and accurate record of things done, a poetry of deeds, or like John's Revelations, of things beheld by an astonished witness of peculiar genius. As the author of the first great American poetic autobiography, he must have actually *done* and seen everything he wrote about. It was autobiographical, right? I didn't drive until I was in my mid-twenties; I was a dedicated pedestrian who walked or took the bus. But mostly I walked. I often carried Whitman around with me, the paperback folded down the binding so it would fit my back pocket. The fold always fell open to section 34:

> Now I tell what I knew in Texas in my early youth,
> (I tell not the fall of Alamo,
> Not one escaped to tell the fall of Alamo,
> The hundred and fifty are dumb yet at Alamo,)
> 'Tis the tale of the murder in cold blood of four hundred and twelve
>   young men.

Eventually I put the dates together—the Alamo fell on 6 March 1836, when Whitman was around sixteen or seventeen—and realized that this was not autobiography but part of Whitman's self-mythologizing: he never claims he was *at* the Alamo but, as "poet of these states," that he was familiar enough with Texas to discuss it. Years later, I learned from Justin Kaplan's biography that Whitman *had* been to Texas, once, but probably had never visited the Alamo. So Walt was not only the Father of free verse and the inheritor of the Romantic tradition of poetic autobiography, but also the Father of Madison Avenue and, like Professor Marvel (aka the Wizard of Oz), one hell of a salesman, or to be less kind, a con artist. In a sense this should not exactly shock his readers, since our greatest novelists have produced protagonists who are con men of the first rank, from Melville to Baum to Dreiser to Fitzgerald. Whitman might have been their life-model, conning Emerson when he published Emerson's congratulatory letter as an advertisement (without consulting the American Plato in advance) for the first edition of *Leaves*. Most delicious of all, he reviewed his own books under assumed names in the pages of the very newspapers he wrote for and edited. His own books—what a guy! Editing a small literary magazine in the early 1970s, I happily followed his example (though not in the pages of my own mag).*

As I learned later, it's one thing to call a person a liar, but nothing at all to call a poet one. So a far more effective and honest way of representing Whitman's misrepresentations would be to note how everything in Whitman occupies not "life" space but print or textual space, with the caveat that in Whitman the text is always the same place—Whitman himself. It is always the same world, just as one's arms are always one's own even when half the length and hairless. The analogy is most apt as a description of *Leaves* because his poetry is always part of the same constantly evolving, growing, and maturing poem. To blame Whitman for his stretchers is to blame the continents for drifting. It is his nature. The historical "inaccuracies"—I'm being polite—are an order of magnitude greater than the one for which one narrow-minded British critic crucified Keats, who accidentally made the wrong Spaniard the discoverer of the Pacific. Keats's excuse was simple ignorance; Whitman's was craven ambition, or if that's too harsh, youthful resourcefulness. Whitman is the great poet of place not because he had been everywhere; his ambit seemed to include New York City, Camden, and Chestnut Street in Philadelphia. Otherwise he seems rarely to have left his house. He virtually never went anywhere beyond the precincts of his imagination.

Thus the whole idea of "place" in Whitman is to some extent bound up in his sense of the poem as *body,* even as embodied geography, whose serial changes are not mere supplements to but fulfillments of an original that continuously matures backward into what it always was. Place is both real and imagined, and space a constant obsession with this poet, who insisted he was not

---

* In what was probably one of his earliest media interviews, if not the earliest, a twentyish Bob Dylan told WYNC radio in 1961 that he was originally from Duluth (he wasn't), grew up in Gallup, New Mexico (he didn't), and had spent years traveling with carnivals (he hadn't).

"contain'd" (a favorite word, used four times in *Song,* along with *contribute* and *enclose* and *collect*) between his hat and boots. Take this, for instance, from the "Preface" to the original (1855) edition of *Leaves.* Saluting America for its magnanimity, he goes on to celebrate its spiritual vastness in more directly figurative terms. "The largeness of nature or the nation were monstrous without a corresponding largeness and generosity of the spirit of the citizen," he writes. "The American poets are to *enclose* old and new[,] for America is the race of races. Of them a bard is to be *commensurate* with a people." To *enclose* is to contain space; to be *commensurate,* a word that will figure so powerfully in Nick's closing descriptions of Gatsby's house, is to be of equal measure. What follows, a full page of names of places and of birds, is the quietly elaborated implication of words like *enclose* and *commensurate* until the terms of the argument become more and more spatial and ambitious:

> [The poet] incarnates [America's] geography and natural life and rivers and lakes. Mississippi with annual freshets and changing chutes, Missouri and Columbia and Ohio and Saint Lawrence with the falls and beautiful masculine Hudson, do not embouchure where they spend themselves more than they embouchure into him. The blue breadth over the inland sea of Virginia and Maryland and the sea off Massachusetts and Maine and over Manhattan bay and over Champlain and Erie and over Ontario and Huron and Michigan and Superior, and over the Texan and Mexican and Floridian and Cuban seas and over the seas off California and Oregon, is *not tallied* by the blue breadth of the waters below more than the breadth of above and below *is tallied* by him. (italics mine)

It's an interesting investment of imagination to believe that the most accurate *tally* of space is verbal. But on he goes: "When the long Atlantic coast stretches longer and the Pacific coast stretches longer he easily stretches with them north or south. He spans between them also from east to west and reflects what is between them." And suddenly the poet is transformed from instrument of measurement, stretching and spanning the continent, to the measured colossus itself—America:

> On him rise solid growths that offset the growths of pine and cedar and hemlock and liveoak and locust and chestnut and cypress and hickory and limetree

and cottonwood and tuliptree and cactus and wildvine and tamarind and persimmon . . . and tangles as tangled as any canebrake or swamp . . . and forests coated with transparent ice and icicles hanging from the boughs and crackling in the wind . . . and sides and peaks of mountains . . . and pasturage sweet and free as savannah or upland or prairie . . . with flights and songs and screams that answer those of the wildpigeon and highhold and orchardoriole and coot and surf-duck and redshouldered-hawk and fish-hawk and white-ibis and indianhen and cat-owl and water-pheasant and qua-bird and pied-sheldrake and blackbird and mockingbird and buzzard and condor and night-heron and eagle.

Even his punctuation—in the original "Preface" his preferred punctuation mark was the ellipsis—suggests that he is giving us a flyover (notice all the references to winged life, to American fowl, pigeon, oriole, coot, hawk, etc.). The central argument, his "thesis" as it were, is that "[the poet] incarnates [America's] geography," which is a wild enough idea on the face of it without adding the fact, for I think it is a fact, that this equation between physical and poetic size, the size of the poet and the size of his subject, is the central element of his truly manic, truly unique poetic faith. When he claims that he contained multitudes, he means it. For Whitman, nothing was "outside" Walt Whitman.

Readers get giggly and nervous before the opening lines of *Song of Myself* and snicker at the conceit that would prompt someone to "celebrate" himself. Lines like "the scent of these armpits' aroma, finer than prayer" are too much even for some poets (Philip Levine, for example). But the preposterous—and all significant poetry is preposterous—may still be beyond disproof; or, to paraphrase Augustine, a thousand doubts do not a truth disprove. Like the average politician, Whitman understood that America's size would go a long way to shaping its politics, the character of its population, and its future. The idea that occupiable space shapes character, later worked up into an historical thesis by Frederick Jackson Turner, whatever its validity worked wonders for Whitman's poetry and would for American literature writ large. The temporal element that dominates Wordsworth, for instance, is replaced by a preoccupation with space, with how American character fills it and is tested by and against it.

To be just, Whitman was not alone among major American writers of the time in drawing an equation between the size of the land and the individual's self-measure, between character and real estate. You see signals of it in Washington Irving, Thoreau, Fenimore Cooper, Emerson, and in Huck Finn's concluding resolve to "light out for the Territory" and refusal to be contained by mere social convention. The Louisiana Purchase of 1803, engineered by that "small-government" chief executive Jefferson, practically doubled the country's size; the outcome of the Mexican War added what would become six states and large chunks of another five to the American West; by 1850, five years after Texas became a state, the country's and slavery's westward expansion were physically complete. American writers—the one possible exception is Poe—have never been agoraphobes, but Whitman stands out as the least of such because his fearless belief was in the poet's ability, or need, to identify with the country's size, and because he takes the idea further than his contemporaries imagined. Yet there is very little essential difference between the claims he makes about space and spirit and, for instance, Turner's discredited speculations on the role of the frontier in the shaping of American character (a kind of biological determinism), or for that matter, what Charles Olson meant in the 1950s when he remarked that America can't be reduced to a kernel culture because "the mass of it is It." Whitman was merely among the first and the most influential geographical determinists to tell an American audience about the uniqueness of its situation, and add that he was the poet who had discovered it. Is this the conceit of the conceited, or the ecstatic cry of joy of the discoverer? Boast or *eureka*?

Reaction to similar passages from the "Preface" depends entirely on a willingness to accept this crucial aspect of his stance, and is far more than a mere "willing suspension of disbelief." Whitman is not only positioning himself as host of his self-narrative but the reader as well. The "Me Myself" announced in section 4 of *Song,* the speaking host of all of *Leaves,* may be taken as a mere conceit, but to Whitman it was no conceit—and certainly neither "mere" nor decorative—but an article of faith. It is no more useful to try to convince Whitman that he was not, as he says, "the man, I suffered, I was there," that he does not "contain multitudes," or that he is not all the speakers whose lives and voices he borrows and migrates into, than it would be to, say, convince Wordsworth that the child isn't the father of the man, or to persuade Dante that the events of the *Divine Comedy* never occurred. These are articles of poetic faith; there are plain, empirical facts, and then there are the greater truths of the imagination. A fact, as Keats said, isn't a truth until you love it.

Which is another reason Whitman remains revolutionary. We live in a cultural moment obsessed with the "truth" of events, with "reality" this and that, that punishes the autobiographical subject for departures from literal accuracy and for straying too far from confirmed or at least reported facts. This vulgar and essentially impossible belief in a reality, or "reality," that can happen unrehearsed, apart from the viewing subject, and then be televised and replayed makes "reality television" not only possible but inevitable, not because people are gullible but because Americans are especially aware of a deep truth about human identity: what we call the unitary "self" is a sleet of memories and feelings shaped by external forces. Its shape shifts, and is as instantaneous and unfixed as those whirling skeins of snow that dance over lawns and rooftops—instantaneous and illusory and ephemeral, in fact. The self is a multiplex of selves, many of which we know only in imagination. Whether life or literature, it doesn't matter. Bob Dylan and Lady Gaga sprang as full-blown from the imaginations of Robert Zimmerman and Stephani Germanotta as did Jay Gatsby from Jimmy Gatz or Holly Golightly from Lulamae Barnes. Fiction and fact have comfortably shared living space in American thought for two centuries (and why some insist on the fluidity of the body and gender and not of imagination and personality is a difficult question). Whitman was if not proving then reminding America of this (if it needed reminding). He had heard a more modest but no less alluring version from Wordsworth. Did either Lucy Gray or "Michael" ever actually exist? Did Wordsworth actually hear a solitary reaper singing away in a distant field? The difference is that Whitman was to include the manifold of real and potential selves and subjects into the hypermingled populations of *Song of Myself,* making it clear that the imagination's creations are at bottom autobiographical.

In his memoirs Yeats admits that as a teenager he used to carry around a copy of *Leaves of Grass* wherever he went. Later in his career he distanced himself from Whitman, claiming Whitman "lacked the vision of evil," or the vision of the world as a staging area of constant conflict; and Whitman himself seems to confirm this when he announces that "there is no evil" in "Starting from Paumanok." But as a young man, Whitman's example of poetic autobiography so impressed Yeats with the fluidity of its apparitions that, when he set out to write his own prose version, he called it *Autobiographies*. It is a quite literal application of Emerson's statement that we are a part of everything we meet—but radically redacted in order to expose the self as not a singularity but a chaotic totality. It says that we are not only *part of* everything we meet but that we *are* everything we meet, full stop. Like a living organism, a coral reef, the "Me Myself" grows, its contents scavenged from everywhere, on a daily basis, and like a fractal its shapes are self-reproducing. It is never possible to tell exactly from where the self actually springs or begins or where it ends. Whitman's phrase "Me Myself" is more than apt because it names an entity that is more ample than any physical self. The American imagination longs for that which is, to quote Nick Carraway, commensurate to our capacity for wonder, and for what it loves—in this case, a parcel of real estate spacious enough to contain the fullest expression of our deepest longings. Which makes sense, since the Declaration of Independence is unique in claiming that Americans possess, as a *human* right, the "pursuit of happiness." What an outrageous idea.

Whitman's imagination of space has everything to do with the compositional "design"—if you can call organic growth a design—behind *Leaves*. This seems odd to say about a book that went through nine editions, but its evolution was probably as preordained as anything in nature—i.e., not at all, or not as far as we can tell. The first edition contained twelve poems, among which was a significantly different version of *Song of Myself*. The punctuation is irregular; ellipses substitute routinely for commas or periods. At key points the text is strikingly different from the versions we see anthologized nowadays. The version we now read, for instance, contains in the present section 3 a reference to a "hugging and loving bed-fellow" who "sleeps at my side":

> I am satisfied—I see, dance, laugh, sing;
> As the hugging and loving bed-fellow sleeps at my side through the night, and
>   withdraws at the peep of the day with stealthy tread,
> Leaving me baskets cover'd with white towels swelling the house with their
>   plenty, . . .

But the original, published a year earlier, unsectioned and titled "I Celebrate Myself," is different:

I am satisfied ... I see, dance, laugh, sing:

As God comes a loving bedfellow and sleeps at my side all night and close on
  the peep of day,

And leaves for me baskets covered with white towels bulging the house with
  their plenty, ...

The addition of the appositive "as God" in the 1855 version thoroughly transforms the moment. It also introduces a note of provocative ambiguity: is it
God arriving like a bedfellow or this bedfellow arriving like God? I don't know
whether the word *basket* already encoded male genitalia by the end of the nineteenth century; it certainly did by the beginning of the twentieth. But as the
poem proceeded through successive (a total of nine) editions, and as the book's
popularity and his reputation grew, Whitman further cleaned it up and revised it.

Whitman's extraordinary poetic belief that the poet was a world unto himself was the necessary fiction that is and remains at the center of his work. To
him, word is to world what the point is to the plane. "Speech is the twin of my
vision," he says in section 25 of *Song*, a spectacularly savvy translation of *fiat lux*
into plainspoken American. There will be no drawing distinctions between the
words this poet uses to describe the world and that world itself. Nowadays, this
willingness to transcend differences that were construed in his own century
as biological—differences of race, ethnicity, class, and gender—has become a
prerequisite. A glance at a list of typical conference topics, for instance, reveals
titles representative of the range of contemporary concerns that the American
academy sees prophesied in his work: "Whitman's 'Libidinous Prongs': Visions
of Self and Nation in the Erotic Landscape"; or, "Averting Penetration: Gyne-
cology and Domestic Space in Section 11 of 'Song of Myself.'" Yet Whitman's
view of the poet as the embodiment of the physicality of his speech, of speech
as a crucial mapping of references and fleshly measures, is too radical for normative academic discourse to study without sounding absurd, and is his most extraordinary "discovery," the assumption that guides all his other transgressions.
Indeed, how can one be said to be a transgressor when in fact one is the both
transgressor and transgressed? How can you stay in your lane when you own
and in fact built the highway, the "landscape" itself?

Whitman does not and did not come to this discovery independently. As
usual, Wordsworth got there first in what Charles Altieri has called the "Words-

worthian scenic model for the formation of selves." The most outrageous example is from the "Intimations Ode":

> Our birth is but a sleep and a forgetting:
> The Soul that rises with us, our life's Star,
>   Hath had elsewhere its setting,
>   And cometh from afar:
>   Not in entire forgetfulness,
>   And not in utter nakedness,
> But trailing clouds of glory do we come
>   From God, who is our home:
> Heaven lies about us in our infancy!
> Shades of the prison-house begin to close
>   Upon the growing Boy,
> But He beholds the light, and whence it flows,
>   He sees it in his joy;
> The Youth, who daily farther from the east
>   Must travel, still is Nature's Priest,
>   And by the vision splendid
>   Is on his way attended;
> At length the Man perceives it die away,
> And fade into the light of common day.

Human beings it seems cannot obsess about space without obsessing about
time. Probably this is one reason Wordsworth's epigraph for the "Great Ode"
was his own short poem "My Heart Leaps Up," whose third to fifth lines, by
successive verb tenses—"So is it . . . So was it . . . So be it"—surround the present with the past and the future in three compact trimeter lines and present
you with a spatio-temporal précis of human growth. Wordsworth's grandest
fiction, his own anxious reaction to his obsession with time, was that our lives'
motions in and through time were like the motions of small boats in lakes and
rivers. Occasionally we are stilled, caught in an eddy or "spots of time," a kind
of time-travel where we seem both in motion and motionless. This meant two
things for Wordsworth: first, life itself is essentially tragic unless redeemed by
recollections of childhood. "Heaven lies about us in our infancy" is a grander

way of saying what most of his poems asked: *why don't things feel the same?* He essentially invents Childhood for the late eighteenth century—the century that also created children's literature—as the period of our lives that anchors us to a primal sense of well-being and happiness, to childhood as "a pure point of origin," in Jacqueline Rose's words, one that will continue to make us happy, or rescue us from inevitable sadness, so long as we can remember it. The second important factor is remembering or, to use Wordsworth's term, "recollection," which is the very means by which we get back there:

> For when oft upon my couch I lie
> In vacant or in pensive mood
> They flash upon the inner eye
> Which is the bliss of solitude
> And then my heart with pleasure fills
> And dances with the daffodils.

The life of the daffodils—or of any isolated element of our physical experience—is recuperable only through some commensurate, reigniting imaginative experience. Memory regathers the daffodils; imagination makes them dance.

Whitman's response to Wordsworth was complex, but it stands out among his contemporaries as the most aggressive, and after Poe and Dickinson, the one least cowed or shaped by reputation and influence. (Dickinson behaves as though she never read him.) Whitman seems the only American of his generation to have confronted Wordsworth without having become either overawed or aggrieved by his power and reputation, which is how or why he taught American poetry how to construct an American poetic autobiography in a plainspoken American that comes far closer to sounding like the "real language of men" than anything in Wordsworth. He gave it its directions, its bearings, its terms of reference, and licensed its general formal waywardness—now lyrical, now dramatic, now a simple narrative—and often over-the-top diction. When he says, for instance, "I celebrate myself and sing myself / And what I assume you too shall assume," he isn't kidding; it is his imaginative translation of the preposterous idea that all men are created equal. The poet's selfhood—what he calls the "Me Myself"—is a continuum that includes all other continua, beginning with you and me. What he believes is what his reader would and *must* believe

because, inhabiting all poetic space-time, Whitman is not temporally bound
as personality always is in Wordsworth, and as such is therefore in some sense
immortal. Maybe this is why he says in *Song of Myself* that "Death leads life forward." What is "down" when there is no "up"?

To paraphrase Confucius, no matter where we go, there Whitman is, "under
your bootsoles." He is not only the poet who waits in the distance, up there
"somewhere waiting to catch you," but both "inside and out," the gambler "going in for [his] chances, spending on vast returns." His occupancy moreover
includes not only all of us but all creaturely existence, right down to "beetles
rolling balls of dung" in section 24 of *Song,* and most outrageously, the sun
itself ("Dazzling and tremendous how quick the sun-rise would kill me, / If I
could not now and always send sun-rise out of me"). And how many times did
I have to read that short poem that he wrote near the end of the Civil War, "A
Noiseless Patient Spider," before I realized the odd and maybe accidental but
powerful syntactical elision between the spider of line 1 and the speaking self of
line 2? The title of the poem and line 1 are the same:

> A noiseless patient spider,
> I mark'd where on a little promontory it stood isolated,
> Mark'd how to explore the vacant vast surrounding,
> It launch'd forth filament, filament, filament, out of itself.
> Ever unreeling them, ever tirelessly speeding them.
> And you O my soul where you stand,
> Surrounded, detached, in measureless oceans of space,
> Ceaselessly musing, venturing, throwing, seeking the spheres to connect
>   them,
> Till the bridge you will need be form'd, till the ductile anchor hold,
> Till the gossamer thread you fling catch somewhere, O my soul.

Line 1 is an appositional phrase: the "noiseless patient spider" is therefore logically (or grammatically) connected to the lyric host, the "I" of line 2, who
speaks. What appears to be a typical "nature poem" about how spiders maintain
their webs is anything but. Not only is Whitman's emblem the spider; in some
sense, he *is* the spider. The poem, if you watch how its logic develops, makes the
obvious comparison of the filaments the spider spins (literally from its gut) to

the only thing comparable in poets, lines of poetry. Whitman, no punster, no explainer, and without much use for irony, avoided making the point overtly by way of a hackneyed wordplay on *lines,* yet it's there all the same. What spiders are to their webs, poets are to their poems; for the poet, the world and the work function as conceptual equals. A spider's creation is a work of organic reproduction, the belly-spun threads holding the spider's world in place; for Whitman, as it was for the poet of Genesis, creation is a speech act. What the filaments are to the spider, a poet's lines are to the word-nets that contain his world. (The word *text,* though it's impossible to know if he knew this, comes from the Latin word *textus,* among whose meanings is spider's web.)

Moreover, and depending on one's view of things (a child's, say), it may not be that tree over there on the right and the pillar holding up the roof on the left and the length of clothesline between the two that is holding up the spider's web. It may be the other way around. Indeed, from a spider or a poet's point of reference, it's the web that connects the world and allows it to communicate with its parts. The world is only there because it is, in a sense, in the way, there to be served, encompassed, enclosed, contained in words commensurate with the body that speaks them. The great irony in calling Whitman "America's world poet" is that the world he celebrates and the nature he worships is his own, as that nature constantly counts off the distance between itself and whatever else there is.

—2004

Rousseau and Romanticism
a Century Later

The conservative reaction against free versification back in the 1980s, which produced the New Formalism, also breathed life into the ghost of Irving Babbitt and *Rousseau and Romanticism,* which turned one hundred in 2019. As a critic, Babbitt has long been out of favor, and though his book was directed almost entirely against the English Romantics of both first and second generations, for Americans the salient fact is that Babbitt was an American critic and educator who was to some unknown extent partly responsible for the outlook of his most famous American pupil, T. S. Eliot. Babbitt's book was published the same year that Eliot's "Tradition and the Individual Talent" appeared in *The Egotist,* and his influence on Eliot's essay (and its reflection in the thinking of Eliot's friend Ezra Pound) was powerful, especially when it came to their conjoint dismissals of Anglo-American Romanticism. Babbitt's role in the education of Modernism's primary polemicists and their attacks against the Romantics usually escapes examination.

Babbitt's thesis was simple: Romanticism, fashioned from an overwrought sentimentality with no ethical basis and out of hyperbolic claims for individuality, imagination, and Nature, was essentially the fault of people like Rousseau, but of Rousseau especially, who renounced original sin and conventional morality and exalted what Babbitt confusingly calls "naturalism." ("Natureism" would have made more sense.) Babbitt's "naturalist" is not a biological determinist like Dreiser; in fact, his prime exemplars are British Romantics. His use of naturalism reminds you how the nineteenth century routinely called Wordsworth et al. "nature poets," and that Lowell, in 1865, either joined in or set off the reaction against Romanticism by condemning the "modern sentimentalism about Nature" as "a mark of disease" and pointed specifically to Rousseau as "the modern founder of the sect." The Romantic whom both Lowell and Babbitt (and to a lesser extent, Twain) disapprove is anyone who celebrates what is most primitive, instinctive, irrational, and fantastic in human behavior. The presence of these "naturalists" was transhistorical and actually not unwelcome until Rousseau attempted, in Babbitt's words, "to set up primitivism as a philosophy and even a religion," undermining the "ethical centres" that for ages had kept naturalism in check. The so-called movement's liberating energy was a conviction that a complete ethical program might be devised around its belief that human nature was the center and source of social and civil virtue—the pure secularist position of 1762's *Du contract social*—thus inverting a millennial-old understanding of political order, not to mention of human nature itself. Babbitt's pietism is on full display as he goes on to accuse Rousseau's followers and essentially the entire Enlightenment of finding in the natural order supernatural forces and of facing nature with an attitude of what Wordsworth called "natural piety," or what Blake condemned as "natural religion." In other words, words other than Babbitt's, of replacing God with Nature.

Babbitt does supply much detail in a testy summation of Romanticism's rise out of seventeenth-century Enlightenment science, which, he argues, turned nature into an object and abstracted the human figure from the landscape so completely that the former effectively replaced the latter. Gradually, the dominos fell. External authority (religion, morality, monarchy) was undermined; responsibility became the project of the solitary sentient individual. Babbitt names Neoclassical theorists like the benign Edward Young as "spirited" but "unsound," accidental pioneers who along the way so totally mistook physical shape for shaping spirit that the imitation collapsed into the copy. People became too completely "human"—overfocused on their own subjectivity—abandoning to science the belief in their "superrational" part or, joining intellectual outlaws like Shelley, emptying Christianity of its preceptive core and substituting aesthetics for ethics. Babbitt reserves the most anger for Rousseau, who redefined society as a contractual rather than a consensual entity. In a sense, he dislikes Rousseau because Rousseau was not Locke. "I am not trying to give rounded estimates of individuals," Babbitt admits, "but to trace main currents as a part of my search for a set of principles." All well and good. Whether his idea rises or falls thus depends on whether the current he identifies solely with Rousseau is actually mainstream.

But it's not, and the book itself rises in incoherence as it grows in rhetorical passion and size (more than four hundred pages in this edition). It is less an elaborated thesis than a network of constantly regenerating antitheses, a compare-contrast essay blown up to book length. The initial, rudimentary historical distinction between Romanticism and Classicism seems to set off a chain reaction of dichotomies that spread through the text: "intensity" contests with "decorum," Romantic "wonder" with Classical "awe," "unity of insight" with "unity of instinct," supernaturalism with naturalism, "hard" with "soft" sentimentalism, and even imagination as either "centrifugal or centripetal," "concentric or eccentric."

I'm sure I missed some. In any events, what results is an epic war between paired contraries doing battle for the soul of the West over the topography named in the chapter titles ("Genius," "Imagination," "Morality," "Irony," "Nature"). The problem is not that the fight is fixed, with (in contemporary terms) the reactionary conservative against the radical liberal. That you might, alas, expect. But you also hope it'll be done with greater art, or at least tact. Yet each contest is resolved by a rhetorical flourish or a paragraph of smug and often flat-footed prose. About halfway through, and with the best will in the world, having got a sense of the book's prose rhythms, I would pause and say to myself, "now watch what happens," and sure enough, it would. Very soon, the style itself seems contaminated by his accountant's instincts, and Babbitt is floating his judgments on that junk bond of flimsy theories, the overbalanced conditional clause ("If [Samuel] Johnson is wise without being poetical, Keats is poetical without being wise"). It's the sort of thing you expect in a classroom dominated by an experienced bloviator. The intensity of his dialectic is unqualified yet protected by his reputation, his institutional affiliation, and his ability to shift focus and escape from any possible objections by deriving another set of antitheses, each of which gets internal support from his maddening habit of turning every complex sentence into a parallelism. In the end, you sense that you're being conned.

Even the most conservative reader will find some of this both overwrought and occasionally vacuous. In Rousseau's writing and personality Babbitt notes "the absence . . . of the note of masculinity" and explains the omission as part of Rousseau's "general readiness to subordinate his ethical self to his sensibility." In other words, the fact that Rousseau was probably some sort of "girly man" means that women are "generally ready" to subordinate ethics to aesthetics—right? That the only truly ethical soul is the completely "masculine" one? Is *nostalgia* an apt cognate for what he seems to be describing as Romantic *longing*, which is, in his own terms, not the Odyssean heroic desire to recover his home, but like Rousseau, Shelley, et al., a license to abandon your wife, get lost in the wilderness, and leave your kids and the utility bills behind? Rousseau was no model parent, but is Babbitt seriously implying that Kant's account of aesthetic freedom is a prescription for Rousseau's abandonment of his five children—a bogus insight worthy of, say, Paul Johnson? Some claims seem to come from the depths of an armchair: for instance, that the unanticipated consequence of Romanticism was "to discredit moral effort on the part of the individual," as if there were no Romantics who quietly dissented from its collectivist urgings or, like Poe or Mary Shelley, who dissented from within. His tendency to implicate by association is so shrilly partisan that at times it amounts to a kind of bullying. "The Rousseauist always betrays himself by arraigning in some form or another[,] 'the false secondary power by which we multiply distinctions,'" he writes, thus placing by way of quotation a real but unattributed splice from Coleridge's *Biographia Literaria*—the passage where Coleridge, not (it's true) all that clearly, distinguishes between Secondary Imagination and Fancy, a passage which means something radically different in context.* Babbitt reminds me of a visiting poet who once interrupted his host's house tour by pointing to his bookcase and then smirking, "Let me examine the contents of your soul." Gotcha! For Babbitt, a reading list is an index of moral personality, a revelation of party affiliation.

Babbitt's soliloquies are irritating, but his scholarship is unnerving given the reputation of his home institution (Harvard). Favored phrasings are repeatedly incanted in vaguely Spooneristic fashion that's supposed to sound clever

---

* "The Imagination then I consider either as primary, or secondary. The primary Imagination I hold to be the living Power and prime Agent of all human Perception, and as a repetition in the finite mind of the eternal act of creation in the infinite I am. The secondary [Imagination] I consider as an echo of the former, co-existing with the conscious will, yet still as identical with the primary in the *kind* of its agency, and differing only in *degree*, and in the *mode* of its operation.... Fancy, on the contrary, has no other counters to play with, but fixities and definites. The Fancy is indeed no other than a mode of Memory emancipated from the order of time and space; and blended with, and modified by that empirical phenomenon of the will, which we express by the word choice" (*Biographia Literaria*, vol. 1, chap. 13, Coleridge's italics).

("the Enlightenment confused noble language with the language of the nobility" comes up at least three times); even more infuriating is the way ideas are
piggybacked on quotations shorn of context, citation, or attribution—an annoying habit that Eliot quickly would turn into a stylistic signature. "The lack
of inner form in so much modern drama and art in general," he claims, citing
no examples, derives from the Rousseauist's "undisciplined" sensuousness. The
Rousseauist "to his aesthetic perceptiveness failed . . . to add ethical perceptiveness because of his inability to distinguish between ethical perceptiveness and
mere didacticism, and so when asked to put ethical purpose into art he replied
that art should be pursued for its own sake (*l'art pour l'art*) and that 'beauty is
its own excuse for being.'" Poor Emerson! After metonymic reduction to the
best line from his "The Rhodora," which Babbitt decontextualizes, misreads,
and never identifies, the Concord Philosopher, an ordained minister, is transformed into the anonymous spokesperson for Beardsley and *The Yellow Book,*
with whom he shares a cell in Hell with Wilde and Swinburne. Here's another:

> In its extreme manifestations romantic morality is indeed only one aspect,
> and surely the most singular aspect, of the romantic cult of intoxication. No
> student of romanticism can fail to be struck by its pursuit of delirium, vertigo
> and intoxication for their own sake. It is important to see how all these things
> are closely related . . . to the attempt to put life on an emotional basis. To rest
> conscience, for example, on emotion is to rest it on what is always changing,
> not only from man to man but from moment to moment in the same man. "If,"
> as Shelley says, "nought is, but that it feels itself to be," it will feel itself to be very
> different things at different times. No part of man is exempt from the region of
> flux and change. There is, as James himself points out, a kinship between such
> a philosophy of pure motion and vertigo. Faust . . .

. . . and on he goes. The line from Shelley is lifted from *Hellas,* an early lyrical
drama. It is part of a longer passage spoken by Ahasuerus, the Wandering Jew,
and it obviously has a different impact and meaning in context:

> . . . this Whole
> Of suns, and worlds, and men, and beasts, and flowers,
> With all the silent or tempestuous workings

By which they have been, are, or cease to be,
Is but a vision;—all that it inherits
Are motes of a sick eye, bubbles and dreams;
Thought is its cradle and its grave, nor less
The Future and the Past are idle shadows
Of thought's eternal flight—they have no being:
Nought is but that which feels itself to be.

The absurdity of crediting Shelley with something said by one of his characters—a *character* in a *verse play,* no less—is or ought to be obvious; and the idea that the line, out of context, is perfectly clear is laughable since Ahasuerus's speech even confuses the character who hears it, Mahmoud. To then leap to imply that William James would agree with Shelley (or Ahasuerus?) is the sort of malfeasance barely forgivable even in the most naïve reader or bubbleheaded undergraduate. This is not argumentation but hocus-pocus; one gets the feeling that this was Babbit's lecture style.

But the man's not done:

> "Whirl is King," cried Aristophanes, "having driven out Zeus." The modern sophist is even more a votary of the god Whirl than the Greek, for he has added to the mobility of an intellect that has no support in either tradition or insight the mobility of feeling. Many Rousseauists were, like Hazlitt, attracted to the French Revolution by its "grand whirling movements."

This is simply silly, the sort of shrill pedantry and pedantic inaccuracy ("like Hazlitt") that gives teaching a bad name. The whack at the French Revolution as he slides out the back door is the sort of tiresome genuflection of the committed Francophobe to Arnold, if not to Burke, and the reference to those "many" unidentified "Rousseauists" reminds me of what Blake had to say about generalizations ("To Generalize is to be an Idiot"). And as the reference slips shamelessly by in the Aristophanic backwash, Babbitt gets away without revealing to the (expectant? confused?) reader that Aristophanes's "cry" is from *Clouds* (lines 381, 827), the comedy that lumped Socrates with Athenian Sophists, from whom Socrates spent his career trying to distance himself, and the play that may even have helped arm his detractors (a group which now includes by proxy Babbitt himself) with the charge of impiety that led to his imprisonment and death. Yet seventy pages later Babbitt is hymning Socrates ("no mere rationalist," "a man of insight"), so either he is trusting that the reader will either understand all his spaghetti-on-the-wall references, untangle the ironies and share in the laugh, or be so awed by the smoke and mirrors we'll pay no attention to the man behind the curtain. Granted, it's probably pedantry on my part to point out such backfires, but it was pure malfeasance to commit them in the first place. As teachers often say to miscreant students, you should have known better.

I did not so much finish as escape this book, feeling a bit like Teufelsdrockh's editor, "mingling feelings of astonishment, gratitude, and disapproval." To appropriate a Babbettian syntactical chord-shape, if his scholarly apparatus was unsound and irritating, his range of reading was extraordinarily wide (if not deep) and generous (if not humane). Only a crank would be so mean-spirited as to toss out, along with his argument and his bloviating style, his stated goal, which was not trivial. As his disciple T. S. Eliot long ago pointed out, Babbitt set out to identify an alternative to the ethical goals of religion that circumvented religion's ethical *content*. "The Greek, one might say, humanized nature; the Rousseauist naturalizes man." And so Irving Babbitt attempted to humanize religion, if not turn it into a partisan pursuit. But since Matthew Arnold had got there first, the attempt could be called late Victorian if it were not so ferociously American—even Emersonian—in its progressive how-to-ism, its real enthusiasm for learning and at bottom its commitment to what we would call nowadays the creation of a literary canon.

Babbitt, does, after all, reveal if only by accident the extent to which Romanticism really is what T. E. Hulme called it—a "spilt religion," a form of philosophical idealism that substituted either Nature (Wordsworth) or Imagination (Coleridge) or Poetry (Shelley) for God but retained religion's conceptual framework. Shelley's own definition of poetry—"Poetry, and the principle of Self of which money is the visible incarnation, are the God and Mammon of this world"—casts aesthetic value in overt scriptural terms and predicts Arnold's claim that poetry would replace religion and, in a vastly different context, Stevens's triumphal "God and the Imagination are one." The text of the discourse is, as usual, Wordsworth's:

> My heart leaps up when I behold
> A rainbow in the sky;
> So was it when my life began;
> So is it now I am a man;
> So be it when I shall grow old,
>   Or let me die!
> The Child is the father of the Man;
> And I could wish my days to be
> Bound each to each in natural piety.

As the bastard offspring of Darwin and Freud, we hardly need to add Blake to find the idea of "natural piety," especially to the pious among us, nerve-wracking. And sprung from what deeply disturbing—because so self-satisfied—view of personal history, only Wordsworth knew. But with almost ritual care (*so was it, so is it, so be it*) he surrounds his past with a delicate arc of tenses for which a rainbow is figurative cause and physical analogue. Can you ever again look at a rainbow and see it as the seal of God's compact with Noah? The rainbow has lost its innocence. From this point it will be the emblem of Wordsworth's compact with that earlier child-self that fathered him. All fathering is from then on self-fathering; it is not Jesus but Nature who loves us, and it's not the Bible but the landscape tells us so. This is the Wordsworth who tends to identify his personal growth with that of the raw real estate he sees and imaginatively populates. No wonder the agitated Keats dredged up the phrase "egotistical sublime" to describe him.

But it is not so clear, reading Wordsworth, that the path back to a source stops at Rousseau rather than Augustine, or leads forward without a detour to dead end at the 1960s and the Haight rather than at the 1980s and Silicon Valley. In fact, you really don't need to set out from Wordsworth at all. The kernel of Babbitt's argument is that Romanticism must be viewed as a moral rather than a strictly cultural entity, a specific mode of behavior that we measure very poorly with period or disciplinary designations; and his point, the accepted one nowadays, is as sound now as it was in 1919. This lucky distinction, however, only frees him to condemn Romanticism while blessing the Romantic, to ridicule Coleridge's *Rime,* for instance, without ridiculing Coleridge, to blame Ahasuerus without blaming Shelley. It's precisely what that other grand blovia-tor, the aforementioned Matthew Arnold, did in 1864 in "The Function of Crit-icism," when he praises Wordsworth's poetry but assassinates him in the same breath by adding that Wordsworth "should have read more books." The tech-nique, condemnation via surrogate, perfected by politicians, opens the range of implication. But a unified theory of culture—which is what Babbitt thinks he is up to—must be more variously and frankly synoptic if it is not to be as comically pathological and preachifying as the Widow Watson's lectures. Bab-bitt's continued cultural visibility is maintained partly by Tory partisans like Paul Johnson, whose 1989 *Intellectuals* was an example of the sort of second-string intellectual flim-flam encouraged by his master's example. Ideological narcissists who find in Babbitt an ancestral voice prophetic of our present trou-bles (nonrepresentational art, BLM, tenured radicalism, secular humanism, the films of David Lynch) overlook how limited he was as a diagnostician of his own and how fast and loose he played with certain facts. Hazlitt, for example, an early enthusiast, later modified his enthusiasm for the French Revolution ("political revolutions are not so well calculated to better man's condition, as during a certain period I, with almost all the thinking men in Europe, had been led to suppose") and was often savage in his estimate of Rousseau, neither of which you'd know if you had read only Babbitt.

Those limitations date the book and eliminate Babbitt's usefulness as a speculative thinker possessed of any real breadth. Babbitt never engages Rous-seau on the matter of his art since he confesses in his introduction not to be about aesthetic or literary criticism; you honestly wonder if he ever read him, or how far he got into *Confessions.* Yet the less trivial matter, that Rousseau vir-tually reinvented the genre of secular autobiography, strikes me at least as trans-categorical in interest as Rousseau's sins against common sense. Rousseau at-tempted "the first description of the paranoia of everyday life," as Charles Rosen put it, and opened the possibility that insanity is itself a condition of modern urban experience. Babbitt might even agree with Rosen, but he would point the facts differently: once the source of insight shifted from God to man, man must accuse the world itself of being mad to convince himself that his individuality is no mere hallucination. The larger problem for Babbitt is that he seems to argue that all "ethical" behavior on the Classical model is self-correcting; the immediate problem, though, is that he ignores how Rousseau *on principle* democratized autobiography, made it the place for both the sick and the sane, aristocrats and us sansculottes, and made it so unembarrassedly *popular* that all subsequent autobiography would be doomed the moment it began to dish out highfalutin moral examples. Rousseau turns out to have been, predictably or not, the progenitor not only of the great, "straight" autobiographies of Ben Franklin and Jefferson and even Darwin, but of *My Daddy the Pedophile* and the more entertaining modern ones—James Frey to J. D. Vance to Cher. The dilemma for you and me is that Babbitt's attention contracts around a figure representative of what is, at best, a limiting case of Romantic philosophy framed by a disciple of the French Enlightenment. The book, as either Wellek or Lovejoy noted years ago, should have been titled *Rousseau's Romanticism.*

I have to emphasize this last point. Babbitt not only overstated the French but bafflingly underestimated the English contribution to Romanticism. True, Wordsworth and Coleridge, of the so-called First Generation Romantics, were supportive of Rousseau and the French Revolution; but by 1797 both were openly defecting from or recanting their radicalism. One recent biography even strongly suggested that Wordsworth was spying for the Crown while in France. (Shelley champions Rousseau as late as *The Triumph of Life,* but Shelley is the most intellectually complicated figure in the Second Generation and exempt from the most reductive moralizing.) Coleridge's early endorsements of Rousseau were never unqualified, and if you can forgive me for excusing Wordsworth from serious consideration—he was a pretty forgettable critic—it is Coleridge's continuing example as a moralist and amateur theologian that agitates against Rousseau's thesis, that stands out as the decisive difference, and that Babbitt, whatever his other omissions, may not be forgiven for having overlooked. The decisive difference between English and French Romanticism is that England had a Coleridge, a Hume, a Wollstonecraft and a Burke, and that France did not. The path back may just as well end, as it began, with Coleridge.

Coleridge's intellectual growth was choppy and fairly disorganized. In 1795, Coleridge is twenty-three years old, a newlywed and a ferocious idealist with

no practical vision, giving lectures to pay for his Pantisocratic exodus to Pennsylvania. He praises "French Freedom" as "the Beacon, which while it guides
to Equality, should shew us the Dangers that throng the road." His radicalism
lasted less than five years. By 1798, he's a twenty-six-year-old father of two in a
bad marriage who no longer opposes England's war with France; a year later he
has dismissed Rousseau's belief in natural goodness and in a letter to his brother
George writes, "Of GUILT I say nothing; but I believe most steadfastly in original sin," adding that his opinions are "untainted" by foreign (read: *French*) influences. And one year later he is toeing the line like a good Lockean, claiming that
"Governments must be founded on property" and dismissing as immature the
notion that just societies could be constructed on Rousseauist principles of personal and natural rights ("that government [is] the best in which the power was
the most exactly proportioned to the property"). By 1802, in his thirtieth year
and four years after the appearance of *Lyrical Ballads,* in a long article in the
Morning Post he compares contemporary France to Rome and concludes that
"Rome," unlike France, "was really an enlightener and civilizer." His assessment
of Rousseau as late as 1809 is hardly unconditional: "In his whole System there
is beyond controversy much that is true and well-reasoned, if only its application be not extended farther than the nature of the case permits. But then we
shall find that little or nothing is won by it for the institutions of Society; and
least of all for the constitution of Governments, the Theory of which it was his
wish to ground on it." In other words, Rousseau's approach to personal morality
as a matter of personal conscience is beyond reproach, but "with what shew of
Reason can we pretend, from a Principle by which we are to determine the pu-
rity of our motives, to deduce the form and matter of a rightful Government?"
The question is a dagger. What works for one may not work for all. Rousseau
himself lays opens his system to exactly the implication that Coleridge cooly
dismisses as basically irrational.

Coleridge's shaping of a specifically English Romanticism is one of the particular critical triumphs of the last century, largely owing to I. A. Richards, but
it is also the discovery that reveals how much of Babbitt, and less obviously
Eliot, is an artifact of the nineteenth. "Coleridge's theory of knowing treats
knowing as a kind of making, i.e. the bringing into being of what is known,"
wrote Richards, who reinvented Coleridge for the New Critics and for his time.
Richards was alive to how much such a theory—really Coleridge's description

of the Imagination, which only if you're being really generous is a "theory"—shared with what, in 1934, was "modern psychology." This blurs what is at the root of Coleridge's departure from Rousseau: he was a devout Christian, and his theoretical writing (particularly about imagination) is explicitly aligned with Christian orthodoxy, an intellectual trait shared by the upper echelons of New Critics like Brooks and Frye. Imagination in Coleridge's description is the second degree of a spiritual isomorphism; it is "an echo in the finite of the infinite act of I AM," the human faculty circumscribed, limited and protected by the divine. As such it proves to be so hostile to Rousseau's assertion of the primacy of the Self, limited only by social interaction, that it's more than just a minor qualification. There have been several attempts, for instance, to characterize the formal influences behind Coleridge's "Conversation Poems," but most readers seem to agree that their contours are exactly *not* Wordsworthian or Shelleyan. Coleridge could not accept the possibility that Imagination was self-sufficient or self-subsisting; his imagination, particularly in those long meditative lyrics, always seems in the end to fly back to his wife, Sara, his son Hartley, or to God. The critic Anne Mellor once argued that "in the future when we speak of romanticism, we will have to speak of at least two romanticisms, the men's and the women's." I suggest at least two others—Rousseau's and Coleridge's.

—1993

The Measure of the Eye

POUND AND IMAGISM

Ezra Pound is too enormous a subject to surround in no matter how encyclope-dic an essay, so I limit myself to early and middle Pound, from *Lustra* through *Hugh Selwyn Mauberley*. I concede the objective validity of the moral issues: Pound's political lunacies blocked access to his poetry (and criticism) for so long and for so many that it's natural to wonder whether the former hasn't perma-nently ended passion for the latter. Two major assumptions, though, precede me. The first is the core insight of Hugh Kenner's *The Pound Era*: "Pound's work, say from *Lustra* to the last *Cantos,* is the longest working-out in any art of premises like those of Cubism." I would put an even finer point on this: those "premises" were found in Imagism, and Pound, early or late, was an Imagist. The two-line "In a Station of the Metro," which appeared first in *Poetry* in 1912 and in a slightly different form in *Lustra,* is the formula that embodies the approach behind longer and more complex works—the works of Pound's own matu-rity, *Mauberley* and *The Cantos,* and work influenced by Pound, from Eliot's *The Waste Land* and Zukofsky's *A* to Olson's *Maximus* poems, to Ginsberg's *The Fall of America.*

A second assumption: Imagism, no matter how congenial attempts to dis-credit it, was the first disciplined attempt to rethink poetry's discursive direc-tions since Wordsworth. What happened to Imagism after Pound rechristened it as "Amygism" is of gossipy interest, but its theoretical implications, especially on poetry as a spoken medium, are not. As Pound himself said, "The great writ-ers need no debunking," and Pound remains one of the great American writers of the English language. To take seriously him and his brainchild, Imagism, is to unpack the visionary background of twentieth-century art and understand why it is so hard, why it seemed so new, and why so many of its practitioners were so pessimistic about its future.

The distance Pound covered between *Ripostes* (1912) and *Lustra* (1915) is a measure of what he set out to escape—Romanticism principally, Symbolism secondly—and the poetic methodology that he would invent and call Imagism. After an education in broad cultural realities—modern technology, Cubism, oriental poetry—the "doctrine of the Image" reemerges as the Ideogrammic method of the 1930s. But Imagism itself is preceded by a cocooning, as it were, from which, if his prose alone is any indication, Pound brought two senses of himself. The first, that he was charged with a pedagogical mission, is, depending on your view of Pound's poetry, either its glory or calamity. The second, that a "scientific" understanding of the art of poetry is indispensable to its production or consumption, leads to an instrumentalist, at times crudely top-down approach to everything, especially art. The instrumentalist theme never disappears from Pound's poetry or criticism; it is, and especially early in the century, the demonic twin of Williams's description of a poem as a "machine made out of words." Both senses, one of the poet's role and the other of his philosophy, appear in "I Gather the Limbs of Osiris" (1911–12). "The artist seeks out the luminous detail and presents it. He does not comment. His work remains the permanent basis of psychology and metaphysics." Throughout the essay he distances himself from "scholarship," meaning institutional learning, by retreating to similar revisionary formulations—capitalizing the phrase "Luminous Detail" in the second paragraph, for instance. His unacknowledged debt to Shelley's *Defense,* to Coleridge, to French Symbolism is undeniable. He is a Shelleyan legislator ("As for myself, I have tried to clear up a certain messy place in the history of literature"—he is barely twenty-six when he writes this), a Socratic dialectician charged with cleaning up public taste by requiring poets and readerships to know things, and at times a doctor ("If a book reveal to us something of which we were unconscious, it feeds us with its energy; if it reveal to us nothing . . . it draws energy from us"). Then, in the section called "On Technique," he seems to find his range: "Let us imagine that words are like great hollow cones of steel of different dullness and acuteness; . . . Let us imagine them charged with a force like electricity, or, rather, radiating a force from their apexes—some radiating, some sucking in." The thing runs on for another one hundred or so

words and makes us wish he would explain his explanation, especially since
he ultimately places the whole passage under erasure ("This peculiar energy
which fills the cones is the power of tradition, and the control of it is the 'Technique of content,' which nothing short of genius understands"). Only his enthusiasm and perhaps his youth forgives its elaborate silliness. By comparison,
the head-scratcher Eliot fetched out eight years later to explain how poetry is
like science—"I invite you to consider . . . the action which takes place when a
bit of finely filiated platinum is introduced into a chamber containing oxygen
and sulphur dioxide"—is almost tame. Not silly, however, is how much Pound
needed a metaphor of precisely this instrumentalist character to mediate the
influences—late-Symbolist, later-Romantic—quickening his own.

Symbolism was a particular irritant. The Symbolist "dealt with 'association,'" "degraded the symbol to the status of a word," conferred on his symbols "a
fixed value." Verlaine and Baudelaire he lumped together, claiming that "neither
. . . is the least use, pedagogically, I mean. They beget imitation and one can
learn nothing from them." Yeats, whose huge presence drew Pound to England
in 1906 and whom Pound, late in 1913, served as amanuensis and collaborator,
was also suspect. A "transparent lamp around a spiritual flame," Yeats called the
symbol, itself the manifest content of what emanates from that other Yeatsian
mirage, the Anima Mundi. But no matter its wider applicability, for Yeats the
definition worked and was productive and consistent with his own practice.
"O Rose, red rose, proud rose of all my days" is a pointer to no real rose at all
but to an abstraction that stands for Ireland, Intellectual Beauty, and whatever
else Yeats wishes.

Pound would have none of it. As late as *The Pisan Cantos* and Canto 83
(1948), Pound identified visionary Symbolism with spiritual evil:

> Le Paradis n'est pas artificiel
> and Uncle William dawdling around Notre Dame
> in search of whatever
>   paused to admire the symbol
> with Notre Dame standing inside it

The French alludes to Baudelaire's *Les Paradis artificiels,* a bitter memoir of
hash-and-opium addiction indebted to DeQuincy: the clear line of sight is

from Baudelaire to Yeats. A *Paradis artificiel* (as Baudelaire titles his first chapter) is at bottom a rhetorical necessity imposed on the world by those who cannot live in it; it derives from a *gout de l'infini,* an appetite for infinity. The world of Verlaine's "Claire de Lune," say, or of Yeats's "Byzantium" are such artificial Paradises, toy or substitute worlds that can teach us nothing about what's real, or what's really important. A symbol, Pound believed, is for this reason potentially destructive, if not evil: it fixes existential value in a word and replaces a physical value with an intellectual (or mystical) one. The Symbolist then proceeds—and the analogy with charging money at interest, or usury, certainly would not have escaped Pound—to circulate the substitution term as poetic currency. "The imagiste's images," on the other hand, "have a variable significance, like the signs a, b, and x in algebra," he writes. The resilience of the image was its ability to resist capture by whatever rhetoric a greedy politician or an incompetent poet might dream up to exploit it.

There is no getting around this last point: whatever his other obsessions, early on Pound was especially obsessed with the exploitation of language, with language used to obfuscate history and the historical record. His faith in the poet as public servant, a central persona in *Lustra,* is what drives his denunciation in *Gaudier-Brzeska: A Memoir* (1915–16) of "the period sentence and the flowing paragraph" as the cause of the fall of Renaissance Italy. "For when words cease to cling close to things, kingdoms fall, empires wane and vanish. Rome went because it was no longer the fashion to hit the nail on the head. They desired orators." The Image was the antidote: it was itself an instrument of vision, a lens. Like a scientist the Imagist learned from history and used it; he was a scientist who dealt in emotions. "I see," said the unidentified Russian to Pound, "you wish to give people new eyes, not to make them see some new particular thing." The vision of this new artist-as-scientist gained focus through the Image, which resisted reduction to the monadic simplicity of the symbol, whether a placard word, a political slogan, or a poetic term.

There's another reason to keep Pound's moral fervor in mind when reading *Lustra*: his obsession with historical memory, memory as written record. He seems at times to regard human history as a faintly imbecilic curator habitually misplacing or destroying the products of human genius and barely kept in line by the artist. One of the "lessons of history," he says in the 1929 "How to Read," is that "maintaining the very cleanliness of the tools, the health of the very matter of thought itself" is the poet's job: "the individual cannot think and communicate his thought, the governor and legislator cannot act effectively or frame his laws, without words, and the solidity and validity of these words is in the care of the damned and despised literati. When their work goes rotten . . . order goes to pot." Durability, he adds, depends on utility, and utility measures your closeness to Tradition. Thus, while aligning yourself with tradition guaranteed nothing—are you listening, Eliot?—in the long run it was less dangerous than fashionable "systematic derangements of the senses" that replace traditional means of knowing with a hermetic vocabulary of sensation, impressions, and feeling "deprived of intellect, and out drunk on its 'lone, saying it is the 'that which is beyond the intelligence.'" Tradition could at least tell you what needed to be done, though it lacked the flexibility Eliot implied that it had in his early essays. Tradition, moreover, according to Pound, is essentially historical memory embodied in books and cultural monuments that no personal apocalypse can touch—hence the lack of flexibility. Pound before *Lustra* had matured a recognition of how much Symbolist aesthetic had achieved: he was never blind to the formal beauty of works of genius, like those of Baudelaire, Rimbaud (both of whom he translated), and Yeats. *Lustra* gave him the opportunity to find out how much of that formal yield Tradition would permit him to carry over the threshold of *Lustra* and into the practice of Imagism and the extroverted art of his maturity.

From the opening page it is clear that *Lustra* is a book with a mission. Just what that mission is Pound suggests in the definition of *lustrum* he adds below the dedication: "an offering for the sins of the whole [Roman] people, made by the censors at the expiration of their five years of office." The poems are ritual sacrifices made by a public official about to leave office; *Lustra* is therefore a public service and a uniquely public book. Satirically brooding over morality, society, and poetry's power to change things, the poems either laugh at their audience or ask it to laugh at itself and are usually framed as envoys directed to twit this or that vested interest and to bring some reforming sense to British taste. Pound is also opening a personal referential domain in *Lustra:* in his correspondence he occasionally compared intellectual to sexual penetration: sexual power was a kind of IQ. As he wrote in a postscript to his translation of Remy de Gourment's *The Natural Philosophy of Love* (1921), which apparently inspired the idea, "the brain itself, is, in origin and development, only a sort of great clot of genital fluid held in suspense or reserve." Successful entrance into another consciousness is, therefore, a kind of sexual victory, a measure of the strength of intellect over stupidity. This attitude never disappears from his work ("The female is a chaos, / the male / is a fixed point of stupidity," he once wrote in a letter to Marianne Moore).

In "The Garden," one of the great lyrics of the last century, the attitude actually matures into keen observation. A young girl is passing a railing in Kensington Gardens:

> Like a skein of loose silk blown against a wall
> She walks by the railing of a path in Kensington Gardens,
> And she is dying piece-meal
>   of a sort of emotional anaemia.

Of several such poems where Pound describes an encounter with a woman, this is the most finished and most suggestively titled. He presents the objects of physical and poetic vision by "super-positioning," to use the word he uses to explain how Imagism works. "The 'one-image poem' is a form of super-position, that is to say, it is one idea set on top of another," so he sets Kensington on the Garden of Eden to prove the poet-physician's diagnosis ("emotional anaemia"). In the five-line "Shop Girl," which appears later in the book—

> For a moment she rested against me
> Like a swallow half blown to the wall,
> And they talk of Swinburne's women,
> And the shepherdess meeting with Guido.
> And the harlots of Baudelaire.

—he reproduces the same figurative vehicle, fragile sensuality buffeted by wind, with a subtle difference. The shop girl is a swallow to whom an ephemeral sensuality clings; the iterated syntactical shape of lines 3–5 turns the poem from satire to elegy without getting stuck in sticky *Ou sont les neiges* reveries. The girl is, after all, a waitress who "brought us our muffins." Yet which of us will not like her "turn middle-aged"?

The young girl in Kensington, on the other hand, is a "skein of loose silk," not even a "swallow" but a thing upon whom the world's impact is not tragic, but inevitable:

> And round about there is a rabble
> Of the filthy, sturdy, unkillable infants of the very poor.
> They shall inherit the earth.

This backhanding of the Sermon on the Mount looks easy, but you wonder what lesser competence might have done with the same opportunity. A fancier, hypotactic approach—"who shall inherit the earth," say, or an exact quotation ("The meek shall inherit the earth")—would have either sounded precious or overdone the allusion. Pound's success is in lifting the poem from the level where it is merely a self-regarding showpiece, the spot where most of Imagism's officially anthologized poetry languished, to permanent and surprising seriousness. After all, it's essentially about a pickup in a public place; what Pound does with it is both unique and anything but vulgar—or sentimental. It was Victorian sentiment that produced this pretty pedestrian, a biological cul-de-sac of exquisite breed and excessive delicacy who is no Eve but an enigmatic mock-up or parody of her. Everything about the young woman is fastidious and overdetermined by a culture reduced to aphorisms and maxims; she is a walking cliché, her poised figure kept upright with corsets and stays. Since earth is no Eden, why should what is sturdy and unkillable not inherit it?

> In her is the end of breeding.
> Her boredom is exquisite and excessive.
> She would like some one to speak to her,
> And is almost afraid that I
>   will commit that indiscretion.

The prosody itself casually rolls to a stop, reacting to the "end" of breeding. London's street rats collaborate in fulfilling the prophecy precisely because what they surround will reproduce only if forced to. Breeding in the young woman's case is an impasse to precisely the eugenic miracle it proposed.

Discussions of Pound's influences, or of any poet's, can come down to checklists of his reading—to material sources—and attract scholarly interests more archaeological than literary. With Pound, a covenantal understanding seems to be at work: his work is the sum of the cultural details identified in the footnotes to the poems, outside of which the author himself hardly existed. Pound is partly the reason for this. "He does not seem to have inhabited his own experience," Olsen said in 1946. But if I am overstating the critical preoccupations of some Poundians, it's only by a little. An allusion like "They shall inherit the earth" is viewed strictly as a source, as writing reduced to the material level of print, where a line or a phrase points self-consciously "backward" to its antecedent(s) and, in a sense, gives its secrets up all at once. Critics like Bloom attacked both Eliot and Pound not so much for their use of the past but for having done so with such demanding self-consciousness that "familiarity with the text" means being familiar with the whole textual "family" it belongs to and returning the prodigal—*Mauberley, The Waste Land*—to the community of the like-minded (or -educated), who maintain the make-believe network of extended literary relationships called Tradition, which at bottom is just another version of our dream of human continuity, Freud's "family Romance." For *source* Bloom substituted *influence*, which points not to the bare thinghood of the antecedent ("Blessed are the meek, for they shall inherit the earth") but to the dialectic of renewal or disaster that happens when two poets (Matthew 5:5; Pound, "The Garden") creatively, which is to say antagonistically, encounter each other. The former was in general Hugh Kenner's position, that which endorsed the full-on image-study; it was the outgrowth of Eliot's influential fable "Tradition and the Individual Talent" (1919), which promoted impersonality, a respect for tradition amounting to near servility, and radical indifference to, even disregard of, "originality." Eliot himself was repeating Arnold's evangelizing for an unbroken canon of values, which seems to be what both meant by Tradition, to which each generation's work is laboriously and unabashedly mortgaged.

Eliot's cameo here, in an essay about Pound, is germane, almost inevitable: Modernism is arguably the godchild of Arnold and daughter of Eliot, with Pound as midwife (of *The Waste Land*), so it's useful to recall Eliot's understanding of how poetry comes to be made. The process is strikingly like the production of scholarship—a continuous and cumulative, hieratic undertaking, with "disinterested" critics acting as an oversight committee conducting traffic flow and ensuring the maintenance and operation of the objective correlative(s). But an antithetical critic like Bloom was bound to view any such reverential stance as either polite nonsense or propaganda—in Eliot's case, Christian propaganda. Poets, Bloom argued, do not collaborate like initiates lining up for the laying on of hands. The assumption that the production of poetry somehow involves cooperation with the very Tradition that is out to get the poet leads to a confusion of the manifest content of the given poem with its latent content, which is what it refers to and which is always prior, greater, "stronger." To take Pound's "The Garden," it's acceptable for a critic like Kenner to superimpose the Garden of Paradise upon Kensington Gardens only so long as the priority of the former is respected and the result is irony, which preserves the distinctions between mental "locations"; but it is less acceptable to assume that the poet wants to overcome the irony and maintain his or her originality, a quality of poetic genius that Eliot refused to countenance, and in so doing to rewrite the Fall, or to send up the Sermon on the Mount.*

On the face of it, *Lustra* is no place for antithetical critics. Much of the poetry is overtly referential and gives itself up immediately, like "Amities," which bittersweetly renounces some of Pound's older, less vital professional friendships, with its epigraph from Yeats, its French allusion, and the six-line coda in Pound's own Latin. The funny "Epitaphs" to the Chinese poets Fu I and Li Po (who "also died drunk. / He tried to embrace a moon / In the Yellow River"), "Our Contemporaries," a send-up of the recently deceased Rupert Brooke that got Pound into minor trouble with Harriet Monroe, and the tetraptych "Ladies," a send-up of the typical Georgian deb ("Flawless as Aphrodite, / Thoroughly beautiful, / Brainless"), are all glibly referential, unambiguous and accessible to the educated reader. Slightly more opaque (and not to say vicious) is "Tempora," where "The Dryad" who stands in Pound's yard, "With plaintive, querulous crying," cries not the name of Tammuz, the god she serves, but "May my poems be printed this week? / The god Pan is afraid to ask you, / May my poems be printed this week?" The "Dryad," to educated gossipmongers, is Pound's code name for H.D., endlessly tortured by a lasting crush on him and for her unrequited need to get published. Like the young girl in "The Garden,"

---

* It would have been even less acceptable a century ago to point out that not even the writers of Scripture were immune from the anxiety of influence. Matthew's Gospel is modeled so closely on the book of Exodus that it qualifies as what Bloom would have called a "weak misreading" of the Old Testament; something similar applies to the opening of John's Gospel—"In the beginning was the Word"—which is a deliberate allusion to and play on Genesis 1:1.

she is ruined by a refinement that is missing the sort of self-conscious irony that Pound in "Epilogues" directs against his own poems, which he dismisses as "seven-days' wonder."

There is, more hopefully, "The Lake Isle," one of Pound's several attempts to exorcise Yeats, either through straight parody or mocking tributes like "Au Jardin" from *Ripostes,* a satire of Yeats's "The Cap and Bells." In "The Lake Isle" Pound asks the gods to send him not to Innisfree but to "a little tobacco-shop," with shiny scales, neat shelves, and "whores dropping in for a word or two in passing / For a flip word, and to tidy their hair a bit." Pound gets Yeats right down to phrasing ("For a flip word, and to tidy their hair a bit"); and the closing is memorable:

O God, O Venus, O Mercury, patron of thieves,
Lend me a little tobacco-shop,
    or install me in any profession,
Save this damn'd profession of writing,
    where one needs one's brains all the time.

But this is Pound merely having fun with Yeats's horror at being related through his mother to the purse-proud Butlers. Notably, the poem's gently satiric turn is nowhere as complex as, say, the way Stevens's "Anecdote of the Jar" flirts with Keats's "Grecian Urn." Parody and satire are on lower rungs of the ironic ladder than where Stevens stood, whose ironies are always philosophical, and who was no satirist. The other influences advertise themselves openly, in epigraphs (Lope de Vega), titles ("After Ch'U Yuan," whose opening line is another Yeatsian echo, "I will get me to the wood"), internal quotations ("Lugete, Veneres! Lugete, Cupidinesque!"), and outright translations (Catullus, "To Formianus' Young Lady Friend").

But in most cases a good raking-out with, say, Ruthven's *Annotated Guide,* or Google, shows that Pound's influences were material *sources* after all, and reminds me of the connection between a fan and his autograph book. Still, this is precisely how critics usually read Pound: winding their way, usually in Kenner's intimidating wake, through Pound's work to disclose the author of a reference or inscription, or to reenact the poetry's cultural complexity while tacitly admitting to its psychological aridity. Psychological complexity can mean many things, though always it is where or when your sense of mortality is touched by the poet's sense of their own—the heavenly hurt that Dickinson says scars us with "internal difference / where the meanings are." If this turns the point around to mean that psychological complexity is flattened out into cultural complexity in Ezra Pound, that scattered bursts of random feeling are reworked into their social equivalents and, like oil spills, are a mile wide but only an inch thick, then the judgment that concludes *The Pound Era* ("Thought is a labyrinth") is not just unintentionally ironic but profoundly or intentionally evasive. In *Lustra* the poetry begins making a full about-face, turning the weakly rendered subjective energies of *Ripostes* outward toward social satire and cultural criticism. There is obviously nothing inherently "unpoetic" about this turnabout. Whether Pound wanted to be solved out of his work by replacing him or his thought with the labyrinthine culture behind it is not the same as asking whether his obsession with written history—or his obsession with memory as written record—so completely displaces subjective interests from *Mauberley* and *The Cantos* as to make those poems, for some, not only uninteresting but not worth the investment of research, and even unreadable.

The reworking of his influences in *Lustra* is a crucial threshold beyond which Pound tended more and more to substitute objective for subjective interests, historical for human complexities—the Image and the luminous detail for the lived occasion, or as he says in *Mauberley*, the "Classics in paraphrase" for the lesser "mendacities" of an era of uncontrolled introversion. Nothing mattered but advancing the art: "Artalone the Weeps" Joyce named Pound's surrogate in *Finnegans Wake,* and the name is apt.

It is with this understanding that readers should approach "A Pact," nine lines of relative inconsequence to critics except as an index of what you do not normally find in Pound—a sense of the importance of Whitman. Donald Davie in *Ezra Pound* (1975) dismisses both Whitman and Blake with a rousing post-Watergate reminder that American democratic traditions were "framed on neoclassical models by assiduous Grecians like Jefferson and Adams," illogically implying that any embrace of Whitman (or Blake) is a rejection of assiduous Grecians and of European influence. Early in his career Pound did see Whitman just that simplistically: "[Whitman] is America. His crudity is an exceeding great stench, but it is America. He is the hollow place in the rock that echoes with his time. He does 'chant the crucial stage' and he is the 'voice triumphant.'

He is disgusting. He is an exceedingly nauseating pill, but he accomplishes his mission." Yet this early essay of 1909, "What I Feel about Walt Whitman," withholds as much as it gives. Moses (Exodus 33:21) was granted the nearest glimpse of the Creator enjoyed by any man when he hid himself in a hollow place in the rock to witness Yahweh's passage: Whitman, if we follow the allusion, is both the hollow and the Mosaic figure representing the voice that is great within us. Even then, what is on Pound's mind is the issue of poetic succession, which becomes a real worry by 1915 and "A Pact." Its famous opening—

> I'll make a pact with you, Walt Whitman—
> I have detested you long enough.
> I come to you as a grown child
> Who has had a pig-headed father;

—carries over the note of exasperation from 1909 while adding the unanticipated Freudian note. But the poem makes an interesting and unanticipated tonal shift:

> I am old enough now to make friends.
> It was you that broke the new wood,
> Now is a time for carving.
> We have one sap and one root—
> Let there be commerce between us.

Behind the poem's chatty directness something more interesting is going on. The breaking of the "new wood" must refer to the revolution that is Whitman's prosody, a revolution, Pound says in a letter of 1931, that "the Concord school" (Emerson, Longfellow, et al.) missed, failing "to see the forest for the trees." The man who insists on "breaking the pentameter" is therefore gesturing to the Father of Free Verse, but the gesture is initially antithetical: "pig-headedness" stands for Whitman's stubborn lack of refinement and freedom from "creeds and schools," whereas Pound is "a Walt Whitman who has learned to wear a collar and a dress shirt," as he says in the earlier essay. All of which explains the poet's hostility, but without revealing why it has been surrendered.

The answer must lie in the immediate textual logistics, i.e., where the poem appears in the book. Eleven poems precede "A Pact," among them "Tenzone," an apology for his own power; "The Garden," his demystification of the Fall; and the three poems titled "Salutation," "Salutation the Second," and "Commission," each of which contain instructions to poems setting out like children from their parent. "Commission," which comes right before "A Pact," opens,

> Go, my songs, to the lonely and the unsatisfied,
> Go also to the nerve-wracked, go to the enslaved-by-convention,
> Bear to them my contempt for their oppressors,
> Go as a great wave of cool water,
> Bear my contempt of oppressors

and ends, "Go out and defy opinion, / Go against this vegetable bondage of the blood. / Be against all sorts of mortmain." This litany of directives is educated in Whitman's lists; and this audience is and was the same audience Whitman targeted. The paternal pose Pound himself strikes leads to his dismayed, or maybe just amused recognition that his detestation of the father is, in its way, pretty conventional. Whence that last line, with its redefinition of the father-son relationship as a business transaction: Walt the Forebearer vanishes into Whitman the Forerunner. The prodigal returns to the father, but only after he has dispatched his own children into the world.

Whitman arrived early and stayed late. In *The Pisan Cantos,* Pound, having found Whitman "in a cheap edition" in a latrine, aligns him with Tradition through echoes of section 2 of *Song of Myself*—

> hast'ou swum in a sea of air strip
>   through an aeon of nothingness
> when the raft broke and the waters went over me,

—from Canto 80, which he reechoes in the *Libretto* to Canto 81:

> Hast 'ou fashioned so airy a mood
>   To draw up leaf from the root?
> Hast 'ou found   a cloud   so light
>   As seemed neither mist nor shade?

Whitman's humility before the natural world brought home the absurdity of those who "feed on the specters in books," and the irony was hardly lost on Pound, sixty years old, in a detention camp in Italy, broken in health, and his library reduced to left-behinds, that it is the Whitman of *Song of Myself* who rescues him "from the gates of death":

> Have you reckon'd a thousand acres much?
> Have you reckon'd the earth much?
> Have you practis'd so long to learn to read?
> Have you felt so proud to get at the meaning of poems?

One canto later, Canto 82 completes the loop of antitheses: Whitman contains a multitude of other poet-outcasts, a Villon, an En Bertrans, a Dante, even in fractured English, that "Fvy! in Tdaenmarck efen dh' beasantz gnow him," meaning Whitman, who is "known" by Danish peasants even while still regarded with suspicion four miles from his home in Camden and from Jenkintown, where Pound grew up. The broken English belongs to Professor Richard Reithmuller, author of *Walt Whitman and the Germans* (1906) and instructor of German at Pound's near alma mater, the University of Pennsylvania. "Four miles from Camden" would place it in downtown Philadelphia, where Whitman was still "exotic, suspect" and a bizarre choice to name a bridge after.*

The surface of Pound's *Cantos* and all of his work after *Lustra,* so overwrought with allusions raw and refined, is a not at all superficial expression of his insistence on a poetry of double accomplishments: a poetry kept honest by history and yet driven by the passion that precedes great understanding. Rarely is that surface more rippled than when it meets Whitman, who really does seem more than historical memory, scholarship, or intellectual passion can comprehend. The work of preservation that Pound carried on breaks through to oc-

---

* The Walt Whitman Bridge opened in 1957 and connects Philadelphia to South Jersey. In an interview with Charlie Rose from 1992, Allen Ginsberg related how the choice of Whitman was fiercely opposed in the New Jersey legislature when it was first proposed. The reasons: "[Whitman's] overt depictions of homosexuality and bisexuality" and "Whitman's work as sympathizing with communist ideals and . . . his egalitarian view of humanity." As an alternative, another Jersey native, Joyce Kilmer, was counterproposed. When it was revealed that Kilmer was also gay, the objection went away. Whitman got the bridge, and Kilmer got a rest stop.

cupy the surface of his art; this privileged relationship to Whitman is one more important and violent—and late—breaking of the surface.

Imagism was essentially an elliptical approach to poetic design, substituting juxtapositional (or "super-position") for connected meanings, and in *Lustra* Pound invents Imagism with the most fully foregrounded example of the habit realized in "In a Station of the Metro"—

> The apparition of these faces in the crowd;
> Petals on a wet, black bough.

The point of any "poem of this sort," he says in 1918, "to record the precise instant when a thing outward and objective transforms itself, or darts into a thing inward and subjective." Poets measure, define, and apportion the critical distance between subjective and objective interests by introducing, reducing, or maintaining that distance. To write like an Imagist meant seeing, say, two different things by synthesizing them but without obliterating their unique, separable identities. It meant overcoming the hierarchies of normal perception:

> With clouds over Taishan-Chocorua
>   when the blackberry ripens,
> and now the new moon faces Taishan

Right through *The Cantos* one can find small and large examples of what Pound has matured from conscious strategy to the new mental habit of perceiving the world doubled—like this passage from Canto 83, where a pair of mountains, China's Mt. Taishan and New Hampshire's Mt. Chocorua, are superimposed. Imagism, whatever your view of it, was conceived as a philosophy of perception, an absolute way of looking at the world.

It was also a fairly characteristic modern rescue operation to free poetic subjectivity from both its enemies (science) and its friends (the literary establishment). Eliot's assertion of an objective correlative (in the 1919 essay "Hamlet"), in emphasizing the existence of an objective, hard, here-and-now world to which poetic imagination is responsive and in which it "terminates," attempts to do the same thing. Here is Eliot: "The only way of expressing emotion in the form of art is by finding an 'objective correlative'; in other words, a set of objects, a situation, a chain of events which shall be the formula of that particular emotion; such that when the external facts, which must terminate in sensory experience, are given, the emotion is immediately evoked." All this about "objects," a "formula," and "external facts" is a bit quaint nowadays, and the passage was once regarded as a permanent contribution to our understanding of the poetic act. But the passive voice of the last clause gives it away: evoked by *what*? The agent is buried in the machinery. We watch Eliot, like Pound, trying to square traditional subjective interests with a new objectivity. (Just try tracking the roller-coaster meanings of "feeling" and "emotion" through these early essays.) Pound's radical departure from Eliot is that the Image foregrounds the subjective and objective directions *simultaneously*—like an arrow with two heads, or what Kenner termed a "vector"—so that (in theory) they coexist in the imagination as equal partners. But there is a world of difference in their semantic directions, between what in Eliot is "evoked" and what in Pound "darts inward." Eliot seemed almost pathologically disinclined to overly approve a poet's subjectivity; even at his most generous, Eliot made subjectivity the property of the poem, teased out ("evoked") not by readers so much as by the poem's magnetic attraction to (or deflection from: it may fail to work) that monster abstraction, Tradition. This explains to some degree the either interesting or appalling platinum wire analogy that he invited you to consider in "Tradition and the Individual Talent," and his claim that "the more perfect the artist, the more completely separate in him will be the man who suffers and the mind which creates." Poets are catalysts; the compounds they work with are emotions; the constitutive material is personal experience.

For all his instrumentalism, Pound was indifferent to or comfortable with the faint fideism of what he himself once called "the Imagist *faith*" (my italics) and its 1913 list of "tenets":

I. Direct treatment of the "thing," whether subjective or objective.

II. To use absolutely no word that does not contribute to the presentation.

III. As regarding rhythm: to compose in sequence of the musical phrase, not in sequence of the metronome.

Way back in 1957 Frank Kermode (*The Romantic Image*) pointed out how Pound's noisiest scientific formulations of poetic strategies or poetic power— "As the abstract mathematician is to science so is the poet to the world's consciousness," from "The Wisdom of Poetry" (1912) is typical—inevitably fall prey to their unacknowledged context of composition. You could compile a small book of extracts showing how obligated he was by the theory and the need to conduct the imagination through the fields that science had claimed and to overcome his own sheepish nostalgia for the summer dream beneath the tamarind tree. Whence the Imagist protocols, which join magical thinking to Ben Franklin's approach to personal self-improvement. Imagism was an oh-so-natively American truce between poetry and science, at once a "conscious aesthetic to fill the place of Rimbaud's intuitions," in Kermode's words, and what Kenner memorably termed "specifications for technical hygiene," which was the way Imagism was generally understood (at least in 1972), which to Kenner was a major *mis*understanding of it. Both the philosophy and the precept derive from the same excited source.

No matter how magical the properties of "the Image," its acquisition, proposed by Pound in typically DIY fashion, looks easy. This, of course, leads to a final, bittersweet irony. What prompts Pound's claim, in *Gaudier-Brzeska,* that "Imagisme is not symbolism" is a contempt for the Symbolists' "mushy technique," which in turn is motivated by an even deeper disgust with Symbolist "rhetoric": "Ibycus and Liu Ch'e presented the 'Image.' Dante is a great poet by reason of this faculty, and Milton is a wind-bag because of his lack of it. The 'image' is the furthest possible removed from rhetoric. Rhetoric is the art of dressing up some unimportant matter so as to fool the audience for the time being." What Pound never foresaw was what would burst from the mercenary brain of Amy Lowell in a year or so: an Imagist how-to manual, where the "tenets" of Imagist theory became confused with the dos and don'ts of imagist practice, which launched a small franchise of Imagist anthologies. By 1915 Pound had already kissed off both movement and its sometime expressions. Years later, in a review of Binyon's *Inferno* in an Italian journal, he was still complaining: "The imitators of the Imagist movement could not comprehend that the 'rules' enunciated by my group in 1912 were by necessity general rules, and that it is not always advisable that they be applied to the poetry of 1930; even less necessary to use them in the presentation of poetry from 1300."*

But the damage was done, and the change was swift. In August 1914, less than eighteen months after formulating an Imagist "doctrine," Pound uncomfortably curtseys to Lowell's planned *Imagiste* anthology. "I should like the name 'Imagisme' to retain some sort of a meaning. It stands, or I should like it to stand for hard light, clear edges." No "democratized committee" can be trusted with it. It didn't matter; in October 1914 Lowell broke his heart again with the ad for her book *Sword Blades and Poppy Seed:* "Of the poets who to-day are doing the interesting and original work, there is no more striking and unique figure than Amy Lowell. The foremost member of the 'Imagists'—a group of poets that includes William Butler Yeats, Ezra Pound, Ford Madox Hueffer—she has won wide recognition for her writing in new and free forms." She tries to make up with Pound, even dedicating a poem to him, with the inscription, "With much friendship and admiration and some differences of opinion." Pound would have none of it. His response is a two-sentence postcard: "Congratulations. Why not include Thomas Hardy?" Later that month, he breaks with "official" Imagism and writes to Lowell, "I don't suppose any one will sue you for libel; it is too expensive. If your publishers 'of good standing' tried to advertise cement or soap in this manner they would certainly be sued. However we salute their venality. Blessed are they who have enterprise, for theirs is the magazine public." In that (long out-of-print) scholarly curiosity, William Platt's *The Imagist Poem: Modern Poetry in Miniature,* Imagism lives on life support, represented by those who did not do the movement a disservice (Pound, Eliot, Joyce, Lawrence, Stevens, Cummings) and by one or two who did. Amy Lowell's free verse contributions—she was normally a formalist—are mannered and imitative ("If I could catch the green lantern of the firefly / I could see to write you a letter," "The Lover"), and at their worst read like poor translations of poorer originals:

* The article, a translation from Pound's own Italian, is reprinted in the journal of the Pound Society, *Make It New* 2, no. 2, https://www.makeitnew.ezrapoundsociety.org/en/volume-ii/volume-2-no-1/conference-mla-2015?view=category&id=15.

Wind and Silver

Greatly shining,
The Autumn moon floats in the thin sky;
And the fish-ponds shake their backs and flash their dragon scales
As she passes over them.

Ignoring what the "theory of the Image" implied—and apart from what "official" Imagism produced—its crucial implications and attendant problems are
indistinguishable from the host of differently problematic, essentially unimportant poems, most simulacra of either Pound or H.D., that it left behind.
Subsequent arguments against Imagism, however, were not trivial. They were
directed either at the suppression of the agent (the narrative host, the "I" of
traditional lyric) or, in the specific of Pound's "Metro" poem, a different and
unexpected concern: what it was supposed to *sound* like.

Two extracts from Pound's prose frame the question, or problem. One is a letter
to E. E. Cummings of 6 April 1933, where the topic is the appearance of a line of
print on a page: "The normal or average eye sees a certain width without heav-
ing from side to side. May be hygienic for it to exercise its wobble, but I dunno
that the orfer [*sic*] shd. sacrifice himself on that altar." After noting how much
of a line he can take in at once, Pound then adds, "but I don't see the rest of the
line until I look specially at it. Multiply that 40 times per page for 400 pages
[. . .]. Mebbe there is wide-angle eyes. But chew gotter count on a cert. no. ov
yr. readers being at least as dumb as I am. Even in Bitch and Bugle I found it
difficult to read the stuff consecutively." The letter reveals an unusual attention
to the appearance of printed words in a magazine like *Hound & Horn* ("Bitch
and Bugle"), where readers have to contend with the confinements of margins.
Pound's decision to attend to the look, rather than to the sound of the line that
he quotes gets support from the metaphor of "wide-angle eyes": the organic
instrument of vision is defined by way of an analogy with the mechanical one.
    The second extract is an aphorism from his *ABC of Reading:* "Rhythm is
a form cut into TIME, as a design is determined SPACE." His aphorism linking

Time and Space expresses the same instrumentalist theme the letter voices, only with more sophistication. Poetic rhythm is harmonized with graphic design through an analogy that correlates Time with Space. Yet what is slightly extraordinary about Pound's view is the corresponding view of language that drives it: linguistic material carries a specific spatial component; poetic materials, to put it bluntly, are precisely *materials*. Words, like marble or metal, have extension and weight; their physical placement or semiotic design is as accountable for their semantic value, what they come to mean, as what they always, or already, mean in the mind of the author ("orfer"). Meaning gets displaced across a "certain width" the eye "wobbles" over.

Just to bedevil Pound the Instrumentalist, I'm reminded of a possible counterstatement from another century: "Allegories are things that Relate to Moral Virtues [.] Moral Virtues do not Exist[;] they are allegories & dissimulations [.] But Time & Space are Real Beings [,] a Male & a Female [.] Time is a Man [,] Space is a Woman [,] & her Masculine Portion is Death [.]" Blake, in this excerpt from *A Vision of The Last Judgment,* would regard Pound as he did Sir Isaac Newton, a "mere materialist," who errs in thinking of space as the accidental by-product of whatever occupies it, as some thing a painter governs and exploits through rationing of canvas or paper, either of which piece of material "is" or constitutes *space.* You Imagists, Blake would say, are bookkeepers who generalize about the relation of an element or thing in one column of your ledger to something on the other through appeal to nothing but arbitrary categories ("Time": "Space") which they treat as "real" things. But since "Mental things are alone real," Blake would find such legerdemain brutal—each item immobilized in its proper class and condemned never to interact with its contrary, and human agency itself buried alive in a syntactical network of passive voicings (rhythm "is cut," design "is determined"). The connecting agent is either remote, impersonal, marginalized, or displaced, at least according to Eliot's objective correlative or Pound's theory of the image. No, says Blake: Time and Space are "Real Beings" (compare the logic of capitalization informing both poets' spellings of *time* and *space*), and their interaction is organic and sensuous. The instrumentalist is lost, displacing creative agency from himself to the materials themselves; the self is sacrificed to history or to whatever blind historical process connects them.

The consequences of Modernism's overall departure from Romanticism are all around us, but I want to emphasize this one particularly, since it really

gives Pound a certain deserved priority. He tended to express relationships between the things we perceive much in the same way the members of a sculptural group are connected by viewers. He goes on to regard words as currency,
as possessed of material weight, and committing the Blakean sin of seeing with
and not through the eye, he spreads his language across the page as though language were sensation, to reproduce a mental effect or "image." To an extent this
accounts for Pound's sensitivity to semiology, as we see exhibited in the original version of "In a Station of the Metro." But his preoccupation with what
can only be called the physicality of words seems uniquely idiosyncratic, even
though later movements inherit it and pass it on with varying degrees of coherence. *Maximus,* for instance, is a thoroughly learned poem but not widely read
partly because Olson's preoccupation with the physicality of language leads to
a kind of gnomic cooing and doting over individual terms that, on closer look,
don't always yield up their significance. It doesn't help that it is owned down to
its very mannerisms by Pound's *Cantos* or that resolving its difficulties is what
used to be called "a German study"—time-consuming but not much fun.

But there are exceptions; while all poets are conscious of words, not all are
necessarily "word conscious" to the degree that words are given a near hieratic
weight. A poem like Williams's "The Attic Which Is Desire," where he frames
the word "Soda" in a square of clearly typed asterisks, is mainly a playful performance about writing technology in the late 1920s and not really about language
itself; as Kenner once remarked, it tells us the poem was written on a typewriter.
Moore built her poems by counting syllables, not metrical beats, and produced
rigorously policed, homegrown forms that let the work absorb, like an artist's
collage, the language she found in books and conversations; but she was no theorist, and her approach to language was untheorized and fairly conventional.
Cummings, for all his hijinks with spelling and typography, was only circumstantially an Imagist, first to last a love poet, and in his way a committed formalist. A generation later, the serio-comic tone that Ammons brought to *Tape
for the Turn of the Year* (1964), a "long skinny poem" he typed on a roll of adding machine tape, was the outgrowth of an understanding of literature as the
history of literary technique, of "substance running / through shapes of itself,
/ itself the running"; but Ammons, to be painfully clear, was neither slavishly
indebted to Modernism nor much influenced by Pound but closer in sensibility
to the Romantics whom Pound routinely condemned.

"To Pound," said the critic Massimo Bacigalupo of this problematic pre-occupation, "a full correspondence between reality and discourse is possible; this elementary mimetic hypothesis he never questions overtly," and as a result, "[Reality] is barred from the *Cantos,* not because it is 'vile,' as Mallarmé would have said, but because the page is the sole actuality, Pound's world is all told in his lines, it is all present, explicit, equally lit. . . . In other words Pound's poetry is primarily matter." Pound occasionally and fondly quoted an axiom from the Code of Justinian: *nomina sunt consequentia rerum,* names are the outcomes of things. The implications of so wholesale an acceptance of this philosophically difficult position on poetry's cognitive or pedagogical value are that there exist unseen connections between a poem's words and the things they name, between the poem's "world" and the "real" one we reenter when we raise our eyes from the page: the way is suddenly open to a hyperconsciousness about language that either masks or substitutes itself for old fashioned self-consciousness, and for a good deal else—from the Objectivists through the Concrete Poets to the L*A*N*G*U*A*G*E poets.

This disjointedness results, moreover, in a break in the relations between Imagist discursive strategies and the way communication "really" happens. This break produces a second result and one that appears so often to be the cause of the difficulty encountered in reading much Modern and Postmodern poetry: discursive materials, the verbs and modifiers that are the connective tissue of narrative, get absorbed, overt links between or among perceptions are suppressed, historical gestures used for exposition are compressed into allusions, precedent contexts are buried in titles or blank spaces (which are after all part of a text's physical design) or in the more in-your-face manner of footnotes, as in *The Waste Land.* So Hemingway, whose "experimental" period begins and (now that one can view his work historically) really ends with *In Our Time* (or *in our time*), buried the details of Catherine and Frederic's lovemaking, in chapter 14 of *A Farewell to Arms,* in the empty spaces between chunks of narration, or simply through implication, as in chapter 16, where Catherine is apparently giving Frederic a pre-op enema, by leaving all parentheticals out of the dialogue (and thereby also getting around the censors). *The Sound and the Fury* becomes instantly both more and less than a regular "novel" with Faulkner's late, 1945 addition of a full appendix to the original 1929 edition when it was later republished by Random House. Then there is David Jones's *Anathemata* (1952), with a lengthy footnote at the bottom of nearly every page. There are surely other examples.

The point is that the aesthetic vision behind the examples is the Imagist one, which is at bottom driven by a view of words as external *things* that stand for, do the work of, the external things they name, and of the poem as a purely print-bred enterprise. That this vision reflects a radical alertness on the part of writers to their private technology (the typewriter, the voice recorder, the camera) or to cultural influences in the widest sense (vaudeville, Cubism, the movies, the record player, TV) is an interest, but not the decisive one. The twentieth century's enthusiasm for a *visual* prosody does not arrive with Imagism: again, Mallarmé (*Un Coup de dés*) and Apollinaire (*Calligrammes*), to take two proximate examples, had already experimented with so-called "visible lyricism."* The question of concern is how far one can share in this awareness and evaluate it in light of formal, not to say technical tradition, or of the past. One wants to know—the average reader or consumer of poetry, if nobody else—how to read poetry impregnated with concerns so "untraditional" and connected so tenuously with the whole concept of reading as to render it beyond "normal" readerly comprehensibility. Does every poem need footnotes? Are you the snob for claiming that you can read Ashbery's "The Skaters" without a trot, or is there something wrong with the education system that produced you and me and probably so few like us? Or are we still talking about poetry and not something else?

Which, of course, is exactly the question Pound's letter to Cummings raises in its advancing of a visual hygiene of the printed word. The question is posed more dramatically by "In a Station of the Metro," which appeared in the April 1913 issue of *Poetry* in a very different form from the way it appears in *Lustra*. I reproduce the original version, where Pound spaces the words apart and stops the first line with a colon:

In a Station of the Metro

The apparition   of these faces   in the crowd:
Petals   on a wet, black   bough.

---

* The phrase was coined in 1968 by Renato Poggioli in *The Theory of the Avant-Garde*.

"In the 'Metro' hokku," he writes to Harriet Monroe, "I was careful, I think, to indicate spaces between the rhythmic units, and I want them observed." This order is stark in its implications: the spaces between phrases are absorbed as units of vision, not of sound, the eye having first been persuaded that each (spatio-temporal) unit rests in isolation from those surrounding it. The eye, in other words, and not the ear governs meaning. Still, it's a poem. So it's fair to ask, What are these spaces supposed to *sound* like? Ask two musicians and you're likely to get two different answers: a sustained note, an extended silence? Those metrical "rules" we learn in school help us to assimilate poetry to anticipatory patterns, patterns that yield listening habits, which are means of enjoying or at least of getting familiar with what we haven't heard before; it's a human instinct. But the rules are, as we eventually realize, arbitrary, and based on dead languages with vastly different rules for weighing sounds and writing poems. So this two-line poem—decisively not haiku—comes without directions, and does so deliberately. The spaces introduce elements we are unprepared to deal with. In place of what we expect—lines of a certain length, and at the least standard physical layout—is a design that distracts us from what we were raised to look for in poems especially, recurrent patterns of sound.

Scanning the first line is useless. It yields either a line of dactylic trimeter (if the scansionist is ready to elide the first two words and swallow the last syllable of *apparition*) or some bizarre enforcement of the pentameter (if he is tone-deaf). But even accepting either of those possibilities, what about

Petals   on a wet, black   bough,

a line clearly less dactylic than spondaic? Making the point this way (to borrow a phrase of Pound's) is to advertise victory by dragging your own heroic corpse around the walls. Each case cancels the next because the poem has deliberately set out to not only "break the pentameter" but to disable the scansion routines learned in ninth grade Latin. Conventional strategies are useless because they are blind to a poem's physical shape—how do we scan *empty spaces*?—yet the unconventional strategy here demanded is somehow too precious, even obnoxious. Is it creditable to give a sonic value to the spaces between the sounds without defining the *duration* of a pause, which is not just a musician's question? Should you drop in spaces of *x*-length between the elements in the manner of poets who inject melodramatic pauses via ellipses to paper over the obvious fact that the line might just as well break elsewhere, a way of dummying technique? The "pause" can be in fact either one of vision or of hearing, what Kenner called, a bit inconveniently, both "perceptual units" and "speakable units," or Pound "rhythmic units." Are they of the same length? And what after all is a "perceptual" unit—one eyeblink, or two?

What, moreover, about that hinted off-rhyme (*crowd / bough*)? And what, lastly, about the most interesting element, the fact that the poem has no verb? The action that takes place between the sight of the crowd and the remembered sight of the petals is unpredicated in the two senses of the term. No one element performs in both lines to bind them: as with Pound's aphorism, agency (human or nonhuman) is suppressed. Nor can single element in the strict sense be inferred from the ghostly sight of the crowd to the recollected petals: what is there about "apparition" to suggest "petals" rather than, say, "raindrops" or "revenant"? No Blakean imagination is at work here: it's been exiled. On one side of the ledger are the crowding "faces," on the other the "petals." What follows the colon is an aggregation of objects physically and psychologically independent of and forever separated from what comes before them. Not only is it difficult to describe what goes on, but it is almost impossible to decide what the precise nature of "description" even means. The destination or direction of what Philip Wheelright, compelled by this poem to neologize and divide metaphor itself into two semantic types—"epiphors" and "diaphors"—is equivocal: the critic cannot say what the poem says because speech and ordinary telling seem to be but a part of its operations. And the outcome, down the generations, is anyone's guess, from Lang-Po to Madison Avenue ("Indigestion? / Brioschi!").

This fussy and overlong analysis mainly demonstrates the scale of real vexation and sheer busywork this two-line poem has provoked among critics in the century since it was published. Aside from the skirmishes among those foxed in their attempts to find a place for it in traditional practice or the taxonomies of metaphor (the A-list includes Northrop Frye, Donald Davie, Hugh Kenner, Philip Wheelright, Terence Hawkes, and by proxy, Aristotle: nobody's happy with "one-image poem"), there is the problem that the poem is obviously about *something,* though about what none is dead sure. Kenner saw a Classical topos in the juxtaposed interior (train station) and exterior (petalled bough), a vague fingerprinting of Persephone's dual chthonian/ouranean nature. Davie takes it to another level of ingenuity with the proposal that the two lines deliberately transpose technical strategies, making the poem's subject its own technique.

It's too bad, because Pound had none of the devices of poetry, speech, rhythm, or measure in mind when he experienced his "metro-emotion." Or so he admits in the passage in *Gaudier-Brzeska* where he recounts his reaction to getting off the Paris elevated one day in 1912 and stepping into the steamy and a crowd of "beautiful" faces. "I do not mean that I found words, but there came an equation [...] *not in speech,* but in little splotches of colour" (my italics). It took the emotion, he goes on to explain, over a year to discover its proper expression, and length. To describe the shaping dynamic, he fetched out "super-position"— we would say superimposition—again either from graphic art or from early cinema. To risk putting too fine a point on it, this slideshow of visionary mattes had no literary precedent. It apparently translated so instantaneously from inspiration into visualized form that you wonder what "reading," here anyway, amounts to, and amounted to for Pound.

The question posed by Imagist practice, apart from the theory, is how authentic a contribution to traditional technical strategies it is. The Imagist looks for arrangements, for controlled environments of words that represent with physical immediacy his meaning, rather than interpretive proxies. So discontinuities of perception spill into the typography or semiotic arrangement; a poem concretizes, and shape alone asserts that a poem is a poem (Williams's "Poem") or that it looks like what it describes (Moore's "The Fish"). The extreme implication of such designs is that each word *is* each perception: to rearrange the signs is to rearrange the things they stand for. It was this implication that decades ago prompted an exasperated George Whalley (*Poetic Process,* 1967) to complain, "I should like to abandon the term 'image' altogether." To the extent to which we understand poems as "linguistic events," Whalley continues, "the element of 'meaning' must enter; and since utterances can only convey meaning as they unfold themselves in time, the element of time must enter. . . . Criticism, aesthetics, and poetics can profitably recognize that poetry is no more accessible than music, and that Poetic cannot operate unless the ear is engaged." Whalley isn't simply whining. "Linguistic events," as Whalley remarks not without reason, "are not themselves sensory": poetry speaks through measures of sensuous time and marks mental "events" in oral memory. "I made it out of a mouthful of air" means that historical memory is not burdened but released by speech in measures vocalized, line by line. A "visual prosody" runs in the opposite direction, and transfers the debt that consciousness paid to living memory to shaping and spacing, to footnotes, allusions, headnotes, epigraphs, formatting, the bare sprawl of signs. The poem is a "linguistic event" at the maintenance level of the page.

Attempts to dismiss the abandonment of traditional form by rendering semiotically unconventional poems like "The Red Wheelbarrow" back into a pair of tamer, "undistinguished lines of blank verse"—

so much depends upon a red wheel barrow
glazed with rain water beside the white chickens—

miss both Williams's point, which is not the narrowly aesthetic one advanced by the New Aesthetes about the persistence of metrical habits, and even their own, with its predictably lumbering reliance on convention and the conservation of so-called rules (what makes a line of scannable pentameter "distinguished"?). At issue is not the state of the art or the silly, pedantic job of romancing Poetry back to metrical health; it's the very status of human thought, which is thrown into doubt once memory shrinks into what it remembers, becomes the physical "burden of the line," and is disengaged from time. The question that Whalley raised remains whether subsequent history is capable of discovering in Imagism something that sustains its most striking innovations.

Five years after *Lustra, Mauberley* (1920) appears as his last attempt to craft a statement of ambition, and Pound's attention is divided interestingly between the technical and the thematic. *Mauberley* is so decisively an outgrowth of Pound's experience as the craftsman of *Lustra* that it may both productively and accurately be considered, despite the distance of a half-dozen years or so, as the immediate outcome of Imagist discipline. Pound was tired of London and everything connected with it and would soon head for Paris, then settle in Italy; *Mauberley* is also a leave-taking. A dozen years later Pound recollected how he and Eliot, disgusted with the old formalism of the Georgians and the New Formalism of the Imagists, "at a particular date in a particular room" "decided that the dilutation of *vers libre,* Amygism, Lee Masterism, general floppiness had gone too far and that some counter-current must be set going. . . . Remedy prescribed 'Emaux et Camées' (or the Bay State Hymn Book). Rhyme and regular strophes." He was always more interested in the arguments he conducts with

the world than in those he conducted with himself, and so produced a poem
that would concentrate his pedagogic passions ("an endeavour to communicate
with a blockheaded epoch") in a revolutionary technical way ("an attempt to
condense the James novel"). Though not *that* revolutionary: Théophile Gautier's *Emaux et camées* (1852) is in rhymed quatrains throughout, like the Hymn-
book that his confidante Eliot had grown up with.

Pound's approach to *Mauberley,* an autobiographical novel-in-verse, joined
his affection for the sculptural energies of Gautier's poetry to Imagism's major insights about juxtapositional narrative. The result is a De Chirico–esque
grouping of some fairly old-fashioned *vers de société* around the career of the
title character. The extent to which Pound was born again by reacquaintance
with Gautier, the Greek of Bion, and the poet who in the long run may be
Pound's truest Penelope, Robert Browning, is remarkable. Structurally the
poem, which is in two parts, is a complicated intersecting (or superimposing) of
two visions, or versions, of Pound himself. Pound as Pound apparently narrates
part 1, titled "E. P. Ode Pour L'Élection De Son Sépulchre," the tomb assigned
by the author to his persona, "Mauberley," who is killed off at the conclusion of
the second part (titled simply "Mauberley"). Each of the two major divisions
contains a series of disconnected portraits of literary personalities, and over the
whole there broods a disembodied cultural ghost, a maskless precursor of the
Tiresias of *The Waste Land.*

Mauberley extends *Lustra*'s moral preoccupations, with the difference that
Pound, seizing the opportunity for narrative, tends to type his "characters." It is
as though "My Last Duchess" had been written by someone more interested in
interior decoration than character, in Claus of Innsbruck's bronze seahorse than
on the life-and-death drama just recounted. Pound goes further in condensing
characteristic gestures of voice or personal details than one would imagine possible in a typical narrative. The two-quatrain sketch in 1:11 that begins

> Conservatrix of Milésien
> Habits of mind and feeling
> Possibly. But in Ealing,
> With the most bank-clerkly of Englishmen?

is in an obvious sense a version of the fate of the girl in "The Garden." All their
breeding reduced to trained instincts, "those her grandmother / Told her

would fit her station," such people end up in conventional suburban domestic settings with dull if uxorious mates. Pound is still puzzling through the consequences of robust sexuality overpoliced by a scrupulous and ever-vigilant self-consciousness. That two of the first line's three words are not in English notches one crucial difference from "The Garden," and the glib, syntactically clipped framing of these conversational rhythms notches another. If not transcripts, these poems are miraculous eavesdroppings into Pound's educated vernacular, with all its polyglot shorthand and mimicry. Like the conventional Imagist poem, *Mauberley* demands a reader with a literary intelligence subtle enough to supply not only the missing external transitions but the internal references as well. At the same time the prosody is formally familiar, the thematic concerns, like those of the *Lustra* poems, social and moral, and the overall effect aphoristic:

> All things are a flowing,
> Sage Heracleitus says:
> But a tawdry cheapness
> Shall outlast our days.

What results is the first of Modernism's long poems that is hard going without footnotes or a concurrent education in learned, Edwardian trivia. This is worth emphasizing: *Mauberley* is a preview, not just of the character but the degree of technical difficulty readers encounter two years later in *The Waste Land*. I would go even further: the latter might have been impossible without *Mauberley,* as a specific application of the same technique and through the labors of its editor. The telling difference, of course, is that the thematic burden of Eliot's poem is far more deeply personal, in that it is about the gradual dissolution of his marriage and not, or only distantly, about his disgust with English society.

The problem of immediate and postponed reference Eliot, of course, resolves with his footnotes, but here and in *The Cantos* Pound ignores it. The best example is from part 1, section 3. Through seven quatrains Pound moves, balancing his dismay with his present against unqualified praise of the past. A "tea-gown"—for casual around-the-house entertaining, uncorseted—is compared to the prized muslin of the ancient island of Kos, a "pianola" to Sappho's "barbitos," Christ to Dionysus, "Faun's flesh" to mechanically pressed communion wafer, and the sixth-century Greek tyrant Pisistratus to our elected "knave or eunuch." All of which merely lead to the final quatrain:

O bright Apollo,
Τιν' ανδρα, τιν' ηροα, τινα θεον,
What god, man, or hero
Shall I place a tin wreath upon!

This is the equivalent of a mic-drop; there really was nothing comparable in English poetry in 1920, when the poem was published. The Greek is from Pindar's Second Olympian Ode, and for those who can transliterate it, these six words—*tin andra, tin' heroa, tina theon*—set the stage for a spectacularly comical pun that reminds you, if you get it, that Pindar's poem is a prayer that in transliteration becomes near comical gobbledygook, so lost is it in its phonetic equivalents. The effect is like watching a sleepwalker wake up in a busy intersection; the past cannot survive unwarped transition into our modernity. Pound wants not only to make the point but, still an imagist, to dramatize it on the usual stage—irony. The result is a kind of radical parody, where each element comments on the other without communicating anything directly to it. The gross foregrounding of the allusion brings history into the "plot" of *Mauberley*. Artists working in other media and adding moustaches to the Mona Lisa or bringing live horses onstage were already using the technique. The problematical difference with *Mauberley* and its successors is that you cannot get the joke unless you know at least the Greek alphabet. Human indifference appears to rise, by the way, in inverse proportion to the scale of difficulty. In the 1988 edition of Ellman and O'Clair's *Norton Anthology of Modern Poetry*, all the key Greek words are in the original misspelled, with the correct letter *gnu* (here and elsewhere) replaced by the look-alike *upsilon*, killing the joke, and the point. Pound would have loved the irony. And on the page devoted to the poem on the current website of the Poetry Foundation, the opening line is misquoted (as "A bright Apollo").*

* In the late 1990s I attended a panel discussion led by the two coeditors of a new anthology of Modernist poetry, who accompanied their talk with fresh copies of their new edition, which they circulated. When one got to me, for the hell of it I went right to the endlessly problematic Pound entries, *The Cantos* and *Mauberley* and their transliterated Greek texts, and behold! The quotations

Another concern, of at least equal importance to the study of how sources
are brought to bear in Pound's work, is why things are being done this way, and
the answer in general has to do with Pound's desire to open the referential dimension so that the poet literally carries on his education in public, not to show
off but to educate his readership or at least whet its curiosity. The larger structures are related by association instead of thematic interpenetration, which is
the way allusions work, squeezing discursive chunks like fireworks into bursts
of meaning. The juxtapositional insight of Imagist poetry, or so one might think
of it, is nothing more than the extension of allusion from the level of the line
to the stanza. At times, as in the instance of Pindar or the allusion to Matthew
5:5 in "The Garden," meaning is teased from one into another context and the
effect is startling. The technique is in evidence everywhere in *The Waste Land,*
a fact that should surprise nobody given that its editor had already tried it out
in *Mauberley.*

In both poems, allusions come with internal as well as external vectors. Part
1, section 1 of *Mauberley* begins, "For three years, out of key with his time / He
strove to resuscitate the dead art / Of poetry; . . ."; section 2, part 2 ("*Mauberley*") opens an internal dimension by echoing the opening of part 1: "For three
years, diabolus in the scale / He drank ambrosia, / All passes, ANANGKE prevails,
. . ." The shared syntactical contours are at the same time alive to differences
between the overlapped figures: "E.P." and his Shelleyan antitype, the discon-
tented "Mauberley," who dissipated his spiritual treasure while Pound strove
to raise the dead. True accuracy concedes subtle differences, of course: Eliot
solves the problem of thematic interpenetration with his persona Tiresias, who
floats above the five sections like a mother ship, by giving each section its own
distinct headline, and by adding footnotes. After all's said and done, *The Waste
Land* is at bottom an expanded dramatic monologue whose original title ("He
Do the Police in Different Voices"), like it or not, is still its most decisive gloss.

---

from the Greek in the selections from *Mauberley* were likewise either misspelled or miscomposed
and had ended up like the Greek quotation of a decade earlier. The anthologists, gently challenged,
sheepishly confessed that they had no ready answer and offered as sacrificial victims their copyedi-
tors, who are always easy to pick on because always "fresh out of college" and never in the room to
confront their accusers. Human indifference may not just rise in proportion to the scale of difficulty
but apparently includes indifference to proofing your own work. On the other hand, a product roll-
out is a product roll-out.

Mauberley, though, is a bit harder to characterize. A correlation of *The Waste Land* and *Mauberley* would notch obvious differences: in genre (dramatic and narrative), point of view, prosody (Eliot's in mixed meters, most *vers librist,* Pound's in more fixed forms), format (Eliot includes footnotes), and especially tone (one elegiac, the other satirical). The decisive differences are thematic and tonal. The clearest example is the apparent coincidence that both poems contain an allusion to the *same line* from Dante's *Inferno*: "Siena mi fe; disfecemi Maremma." In Dante's original, the lines are spoken by Pia de Tolmei, whose husband, the Duke of Siena, murdered her in their castle: "Maremma," her hometown, "made me, and Siena," her husband's home, "unmade me." Eliot's translation of the line is nothing less than brilliant high parody—"Highbury bore me. Richmond and Kew / Undid me"—to which he adds a simple pointer to "Dante, *Purgatorio* V:133." Pound instead uses the line as the title of the portrait of a certain "Monsieur Verog":

Siena Mi Fe, Disfecemi Maremma

Among the pickled foetuses and bottled bones,
Engaged in perfecting the catalogue,
I found the last scion of the
Senatorial families of Strasbourg, Monsieur Verog.

John Espey reveals that the model for Verog is Victor Plarr (1863–1929), friend of Yeats, fellow Rhymer and biographer of Lionel Johnson. The poem fills four quatrains with "Verog's" reminiscences and ends on a bittersweet *salùt*—

M. Verog, out of step with the decade,
Detached from his contemporaries,
Neglected by the young,
Because of these reveries,

—which suggests to whoever, assisted or not by notes, has unearthed Dante's presence in the poem, that Plarr/Verog was "seduced" from Strasbourg to England and "unmade" by the change, but remained a decent enough representative of his age in the end.

Two years later, a reader turns from Pound's to Eliot's poem and sees this:

Trams and dusty trees.
Highbury bore me. Richmond and Kew
Undid me. By Richmond I raised my knees
Supine on the floor of a narrow canoe.

The result, in Pound, was social satire; in Eliot it is an intimate, bitter commentary on human sexuality. In Pound's, Pia's story is a bare road marker pointing to a source. In Eliot's, she is a major index to his poem's radical "undoing" or ironic reduction of the present and an expression of the decay of heroic and moral value over time. Like Pound's use of Pindar, Eliot's Englished Dante produces a terrific pun ("Undid me"); but unlike Pound, Eliot positions Dante in such a way that Pia is absorbed into Eliot's proxy, a girl seduced in a canoe, and frames the confrontation of past and present as a moral tragedy without surrendering Eliot's lasting, very American and deeply personal obsession in *The Waste Land* with the rootlessness of human desire, which for him explained the violated character of modern sexual pleasure. By simple contrast, Pound let the line resonate in both directions, neither containing nor excluding any meaning that would cling, and thereby highlighting Pound's own lasting obsession, the obliteration of historical memory and resultant cultural decay. His technique points outward, always toward the readership with which he could never break off lecturing, berating, attempting to educate. Unlike Eliot, whose personal disgust with what he describes seems evident, with Pound the personal element is deferred and absorbed into a persona, and then into history. By 1939 Pound will be scolding Eliot for surrendering to depression over the coming war by laying down *The Criterion*. As David Moody writes, Pound had "become preoccupied . . . with the paradox that while *The Waste Land* was a work of genius, it was yet one which threatened to negate what he held to be the essential work of genius," which presumably was to advance the cause of civic health. Powerful displays of personal feeling and expressions of "personality" defeated him.

For all of its satirical compression and experimental enthusiasm, *Lustra* ends on a note of earnest nostalgia for the past. "Provincia Deserta" is one of those rare poems (another is "Villanelle: The Psychological Hour") where Pound nearly exposes areas of the personal life he spent his career retrofitting as either cultural agenda or political insight. The poem is a rumination over a walking tour he made through Provence in 1913, but given the satirical beat of the rest of the book, his earnestness seems, at least at first, strained, or misplaced. The educated tourist Pound wanders around looking at what is and is no longer there, and the poem moves by an unusual, peripatetic logic of predication. Line after line begins with "I have walked" or "I have seen" or a similar expression. The tone in fact is formulaic, a series of declarations with an eerie likeness to the visionary syntax of Enoch's Gospel or Rimbaud's *Le Bateau ivre,* where the rhetorical emphasis evenly divides between subject and object, Seer and what he sees at once. So each line names something observed or heard, but unusually for Pound, each leaves the reader's attention suspended. Is it "the stream full of lilies" and/or the fact that Pound "peered down" into the stream that is important? The goal of all this irresolution is not immediately clear. A sentimental journey? Because there *is* in fact something about it that is painfully nostalgic, especially the ending:

> So ends that story.
> That age is gone,
> Pieire de Maensac is gone.
> I have walked over these roads;
> I have thought of them living.

Like his hero Browning, Pound was one of those poets who can feel nostalgia for a past he never actually experienced. In a book where the poems are in troubadour fashion directed to "go" here or there as though they were children, *walking* is a word alive with suggestiveness, and a prosody that ladders line by line down the landscape is imitating right down its tone Pound's own careful ritual of rediscovery in Provence. More to the point is that this book dramatizes Pound's discovery of his own multiple poetic fatherings and by that much feels suddenly prepared to be "let in," admitted to the tradition whose best sights and sounds he has prayerfully repeated. For him, these are not places but shrines; "I have walked," he says, roads that are both the country roads of Provence and the paths of traditional virtue, and all along he has thought of them "as living." Now then, we might imagine him thinking (though not saying aloud), *now that I have done this, I would be made part of it.* It's a curious echo of Keats's desire to be "among the British poets" after his death. *Let me in.*

There is an element of pathos surrounding the Imagist project's slow evolution into a neurotic fixation on historical continuity and a concurrent anxiety over a history emptied of meaning, into a province deserted by what gave it meaning in the first place. History to Pound was the opportunity that Nature was to the Romantic, a chance to wrest the personal from the impersonal. None seized it with greater passion than he or most of the American poetry that succeeded him and that we remember—Crane in *The Bridge,* Williams in *Paterson,* even poems less well-known nowadays, like Robinson Jeffers's *The Double Axe,* Benét's book-length *John Brown's Body,* or Masters's still lovable *Spoon River Anthology*. American poetry *primarily:* Modernism is a provocation to rethinking terms like authenticity, intention, historicity and personality from that distanced and long-exploded perspective of "impersonality," itself the child of what Arnold confidently celebrated as "disinterestedness." Pound's provocation, and Eliot's too, came from an American preoccupation with rootlessness and our own historical legitimacy. It is why Hugh Kenner titled one of his last and best books *A Homemade World*. To think of tradition the way Nick Carraway thought of personality, "as a series of unbroken gestures," was a blessing reserved for those whose ethnocentric sleep was undisturbed by the nightmare of immigration and emigration, rootlessness and nomadism that at some point has intercepted the work of every important American writer. America's history has wounded its writers into feeling deep self-consciousness about origins and, in a writer like Pound, produced an impossibly naive goal: the objective recording of history, history as it "really" was, a disastrous goal for a poet working in the medium most overdetermined by subjectivity. "For the moment," said D. D. Paige, editor of his letters, of the correspondence, "I wish to emphasize its impersonal quality. His letters do not concern themselves with 'private life'—with what he scornfully calls laundry lists'—but with the health of the arts." And so it was and remained throughout his career. At the same time, and like every other twentieth-century American writer who consciously or not has followed Shelley's lead, Pound's worry about the "health of the arts" came down to an obsession with poetry's epistemic value, about what it "knows," about the kind of information a poem might expedite to a public in desperate need of the truth and that he envisioned, and with terrible urgency, seducing to his side.

—1992

Brinkmanship

HART CRANE

When in "Words for Hart Crane," a sonnet from *Life Studies,* Robert Lowell named Hart Crane "the Shelley of our age," Lowell meant it as praise, not blame, though part of the reason must have had to do with what Crane's work and personality shared with Shelley's. Both wrote poems described variously as difficult, inaccessible, or in Crane's case, incomprehensible. Even Crane himself once said in a letter, only half-jokingly, "I practice invention to the brink of intelligibility." Both poets, moreover, had bad reputations—Shelley, the atheist who abandoned his first wife for Mary Godwin and who seemed always in flight from something, shedding a son along the way; Crane, the perpetual drunk who was both a closeted gay and an admirer of Whitman and, by the law of aesthetic commutation, of Romanticism. Shelley was the airhead who actually took Plato seriously and whom Arnold mocked as an ineffective angel "beating in the void his luminous wings in vain"; Crane, according to Yvor Winters, was "a poet of great genius, who ruined his life and his talent" by following Whitman, and a retrograde formalist who enthused over the wrong Elizabethans. Both had powerful fathers and iffy educations: Timothy Shelley was a peer of the realm, H. C. Crane a wealthy candy manufacturer who invented the Life Saver; Shelley was kicked out of Oxford, and Crane attended Case Western for one semester before bolting for New York.

Crane's career began on a high note. *White Buildings* attracted positive attention when it appeared in 1926. But *The Bridge,* published in 1930, was generally panned, and Crane was personally backstabbed in print by Yvor Winters, whom Crane had regarded as a friend, for what was once held as academic gospel but now seems the dumbest of reasons ("the impossibility of getting anywhere with the Whitmanian inspiration"). Two years later, when Crane committed suicide, he seemed on the verge of being totally forgotten. There was a

Collected Poems edited by Brom Weber in 1933, but it was a mess, riddled with typos and mistakes. Harold Bloom, in *The Visionary Company*—titled after a line in "The Broken Tower"—helped to energize the movement to recuperate his reputation in the early 1960s. In 1972, under who knows what compulsion, Liveright reprinted *White Buildings* by itself and corrected some of the typos. But in a new preface the poet John Logan enthusiastically misquotes line 4 of "Voyages II" (as "Her vast undinal belly moonward bends"). So much for proofreading. Fourteen years later—in 1986—Marc Simon's edition appeared, the only one free of sloppiness and at least attempting to be authoritative. Crane had by then been dead for over fifty years.

White Buildings was an uneven affair. The work at times seemed confused, overwrought by influences that were blocking him, crowding him out, disallowing him a place to stand in his own work. Everywhere he looked he saw luminaries like Eliot and Pound retreating behind masks (*Personae* is the title of Pound's 1926 collection of short lyrics) or "personality" dissolved and reassembled in exploded dramatic monologues like *The Waste Land,* which both impressed and depressed him. Formal models were out of fashion and being replaced or displaced by free verse and "experimental" forms. If you found in the literary magazines like *The Egotist* something that rhymed, outside of Cummings or Lowell it was probably light verse or unintended self-satire. In place of traditional "unmasked" lyrical vehicles, you had "one-image" poems pitched from odd or highly mannered angles. "Personality" was something you satirized, ironized, objectified, decomposed, or in any event, fled from, unless, that is, your name was Yeats or Hardy. Eliot seemed to believe that personality was a thin composite of personal anxiety and external culture, an embattled interface between inside and outside and something a writer had to "escape." One reviewer cracked that Eliot's first-person singular was the least personal pronoun in the language. Modernism was no country for Romantics.

This was especially so for an autodidact like Crane. He had no literary connections and not much of an education past high school, so his workshop was the library and the magazine rack at the nearest kiosk. Personality was not to him what it was to Eliot—the work product of culture, and from Eliot's point of view, a decadent culture—but a pitched battle, a competition between memory and desire. Just as Blake had to cook up a personal mythology, Crane had to devise a method for dramatizing that competition and turn it into a conversation without its becoming a psychomachia with symbols as the puppets and allusions as sandwich boards. So six of the twenty-three poems in *White Buildings* are staged as antiphonal exchanges between fictive others, Crane's better, recollected, or experimental selves.

It's impossible in an important writer to peel the how from the what, rhetoric from form; the rhetoric is always the structural outgrowth *of* the form. So the antiphonal, call-and-response mode became Crane's way of representing not the self's "fragmentation," which was the mode then fashionable, expressing itself in sophisticated personae and dense ironies, but its fluidity, a means of organizing a dialogue between what Yeats, stealing the terms from Shelley, called self and antiself. In Crane's poetry, imagination's sensuous complement is desire, and it is always physical desire, and always associated with his mother. What blocks desire is memory, which he habitually associated with his hated father, C. A. Crane. By the time Crane matured all this into something like a personal structural principle, the ironic objectivity and sham "realism" of many of his early poems had disappeared along with the mannerisms associated with Modernism. He had to grow out of them to grow into himself.

At the outset of his public career Crane left Cleveland and the family business, then dropped his given first name (Harold) to take his mother's maiden name (Hart) instead. Crane punned freely and often on both the words *heart* and on his mother's first name, Grace, in his poetry. It was a roundabout way of eliminating his father, or at least—if that's too dramatic—of bridging masculine and feminine identities, of uniting his memory of a confining past to desire, which liberates. The closing poem in *White Buildings,* arguably his masterpiece, is the six-part lyric *Voyages.* Its subject is love and closing the distance that separates lovers, and the structure of its first two sections is another kind of bridge, one joining the poet he was to the one he was becoming.

Crane's parents divorced in 1917, and for the next seven years he would hop back and forth between Cleveland and New York. But as a teenager stuck in Shaker Heights he was under the influence of Pound, Imagism, and especially Eliot. The narrative of his struggle against their influence, brief as it was, is in its way impressive. He had no degree from high school or college; his classroom was own bedroom, where he read the exploding number of little magazines that were appearing all the time. His apprentice poetry is filled with then-current modern (not yet Modernist) gestures—the copybook Classicism, the epigraphs in a Greek he couldn't read or by authors from the Latin class and the high school he never graduated from (he dropped out when his parents divorced), along with the echoes from Eliot's mostly rhyme-free, *vers librist* early lyrics, the lapses into Pound-speak—it's all there. He had to stop sounding like an Imagist before he could sound like himself, doubly difficult in the case of a closeted gay twenty-something in the Roaring Twenties who was still living in his parents' home and longed to move to New York. It would take him half a decade to admit to being bored with Cummings's typographical razzle-dazzle, Eliot's tedious, mopey whining, and Pound's satirical ironies and constant lecturing.

You see the beginnings of a shift in style and ambition in "Porphyro in Akron" (1921), an odd three-part practice piece that never made it into *White Buildings*. The fairest description of it is charming but confused. It's an attempt at a "persona" poem, where Crane aligns himself with Porphyro, the pagan seducer from Keats's *The Eve of Saint Agnes*. Section 1 is filled with layers of arch observations about American culture; section 2 is a chatty description of a Sunday afternoon among working-class immigrant families, with homemade applejack on the table and fiddlers at the front door speaking broken English ("One month,—I go back rich. / I ride black horse . . . Have many sheep"); and section 3 ends back where it began, in Crane's bedroom, where he's reading Keats and recollects a line from a French lullaby sung to him by his mother ("Connais tu le pays . . . ?"). In the end the combined tug of Keats and Grace Hart Crane pulls him back from the brink of a gooey, sentimental pomposity. The last two lines are an admission that "in this town, poetry's a / Bedroom occupation."

It's no wonder he never revised or included "Porphyro in Akron" in *White Buildings*. The poem is a failure, if an earnest one—of technique and self-enactment—down to the smallest details. That line break between the article and the noun in its concluding two lines, for instance, betrays the run-of-the-mill, mannered period technique that was falling in love with the jolting enjambment, meant to emphasize what followed or to copy the spontaneity of real conversation, and with the "broken" pentameter. Even the subject matter, for him, is odd. He never shared Pound and Eliot's prissy contempt for American provinciality; he could never have been an ex-pat, which is confirmed by his identification with Keats, the least cosmopolitan of the British Romantics. At the same time, Crane was never what's called a local colorist; the opening of "The River" section of *The Bridge,* which is otherwise a rhymed wonder, shows how bad he was at dialogue or dialect. So the subject matter alone grounds whatever rhetorical flights he might have had in mind and suggests that the distance between himself and Keats's Porphyro is permanent since the poem's structure and Crane's personality—he was never comfortable using a persona— doesn't allow a fusion of the two. Keats's Porphyro becomes a self-effacing iro- nist; Porphyro is more or less Prufrocked. Eliot's early poetry up to *Ash Wednes- day,* or to the point where his work was kidnapped by religion, is all about masks and irony. But Crane was never much of an ironist either:

> Akron, "high place"—
> A bunch of smoke-ridden hills
> Among rolling Ohio hills.

What would be backhanded pedantry in Pound becomes the self-consciousness of a twenty-year-old painfully aware of his lack of a formal (let alone Classical) education. ("Crane's mind was no bigger than a pin, but he was a born poet," Cummings supposedly said.) The flat diction and looped-in dialogue of section 2 owes everything to Pound. The biggest giveaway is the cadence. Here's Crane:

> And some Sunday fiddlers,
> Roumanian business men,
> Played ragtime and danced before the door,
> And we overpayed them because we felt like it

The anaphora and the forced bravado echo Pound in a contemporaneous poem like "Salutation":

> O Generation of the thoroughly smug
>   and thoroughly uncomfortable,
> I have seen fishermen picnicking in the sun,
> I have seen them with untidy families,
> I have seen their smiles full of teeth

and heard ungainly laughter,
And I am happier than you are,
And they are happier than I am,
And the fish swim in the lake
            and do not even own clothing.

Two poets describing the same experience—of getting down and dirty with *das Volk,* of nearly going native. But the tonal difference is sharp. Pound, I think, may very well be remembered as a Catullus with major ambitions, a satirist or a social anthropologist, who always gets close to but doesn't want closure with his subjects, either toothless fisherman or their untidy families. The only reason Pound mentions them is to position himself between their candid crudeness and the pretension of the British upper classes.

Crane, though, while he does his best to get close to those "Roumanian business men," instead comes off as overeager and condescending—the rich brat from Shaker Heights whose father owns a candy factory. Plus, the satirist is in his heart always a moralist by default, if a passive one who never moralizes openly. In his best lyrics, like "The Garden" or "Salutation," Pound is the lovable wiseacre you forgive because he can make you laugh, or think, and in the long run who is basically harmless, Stein's "village explainer." The trick of successful satire is to bluff and never reveal your hole card, to condemn without seeming to, so there is never a question of closing the distance between you and your target except through a persona, essentially a prophylactic. The same is true of Eliot, who sounded most like himself when he pretended to be Prufrock, Tiresias, or Gerontion. Unmasked in, say, the *Four Quartets,* he sounds like a church deacon who has read but hasn't totally understood T. S. Eliot. But ironic distance, poison to the lyricist, is most easily gained through masks: irony is a form of negative emphasis that inevitably produces a lasting sense of in-betweenness, diffidence, even inaction. Some sensibilities, like Crane's, or Stevens's in unconvincing poems like "The Comedian as the Letter C," not to mention Whitman, never master the modality, and instead of sounding ironic, they sound indecisive. The indecisive will never own their poems.

What rescues Crane (though not this poem) is Keats: "Full on this casement shone the wintry moon, / And threw warm gules on Madeline's fair breast, / As down she knelt for heaven's grace and boon." The three lines from *The Eve of Saint Agnes* are a life preserver, and the name Porphyro a synecdoche for Romanticism and everything about it that Crane's soon-to-be-shed masters declined to acknowledge; otherwise, the allusion adds nothing to the poem. It merely cushions it against the weak irony of section 2 and leaves you wondering if Crane/Porphyro had a good or bad time with those immigrants. Madeline's prayer for "heaven's *grace* and boon" leads to the liberating entrance of Crane's mother, Grace Hart, who is on the other end of that life preserver pulling in her only son. Crane could never resist the chance to pun, silently and lovingly, on her first name.

Voyages is a sequence of six lyrics commemorating Crane's love affair with a Norwegian sailor, Emil Opfer. It is the last and best poem in *White Buildings* and as erotic and revealing as it was possible for a gay twenty-something New Yorker to be in the mid-1920s. Crane's love life may or may not have some bearing on the way the sequence came together, not at once but in stages, between 1921 and 1926, when *White Buildings* was published.

"Voyages I," the opening poem in the sequence, is the outlier, probably drafted while Crane was still living in Cleveland. It is a reworked version, to what extent is not known, of an earlier draft of something called "Poster," a poem both unpublished and undated. My guess is that it is from somewhere around 1920, probably written after Crane quit high school but before he settled in Manhattan and went to work briefly as a copywriter. "Poster" stayed in a drawer for some five years until he salvaged it for *Voyages*. There, retitled as "Voyages I," it opens the sequence in a way that's remarkably flat and uncharacteristically uncomplicated and so hardly predictive of where it would lead or the rest would go:

Above the fresh ruffles of the surf
Bright striped urchins flay each other with sand.
They have contrived a conquest for shell shucks,
And their fingers crumble fragments of baked weed
Gaily digging and scattering.

And in answer to their treble interjections
The sun beats lightning on the waves,

The waves fold thunder on the sand;
And could they hear me I would tell them:

O brilliant kids, frisk with your dog,
Fondle your shells and sticks, bleached
By time and the elements; but there is a line
You must not cross nor ever trust beyond it
Spry cordage of your bodies to caresses
Too lichen-faithful from too wide a breast.
The bottom of the sea is cruel.

This is *Imagism for Dummies,* the kind of thing that ordinarily might have come out of an MFA workshop, had there been such things in 1922. With the exception of two lines—the astonishing lines 7 and 8—the syntax is flat and the impression it leaves deadening. But for that electrifying couplet—"The sun beats lightning on the waves, / The waves fold thunder on the sand"—"Voyages I" is an evasion, a young poet impersonating his influences and pretending to be "modern," a trick he fortunately never mastered. Its main attraction is that it is everything Crane's later poetry would not be: immediately *accessible,* "reader-friendly." Otherwise, "Voyages I" is a dud, an exercise in chatty description in a nonchalant idiom, sixteen lines of ho-hum lyricism that end with the preachy and pretentious "The bottom of the sea is cruel." Note, too: the first-person singular appears only once, in line 9. Again, it's classroom fodder, a homework assignment.

Which makes you wonder where that mind-blowing couplet came from: its denser diction and syncopated syntax are the first signs of the poet of *White Buildings* and of the poetry Crane will write later. In two lines he gives you a compressed description of the cycle of sunlight hitting ocean water that absorbs all four Renaissance humors: fire and air (*sun, lightning*), water (*waves*) and earth (*sand*). The movement is visual, kinetic—sunlight hitting the water's surface, breaking it, resurfacing on the sand. Of the fourteen words, moreover, twelve are unbreakable Saxon monosyllables. The details lock into the process they describe; they are interconnected, panoptic, iterative, and cyclic. The whole is one huge descending gesture (sun to water to shore) toward nature's violence (lightning and thunder), music (the sun *drums* the water; the percussion produces synesthetic *light*), and even food (*beating* and *folding*). And putting the couplet back into context, the ear hears—

And in answer to their treble interjections
The sun beats lightning on the waves,
The waves fold thunder on the sand.

—a loose-limbed alexandrine suddenly contracting into two lines of eight- or nine-syllables of tight catalectic pentameter that pull you up short after the singsong iambics that introduce them. Read aloud, the momentum of all those piled-up long vowels (be*a*ts, l*i*ghtning, w*a*ves) and doubled consonants that lengthen the short vowels (s*u*n, *th*under, light*n*ing, s*a*nd) works like a drag-chute.

My sense is that it was this astonishing couplet alone that prevented Hart Crane from throwing "Poster" in the trash; sometimes poets find their voice in unexpected places and then mislay it. It's tempting to guess that Crane at first probably didn't realize this was or that this would be his voice, his "sound." Nothing in the ambient literary culture came close to expressing a natural process the way this does—not at a safe ironic distance, where the evening sky looks like a man etherized on a gurney, but intimately, organically, erotically. This brings you close to a notion at the core of Hart Crane's poetics: all thought is essentially metaphorical. Thought and metaphor, which together form the language of feeling, cannot be easily pulled apart, if at all. The object is the subject; and "objectivity," along with the modish, estranging ironies it invited, he wanted nothing to do with. Neither did Keats, whom he idolized, as well as most Romantics excepting Byron, Blake through Yeats and Swinburne, Stevens, Williams, and beyond. The core curriculum of the poetic culture that surrounded him was therefore useless to him, though he didn't know it yet. It embraced lyricism that analyzed and discriminated, alluded and parodied, offered the lyricist an optional mask, and generally balked at such intimate conjunctions, or what Crane calls, in "Voyages III," "infinite consanguinity."

The biggest shock is how Crane pivots from that last line of "Voyages I" to the first line of "Voyages II":

—And yet this great wink of eternity,
Of rimless floods, unfettered leewardings,
Samite sheeted and processioned where
Her undinal vast belly moonward bends,
Laughing the wrapt inflexions of our love;

Even a tone-deaf reader, moving from "Voyages I" to "Voyages II," hears, if nothing else, the alteration in diction and intonation leading to the impassioned personification of the ocean, "this great wink of eternity." Then there's the punctuation. The dash, always a mark of breaking or bridging, identifies "II" as a continuation of "I," but the continuity is totally different in register, a Cinderella before-and-after. "And yet" announces not quite a reversal but a pumping of the brakes, somewhere between a contradiction and a qualification (what the manuals call a *catachresis,* a breaking, and *chiasmus,* or mirroring). From here on through the next five sections, the *Voyages* sequence loses interest in everything except what's most deeply subjective and erotic.

I remember reading *Voyages* at seventeen and wondering, as I got to "Voyages II," what had just happened. I was infatuated with Housman, Hardy, and Dickinson, finding my way through Whitman, just discovering Pound; I knew something about syntactic displacement and Imagism's so-called juxtapositional method. What I didn't know at the time is that Crane had gone back to something he had started and discarded five or six years earlier, a draft he hadn't been able to publish or had found so weak it held no clue to his future. A dropout, I was simultaneously reading the essays of that other, highly distinguished dropout, R. P. Blackmur, and chastened by his testy judgment of Crane. Blackmur lumped him with the (then, as now) vastly underrated D. H. Lawrence, saying, "Each is a blow in the face but neither can hit you twice," his larger point being the same as Eliot's vis-à-vis Shelley, or others' about Salinger—the sooner you're over them, the better. Naturally, the Crane whom Blackmur celebrated was the one who didn't delight in "obfuscating"—namely, the Hart Crane of slighter work like "Praise for an Urn" and "My Grandmother's Love Letters"— but mostly Crane's work drove him to condemn him as a "great failure," the manqué you made allowances for. He charged Crane with duplicity, then doubled back and blamed the obfuscation not on a deliberate plan but on sloppy work habits, the nature of which, unlike the tenured character assassins (Samuel Hazo, Winters), he implied but did not detail.

A year later, I read Unterecker's pioneering *Voyager: A Life of Hart Crane* and found out what Blackmur was getting at. Here's the scene: Crane goes to his room, already with something of a buzz, then settles in with his typewriter, a quart of Dago red, and a record on the Victrola. Typing to the rhythm of Cuban salsa or American jazz, he storms drunkenly around declaiming the poem and occasionally going back to the typewriter to change this or add that. I revered Blackmur (and still do). He was one of the few critics of the 1950s who said what was on his mind and wasn't owned by the academy or the publishing houses. Even when I struggled to disagree, I loved that he was blunt and hardheaded and often correct and not afraid to be dead wrong. (His essay "Lord Tennyson's Scissors" is a whole course in creative writing.) But by then I had begun to revere Crane, too, and had come under the influence of Crane's music, which was an intoxicant more powerful than Blackmur's prose. It was heady, rich, sexy, and unforgettable; it was metrical, like the other marginalized "formalist" I was discovering, Wallace Stevens; and it insisted on being read aloud. Without knowing it, I had been reading section 2 of *Voyages* so much I memorized it, which usually means one cannot stop *hearing* it. Obscure or not, with Crane a poem's intelligibility or "accessibility" is basically irrelevant because his music, like a good deal of what we love because it is so dangerous, can be so powerful.

What happened between 1921 and 1925, between the composition of "Voyages I" and "Voyages II," is that Crane leaped, from "Voyages I" and that stillborn last line, which is all tied up with memory and ancestral wisdom, into the "great wink of eternity" that begins "Voyages II." This was not just "revision" but convulsion, a radical break. A transformation of style is a transformation of personality—"le style est l'homme meme," de Gourmont said. You cannot change your style without changing your life. Even though it may come about suddenly, while, say, revising, it is more than "revision," as it is understood; revision is what happens when so-and-so confronts pages of line-edits and revisits something his peers just loudly praised or meekly trashed, or an editor had just queried. Crane's example was a more complete transformation, accomplished in isolation and not the result of collective commentary or wise advice. It's when a writer becomes the reader over his own shoulder, or becomes his own editor, and leaps over himself, a self-invention or self-parenting so complete that to say simply that so-and-so's technique had "matured" or that she had absorbed her "influences" just will not do. It can, I suppose, result in a change in technique or greater technical refinement, but technique seems to have little or nothing to do with it. We don't know when Emily Dickinson matured into the writer of a poem like "There is a certain slant of light," or even if the transformation I'm talking about occurred, though I'm assuming it did. But it certainly never made her into a supreme technician; she was too busy doing housework to worry about meter or master the *abab* quatrain or finish (let alone polish) some poems or hunt up a rhyming dictionary. But her departures, those failures that broke the hearts of grammarians and pedants who cleaned up her work and added and subtracted punctuation and made her up to look like Shirley Temple on the cover, all that now seems a small part of her greatness. Nor do material influences as such seem to matter all that much. Is "Gerontion" a great poem because Eliot had read and "absorbed" Laforgue or because he loved vaudeville? Is *Song of Myself* the product of Whitman's reading of the Psalms or the hours he spent at the opera? Marianne Moore loved baseball; Stravinsky loved *Gilligan's Island.* Go figure.

"Poster," which became "Voyages I," was—and Crane must have known this—basically an exercise in mannered description, and except for that single couplet, little but sixteen lines of tuning up, throat-clearing. The last line is finger-wagging, a mini-lecture: "let me explain myself just in case . . ." The lecturer draws a line in the sand ("there is a line / You must not cross") and tells nonexistent kids not to cross a nonexistent border. But there were no "brilliant kids" playing with a frisky dog, only Crane telling himself that a "line" had to be crossed. It was a line he had drawn for *himself,* though he probably didn't know it at the time, or at least until he crossed it, as is the case with most artists. On the other side was maturity—of rhetorical pitch and tempo, of lyrical structure—where he would find his own voice and, under wraps as it were, or as others have pointed out, in the drag of high artifice and conventional form, where he would learn to admit his own sexuality into his work. "Voyages II" is a signal flare: I am up here now, I have left that behind, *I have broken through.* Textually, if we need more than intuition to convince us, there is that dash, the "line in the sand" that he vaults over, that introduces "Voyages II." What follows may look like an afterthought to what you just read, or so he seems to be saying. It's not. It's *a corrective,* a violent reaction against those sixteen lines of tedious pedantry with only one couplet to save them; a corrective announced first by the dash, then two successive coordinate conjunctions that, so paired, seem nearly redundant until you speak them aloud: *And yet.* Each word receives some stress when vocalized (despite that short vowel, try reading the line without pausing after *yet*). And yet *what*? The answer is "this great wink of eternity." The actual sea has been replaced, suborned in an act of, at the time, preposterous metonymy.

The syntax and prosody of "Poster" even after its resurrection as "Voyages I,"
reflect the kind of work Crane would have been reading in 1920, the not particularly memorable, slack, free-verse performances of the Sandburgs and Lowells.
Crane not only declines to break the pentameter, but like that other renegade,
Wallace Stevens, he embraces it. Here, then, is "Voyages II," in full:

—And yet this great wink of eternity,
Of rimless floods, unfettered leewardings,
Samite sheeted and processioned where
Her undinal vast belly moonward bends,
Laughing the wrapt inflections of our love;

Take this Sea, whose diapason knells
On scrolls of silver snowy sentences,
The sceptred terror of whose sessions rends
As her demeanors motion well or ill,
All but the pieties of lovers' hands.

And onward, as bells off San Salvador
Salute the crocus lustres of the stars,
In these poinsettia meadows of her tides,—
Adagios of islands, O my Prodigal,
Complete the dark confessions her veins spell.

Mark how her turning shoulders wind the hours,
And hasten while her penniless rich palms
Pass superscription of bent foam and wave,—
Hasten, while they are true,—sleep, death, desire,
Close round one instant in one floating flower.

Bind us in time, O Seasons clear, and awe.
O minstrel galleons of Carib fire,
Bequeath us to no earthly shore until
Is answered in the vortex of our grave
The seal's wide spindrift gaze toward paradise.

Pound had insisted, against the Symbolists and Yeats specifically, that the "natural object" itself was always the "adequate symbol." But what are "crocus lustres"? Where do you find "poinsettia meadows"? What is a "sceptred terror" or a "minstrel galleon of Carib fire"? And do you mean what I *think* you mean by "wrapt inflexions"—two bodies jungled up in bed and wrapped in each other— and if so, why not just say so? You can only imagine the alternate universe where Pound (deeply baffled, agitated) supplies (cranky, obscene) marginal commentary to this poem the way he did for *The Waste Land*.

As for what the lines come to mean, the music is so overpowering that the "why of it" can wait, seems nearly irrelevant. For one thing, the lines, yes, actually *scan,* or rather, they nearly convince you that scansion has a value more than pedantic (though it doesn't). You cannot, or at least I can't, speak line 4—

Her undinal vast belly moonward bends,

—and race through it or run through that comma stop sign into line 5. There are too many long vowels and paired consonants holding you back, a fact that explains Crane's subliminal choice to front-load the noun *belly* with "undinal vast" rather than the way it was once misprinted, "vast undinal," which leaves a hole, or two empty feet, in the line. As blank verse, it's nearly Miltonic. It's a fat sound, a *thick* sound, hefty but without any Miltonic Latinizing of syntax or diction. The stroke of musical genius was stationing *undinal* and *moonward* at either end of the line. Both take about the same length of time to speak, giving the line equal weight fore and aft. The word *undinal* (from the Latin *unda,* "tide" or "wave") you would probably not expect to find anywhere outside of the Loeb translation of Catullus (*tunditur unda,* carmen 6:4), certainly not in an Imagist poem. Yet look at it, and how it works here: You not only "feel" the description, you endure it, experience it syllable by syllable, through the length of the line. The agonized physicality of the sea's bending—or its *being bent* by the moon—is concentrated in that triumphant pile-up of *n*'s and *r*'s and *d*'s. One reason Crane was an outsider is that he didn't always *sound* like his contemporaries, which was, again, the problem that faced Stevens, that other polished formalist with an ear and a fondness for traditional meters.

As for "meaning," this is admittedly not "The Red Wheelbarrow," which is just as memorizable and as difficult in its own very different way. The sea is "eternity," true, but it's also a "wink" of eternity—it flirts. We look; the eternal sea winks back. It winks because it is seductive, female, and fecund, and also because of light striking the surface, which is like *samite,* silk sheets. The sea *winks* at the traveler and the sun and possibly the moon, too. The traveler is no Odysseus, whose venturings were over a finite sea. Crane's sea is both the literal thing and eternity itself, which comprehends history, memory, and authority. The sea "laughs" and "laughs off" or laughs "with" the lovers, who are "wrapped" up in each other—both wrapped together and enraptured, one of the poem's more successful wordplays. ("Penniless rich palms" is a dud, and far less successful.) And when you come to line 4, that undinal womb bends upward in longing or in labor, and the poem turns into a delivery, a birthing.

Crane's compositional routine, stoked by wine and music on the Victrola, destructive or not, must have had an obvious and not-so-subliminal impact on his poems. The impact was not merely subconscious: there are allusions to music all over "Voyages II," beginning with *inflections* (line 5) and *diapason* (line 6), the simultaneous sounding of all eight notes in the scale. The word *diapason* is a bridge backward to at least four musical references in "Voyages I"—*ruffles* (a drummer's pressed rolls on the snare—as in Sousa's "Ruffles and Flourishes"), *beats, cordage* (not only cords of wood but a pun on a musical *chord*), and *treble interjections* (which tells you that there are at least three children on that beach). "Voyages II" grabs and summarizes their referential power in the climactic "adagios of islands." The sea's sheet music, meanwhile, is scored on "scrolls of silver"; the sea composes in one medium, its own, and reshapes another. By the end of the first five lines the poem has redeemed the potential of "Voyages I" and reclaimed what got lost in a clutter of inane, cheesy phrasing ("urchins contrive shell shucks") and predictable rhythm.

The *Voyages* sequence is above all erotic, and stanza 5 of "Voyages II" a complex minihymn to sexual love. Crane had no qualms about personifying things even in his earliest work. Eliot implicitly makes fun of the habit in the opening three lines of "Prufrock"—the sad-sack narrator looks at the evening sky and sees himself gassed unconscious in, say, a dentist's chair—and Pound had mocked the Georgians for overindulging in it as a bad habit. When you personify you implicitly talk to the object as if it can talk back; the animistic instinct is as old as the race itself, an artifact of an earlier vitalism when people talked to the sky and the sky replied. The objection to personification is that it

denies the object, "the adequate symbol," its objectivity, closing the actual distance between the human subject and phenomena and implicitly subordinat-
ing the latter to the former. Worse yet, personification is and was the stylistic
signature of the Romantic sensibility. To borrow from Buber, it implies that the
thou which Shelley invokes in "Ode to the West Wind" is actually listening to
the *I* of the odist who is doing the talking; it is what people do when they pray.
Crane was always an enthusiastic namer and exalter who had picked up Keats's
and Shelley's habit of direct address—"Thou wast not born for death, immortal
bird," or "Be thou me, impetuous one"—and this habit of direct address is the
exponentially more mature, not to say nervier complement to the antiphonal
call-and-response mode of slighter poems, like "Porphyro in Akron." It pops up
in "Voyages I" when he addresses the kids on the shore in that lame last line;
in "Voyages II," though, it pops up and stays up, right there in the foreground.
He addresses the reader ("Take this sea"), his absent lover ("O my Prodigal"),
a composite reader-lover ("Mark . . . hasten"), and those "minstrel galleons,"
which are preceded by a climactic double appeal: "Bind us . . . and awe [us]."
At which point he can only be addressing some culminating twin reader-lover,
with "eternity" looking on. All the poem's encirclings and enwrappings and
enclosings come to rest: the "wrapt inflections"; the "turning shoulders" that
"wind the hours"; the enclosing of the "floating flower." The completion takes
place "in time," human time, and in measures counted off on the pulse and by
the motions of the sea.

No wonder Crane asks—or mandates: it's hard to choose—that he and his
lover be bound and awed at the same time. "Voyages II" is a vision of paradise
on earth. I still wonder at those last lines:

> Bequeath us to no earthly shore until
> Is answered in the vortex of our grave
> The seal's wide spindrift gaze toward paradise.

How do we understand such tricky wording? "Bequeath us to no earthly shore"
might mean, *do not let the voyage end,* but a bequest is often made by one about
to die, so what follows the word "until" sets the limit of the voyage as death itself. "We," that is, are the two lovers, the object of the bequest, which seems to
be the point of the next line. But that line is made ambiguous by "the vortex of

our grave." A grave is a grave, a vortex is a vortex, but this is a grave that is also a "vortex." Plus, a vortex is active, violent, cyclic, even tornadic, like the sun beating lightning on the waves. It is the life-cycle itself. So going down, grave-ward, is actually a Whitmanian going forward, and the "vortex" is a cradle *and* a grave. The "paradise" toward which the seal gazes is the one the poem describes and that we have been gazing at as well. Its gaze is "wide" because it is a measure of desire. It is the "answer" to what the poem has been praying for, total *de-creation*, when our gaze will be wider and emptier than the seal's, will be purely creaturely, and we will die a purely creaturely death. Crane's vortex is ambiguous, but ambiguity like this is productive and, in its way, thrilling. "Death leads life forward," Whitman, America's premier sensualist, declared in "Out of the Cradle." Crane goes one better. Life and death are one motion, moving us in four directions at once, backward and forward, up and down, toward a source that is earlier than history and that never stops repeating itself.

—2018

Owning Wallace Stevens

Anybody remember Hugh Kenner? Charles Altieri's new study of Wallace Stevens* brings to mind, and back into the light, the competition, once thought settled, over Stevens's reputation that got underway with Kenner's offhanded dismissal of Stevens in *The Pound Era,* his 1973 study of Modernism that Charles Altieri, in his new book, calls "magisterial." Not that Altieri agrees with Kenner's assessment; yet Altieri raises again the issue of what Stevens and his work really is about, from whence it came, and the often-vexed critical tradition that has taken shape around it since the late 1960s. What do we know of a poet's moral imagination? Where do we find it, if at all, in Stevens?

Kenner claimed that, of the five major American Modernists he discussed—Pound, Eliot, Williams, Moore, and Stevens—"Stevens alone concerned himself not at all with *paideuma,*" or culture, and so he failed to make Kenner's final cut. The Greek word *paideuma,* adopted as the name of the journal of Ezra Pound studies and related to the title of Jaeger's great three-volume study of ancient Greek education (*Paideia*), loads his argument: unlike Pound or Eliot, promoters of Western culture who each produced an essay collection to mourn or celebrate it (Pound in *Guide to Kultur,* Eliot in *Christianity and Culture*), Stevens seemed oddly incurious, even unserious. His was "an Edward Lear poetic, pushed toward all limits," Kenner argued, to be remembered for "the ithy oonts and long-haired / Plomets" that pepper and pockmark his work. His poems lacked referentiality and his world was "empty of people . . . because [Stevens] is in the Wordsworth line . . . confronting an emptied Nature." Whenever Culture made its way in to Stevens's work, it did so as incidental, not centrally, but as accessory, like a dropped name in a conversation.

* Charles Altieri, *Wallace Stevens and the Demands of Modernity: Toward a Phenomenology of Value* (Ithaca, NY: Cornell University Press, 2013).

Reading Altieri's intriguing analysis of "The Man with the Blue Guitar," spread over several chapters, reminded me of Kenner's chilly assessment of the same poem from *A Homemade World* (1975), where Kenner gathered the leftovers from *The Pound Era:*

> "The Man With the Blue Guitar" ... takes off from the Picasso of the blue landscapes and emaciated harlequins, and offers the unplayed music, silent speech, unstateable statement which, obligated by the pressure of Picasso's vision, might be expected to issue from a guitar in a painted universe. ... The painter's works cling to its dimension, the visual, and share its muteness. Pictures do with the visible universe what poetry once did with the universe the visible universe superseded, the universe of speech, which traced everything to the logos and heard everything informed with divine and human voices. ... So Stevens allows the painter to precede him, performing the first selection, the first arrangement, the first concretion of images.

And Kenner wasn't done. Stevens's Modernist credentials were suspect. There were embarrassing allegiances (Wordsworth, Whitman), tell-all prosodic habits (Miltonic), and of course the silly, gassy neologizing. But all stylistic differences aside, Stevens's poetry probably made Kenner, a devout Catholic, squeamish. "Every agnostic supposes he is the first," Kenner remarked of "Anecdote of Canna," "and Stevens talk[s] as though his theme were the agnostic's plight. ... Matthew Arnold was saying similar things in 1880." The reference is to Arnold's claim that poetry would one day "replace" religion, a claim that by 1930 had begun to make his disciple Eliot so nervous that Eliot was no longer willing to allow Arnold a free pass into the sacred wood.* So he corrected him by adding a typical qualification: "Only when religion has been partly retired and confined, when an Arnold can sternly remind us that Culture is wider than Religion, do we get 'religious art' and in due course 'aesthetic religion.'"

Kenner's is nevertheless a crude put-down. Stevens, he implies, was going through continuing adolescence, a Shelleyan loss of faith, and advertising it in

---

* Wyndham Lewis's late judgment on Eliot: "Anybody with a tongue in his head, anyone certified born of woman, indeed any son of a bitch, can assume the laurel, as far as Mr. Pound is concerned— ... but for Mr. Eliot it is a matter of some moment to know if he has politics, and which; and, still more, what his theology may, or may not be."

poems like "Sunday Morning." The one-two punch of "agnosticism" followed by the reference to Arnold says a lot. Kenner found in Stevens only a highly refined aestheticism and a lack of moral seriousness. At best, Stevens got stuck in late French Symbolism and ended an art-religionist; at worst, he was Ogden Nash posing as a High Modernist, a dilettante who wrote nonsense verse. Unlike Yeats, who got himself unstuck from Symbolism in middle age (around 1907, with *In the Seven Woods*), or Eliot, who raided Laforgue for the rhetoric of *Prufrock and Other Observations* then retired Symbolism for good, the benighted Stevens was left gesturing at the things of the world as if they were the leavings from the poet's continuous self-revelation. Only the gestures remained, and if they evolved, they became postures, the work attempting but failing to avoid self-referentiality. Even early Stevens disappointed the fussy Kenner. In "Thirteen Ways of Looking at a Blackbird," Kenner writes, "[e]ach of the thirteen different ways of looking at a blackbird is a way of playing with the word blackbird, setting it in a miniature context, bounded by the shape of a stanza or the rules of a sentence, exactly as a painter might play with the shape blackbird, placing it somewhere within his rectangle among a gamut of accessories: trees, houses, glass coaches." "[A] way of playing," in other words, but hardly serious play. Similarly, "The Man with the Blue Guitar" is a so-so exercise in art criticism, a giddy adaptation that survives only because people can Google the painting. Again, Kenner: "since Wordsworth's enterprise foundered it has been the painter who has developed the only feasible relationship of the sole man to the mute universe."

At this point—and to advance the narrative—enters Harold Bloom, whose study of Stevens, *Wallace Stevens: The Poems of Our Climate,* was published three years after Kenner's study and is virtually a direct response to Kenner's hot embrace of Pound and Modernism's right wing. More than any critic behind the rehabilitation of Romanticism, Bloom reinstated Stevens and prized all that Kenner condemned. Bloom's approach might be, for simplicity's sake, reduced to this: a poem's meaning is always another poem: "A poetic 'text' . . . is not a gathering of signs on a page but a psychic stage upon which authentic forces struggle for the only victory worth winning." Most important, Bloom revealed that Stevens's "agnosticism" was not that at all, and that it had nothing to do with Arnold, "art-religion," or aestheticism. Rather, it was a test of psychic strength, what he characterized as the solipsistic stance of the major poet struggling to overcome the authority of the past. No coincidence, then, that Bloom reads the same poems that Kenner dismisses and comes to wildly different conclusions.

So, Bloom argues, "Sections I–IV [of "The Man with the Blue Guitar"] are the poem's opening swerve away from its own origins, *which have little to do with Picasso's painting* . . . and much to do with Romantic poetry, particularly with Shelley in his final year, 1822, writing poems to Jane Williams, one entitled 'With a Guitar, To Jane'" (my italics.) Occasionally the confrontation gets down and dirty, even personal:

> Despite several recent attempts to baptize Stevens' poetry by neo-Christian critics, a proper translation of *It Must Give Pleasure,* as of the rest of Stevens, could be: Christianity, as an unchanging fiction, has ceased to give pleasure, in that it has ceased to give poetry. . . . [P]leasure, for Stevens, as I said earlier, is a strong poet's pleasure, which is priority. . . . Hugh Kenner, out of his general distaste for Stevens, unamiably observes that Stevens, like every agnostic, wished to believe that he was the first agnostic. I suspect that the burden here for Stevens, here as elsewhere, is simply Whitman.

Kenner, a devout Catholic, had no choice but to misread (weakly) Stevens's deliberate dissent from High Modernist practice—from its emphases on juxtapositional structures (what Pound himself called "super-position"), open, nonmetronomic prosodic habits, allusiveness, and the reliance on myth (or "mythopoesis")—and view it as unforgivable. And the reason, of course, is that Kenner had repeated the same mistake that every New Critic up until 1977 (when Bloom's study appeared) had been making by following the lead of Pound, who in turn had followed Arnold in reading the Romantics out of meeting, especially Wordsworth ("Wordsworth is a dull sheep," Pound says in a letter), Byron sloppy ("Byron's technique is rotten"), and Whitman an embarrassment.[*]

---

[*] Professional critics always have the same arguments even when changing the terms. Take the following case, a back-alley brawl between R. P. Blackmur (*Language as Gesture,* 1954) and Yvor Winters (*In Defense of Reason,* 1947). Blackmur, ever the gadfly and then and now a better critic than Winters, had a feel for language at the molecular level that allowed him to overlook what Winters condemned—Stevens's poems' tendency to be "about" nothing. The author of what is still among the best introductions to late Modernism, *Form and Value in Modern Poetry,* in the deliberate wildness, even goofiness, of Stevens's work Blackmur saw exactly the habit that enabled him to mature from

Bloom's program has been out there for fifty years and needs no recap: a poem is an act of repression, an "achieved anxiety"; what is repressed is never bare "textual" evidence, and cannot be recovered by tracking down allusions and archetypes in myth and in the history of form, and certainly not in working through the footnotes, compiling concordances and crawling through the biographies of the great. A work like John Livingston Lowes's *The Road to Xanadu* (1927), subtitled "A Study in the Ways of the Imagination," was a classic New Critical image study that sought to unpuzzle Coleridge's "Kubla Khan," and altogether fun to read. Amiably written, reprinted into the 1950s, it nevertheless ends where it began, in mystery, detection without a clear solution, and it tells us less about the ways of the imagination than about the energetic labors of exegetes and their materials. So, where Kenner sees "The Man with the Blue Guitar" as inspired by a material source ("the obligating pressure of Picasso's vision"), Bloom sees a deliberate bypassing of or "swerving" away from any mere *source,* such as the picture by Picasso captured in Stevens's title. Stevens's swerving tack decreases the actual source or point of reference in order to re-create it and enter "the triumphant solipsism or isolation that allows [him] to cross into the pure irreality of his Sublime." Translation: there are no material "sources" to sniff out in the case of Stevens or of any great poet; the transition from the object as a limitation of vision (a mere "source") to a powerfully absorbed (or "solipsized") intensification is the poem itself. The poem exists in a virtual state between subject and world, but its truth is always personal, or rather interpersonal, as between sons and fathers, or the living poet and his influences. By comparison, for Kenner and the New Critic, because history runs downhill and only in one direction (Athens through Rome to London to, we gather, Armageddon), culture is a continuum, and the goal is *paideuma,* that ponderous updating of Arnold's "the best that has been thought and said in the world," which leaves the individual poet stuck having to choose which tradition to pursue, the expressive (Romantic) or the mimetic (Classical). Bloom takes the more radical Nietzschean tack: the poem, and the lyric poem especially, is a competition (his

---

the sour poet who wrote "Comedian as the Letter C" to the poet of *Notes toward a Supreme Fiction.* Winters's dislike of Stevens, in contrast, seems a twisted continuation of his grouchy condemnation of *The Bridge.* Winters hammers Stevens for being engaged in self-parody and prophesies what Kenner had to say a quarter century later.

word is *agon*) between what we feel and what is real, a staging of the struggle between self and world, which *is* morality.

If all of this seems a long way of getting around to Charles Altieri's new book, it is partly because Altieri seems involved in a salvage operation, at the very least in intervening in this dustup over Stevens's reputation between the (old) New Critics and antagonists like Bloom et al. His book happens to be, not incidentally, the second critical study that has come my way in the past six months concerning Stevens and his "ethics" (a word that appears in their subtitles), or his lack of them. Each seems part of a larger moral undertaking within the context of Modernist scholarship to rehabilitate the poet for a younger readership disturbed by the work's failures or refusals to register its context of composition, ever to mention politics or the violence of the world around it.

There is also Stevens's uneasy relationship with his own contemporaneity and its politics, and specifically to World War II, which he somehow managed—unlike every other major poet of his generation—not even to mention in his work, except obliquely. With the exception of the unexceptional *Owl's Clover,* which is not included in the trade edition of *The Complete Poems,* Stevens's poetry acknowledges only indirectly not just global politics but the two major world wars he lived through and that chronologically frame the bulk of his work. We recall how Robert Graves castigated *The Waste Land*'s maudlin serenading of the collapse of a world for which Eliot, who spent World War I working in a bank, did not do battle; but at least Eliot acknowledged both that war and the one that followed, which he spent in London. So did Pound, in an exceptional passage from *Mauberley,* H.D. in *Trilogy,* Williams (whose two sons served in the Pacific), Cummings ("Plato Told"), and even Marianne Moore ("The Fish"). Their work, while not strictly partisan or "political," showed at least some bare awareness of ambient history. The irony is that where you find the ethical sense most dominant in the work of major Modernists—Eliot, Pound, and Yeats— you are embarrassed or put off by its expressions, or to be blunt, are dismayed that the latter two were clearly fascists and arguably, Eliot too. But other than scattered, coolly aloof nods at contemporary events, Stevens seemed indifferent to them. You think, say, of the coda to "Notes toward a Supreme Fiction"—

Soldier, there is a war between the mind
And sky, between thought and day and night

—where the poet's struggle to unite pathos and ethos is compared to actual
"war," or how in the next stanza he compares soldiers marching in a military
parade to a poet's own "Virgilian cadences, up, down / Up down," and still you
want to ask, are you kidding? Written the same year as Midway, Guadalcanal,
and Stalingrad, and this all you have to say?

Altieri's "project" (to use his word) is to reposition Stevens within Modernism without binding him to its technical agendas or its for the most part reactionary politics. The problem with Stevens (though this is not something Altieri
mentions) is the same that critics of Hart Crane have faced: positioning him in
the Modernist canon and coming up with a more convincing and more eupho-
nious tag than that clunky term from the 1980s, "Romantic-Modernist"; free-
ing the work of the taints of aestheticism, "impressionism," know-nothingism,
and dilettantism; and identifying its ethical center and how it constitutes a way
of thinking ethically and morally about the world. The task is difficult, and at
times nearly impossible to map clearly, but his process, which entails some invented terminology, a terrific discussion of metaphor, and a final, puzzling diva-
gation on Wittgenstein, assigns Stevens and his work a varying in-betweenness,
where the phenomenological problem posed by the Romantic lyric—becoming
the subject of one's own subjectivity—is renegotiated and viewed as a much-
intensified form of irony.

So, while Stevens borrows from the Symbolists, and while "we can see in
symbolism a lineage for much of *Harmonium*," Stevens was never a Symbolist,
partly, Altieri argues, owing to his reading of Nietzsche. According to Altieri,
"For Nietzsche, the ethical is wrong from the start. It entails separating human
life into domains like ethics and aesthetics, which then must posit some external criterion that has the authority to make such divisions." Nietzsche's solution
was to collapse morality itself into "the concept of 'art,'" conferring on art real
epistemic value. While Altieri cannot quite go so far as to join Hallam and the
expressivists and their great original, Shelley, in idealizing poetry, he can add his
voice to Nietzsche's in claiming that it constitutes a form of moral knowledge.
This puts vast space between Stevens and Arnold and Arnold's apologetic double, Eliot, for whom a poem mirrors an objectivity that gives pleasure but has

no essential truth-value. A poem is somehow both—an affirmation of value that proceeds, in Stevens, by saying *no* to any fixed, positive value.

To complete this series of commentaries on "The Man with the Blue Guitar," I give Altieri's:

> To be truly modern, "The Man with the Blue Guitar" suggests, in contrast [to "The Idea of Order at Key West"], is to develop negative forces that do not give up their resistance to any form of positive meaning. In particular the poem offers an interpretation of Picasso's "destructions" stressing two fundamental kinds of violence. First, the poem never quite realizes attunement with nature except under the guise of the will of the guitarist. The various voices and moods and levels of diction aggressively pursue their own powers. So the work has no choice but to stage modernist juxtaposition as its basic composing of the senses. Here Picasso's influence entails the destruction of any kind of fluidity or casual expansiveness of mind because those traits would appear as simply an effort to tie the imagination to an outdated rhetorical means of presenting artworks. Second, Stevens' version of Picasso's modernism seems to require the total suppression of the old gestures of understanding that might also be considered outdated rhetoric.

Altieri's care in preserving some crucial distances and differences is impressive, principally those separating the Modernist contributions ("juxtaposition") from the Romantic ones (those "old gestures of understanding" nature) and, second—though this is not part of his enterprise—the difference between Freudian anxiousness over influence and what Kenner meant by "source." "The Man with the Blue Guitar" in Altieri's reading, with which I agree, is a subtle, nearly Po-Mo parody of Modernist "juxtaposition" performed through its prosody. Couplet follows couplet in so robotic a way it turns the result into a herky-jerk absurdity. The pentameters are cut down to tetrameters, the anticipated rhyme scheme randomly short-circuits itself, and the lines stiffen into rows of manic parataxes—anaphora gone crazy. Speaking them aloud, a reader comes away thinking less of the couplets of Pope or of Picasso's painting than of Dr. Seuss: "They said, 'You have a blue guitar / You do not play things as they are.' // The man replied, 'Things as they are / Are changed upon the blue guitar.'" The poem is not only one of the most estranging works of Modernism but a hybridization of conventional irony: the poem's target is *itself* and its technical and cultural resources—in other words, what Eliot meant by Tradition and what comes of following it blindly.

Altieri's approach is disciplined. He reads not just Stevens but the whole of Modernism through the doubled perspective imposed by considering the lyric poem as a phenomenological event. He terms that approach, with its self-ironizing potential, "aspectual" thinking, which is a "perspectivism [turned] inward so that it [does] not express a point of view so much as enable a continual exploration of resemblances[,] allowing a particular subject to participate in what it perceived." Substitute *subjectivity* for "perspectivism" and you have the High Romantic lyric mode, where nothing *is* but as it might be viewed through the intricately evasive *as* (the unvoiced pun buried in *aspectual*), *like,* or whatever device introduces an imaginative figure. The Imagist discovery, by way of contrast, was to create a field of metaphoric tension in which the tenor and the vehicle remain in equipoise. The result is that neither is given ultimate priority. Stevens's approach, on the other hand, forces Altieri to increment each application of "aspectual thinking" with a new twist or nuance and to add explanatory layers, which are helpful but not always clear and lead to some laboriously unclever asides: "Aspects," as he says in a particularly jaw-breaking moment ("Aspectual Thinking"), "are the 'asness' of participation that gives the 'is' its force as realization," which seems an overworked way of saying that figurative language is a special case (or a particularly tricky setting) of consciousness's awareness of itself and that Stevens's poetry plays out this self-awareness on the page, by accumulating verbal figures or vehicles pointing to some provisional, shifting tenor. The *aspectual* opens the range of reference to the other arts (the multiplied perspectives of Cubism, for instance, as well as film), as I suppose it must: the word's etymological root is related to *seeing*. The clear implication is that Stevensian technique stages its engagement with Modernism as an end-around Modernist practice and its positivistic embrace of objectivity.

At the same time, the traditional shapes that metaphors take, "the old gestures of understanding," are also altered or "suppress[ed]." Instead of the conventional stop signs, such as *like* or *as if,* a Stevens poem often performs its meaning in a manner that straddles the metaphorical and the analogical, often by a stacking of appositives, decoupling the vehicle from the tenor, sometimes by omitting the tenor altogether, and sometimes through exactly the odd, distracting sound effects that Kenner mocks and later Yale critics, namely Hillis Miller, defend. (Among the incidental pleasures of this book is Altieri's attention to the nuances of prosody, to how a poem actually sounds.) Stevens's practice flirts with the notion of language's transparency and at once negates it. Altieri calls this "a way of attaching the mind to the world that does not submit to description," and, in *Harmonium* especially, the result is a sense of there being "no aboutness" to the poems. Yet description is always "of" something both independent of the describer and dependent on him, for which reason it is exactly the "aboutness" of his poetry that is at issue. What's implicit is that "there is / No way out of the problem of pathos vs experience," as Ashbery says in "Self-Portrait in a Convex Mirror." A poet must commit himself either way to a life of feeling or a life in the world. What, then, is the status of ethical representation in a Stevens poem with respect to the Modernism that surrounded it?

"I desire . . . to resurrect the art of the lyric," a thirty-something Pound wrote to Margaret Anderson in 1918; "I mean words to be sung." The two words here that stand out are *art* and *sung,* either of which links Pound to traditional mimesis and rhetorical practice. As Altieri sensibly notes, "Neither Williams nor Pound could suffice as a model." What was required was a way of "reading against traditional assumptions about lyricism"—the foregrounding of the lyrical host or "I," for instance—"because the agency involved is not overtly expressive but embodied within shifting relations between sensation and abstraction." And what follows for Stevens was a period of vigorous and continuous naysaying, a sustained refusal to use the time-tested resources that staged the epistemological situation, the ways that we know the world, in the usual ways—the subject cleanly severed from the object world or left in Imagistic equipoise with it. Here is Altieri's application of the *aspectual* to Pound and Stevens at once:

> The aspectual can be fully present only if we recast modernist expectations about the image. The image cannot be a picture of fact. More important, the image cannot be the primary evidence of the power of imagination in the world because even the fusion of imagination and fact that Pound idealized creates a *fixity* and self-congratulatory emphasis on the privileged moment that mistakes the potential force of an ideal of participation. One might say that the Poundian image celebrates the result of specific acts of participation. But that image also has to point to itself as the fulfilling of a chain of impressions and

desires that produces an object now ultimately outside of ordinary time. Stevens cannot quite deny that there is a timeless dimension to art. But he can recast that dimension so that it is seen to result from an act of self-reflection on and within process.

This is, in fact, pretty close to a perfect description of the basic Imagist assumption of the transparency of the sign. In *Gaudier-Brzeska: A Memoir,* Pound claimed that the point of Imagism was to offer the world a new way of looking at things and not at *a specific thing.* Instrumentalist to the last, he insisted that the Image resisted reduction to the simplicity of the symbol. This was Pound's way around the problem of recovering a belief in imagination as inherently a supersensual faculty, Coleridge's "echo in the finite of the infinite," or in Anima Mundi and the occult, which is where Yeats locates it. Which, of course, raised another problem, spied out long ago by Frank Kermode: the "self-congratulatory emphasis on the privileged moment," as Altieri points out here, is and has been the burden of the lyric poem since Wordsworth. It created a tricky situation, then, for the Modernist who happened to think it through, either inside or outside of his poetry, and Pound never did. Pound, who tried to free himself completely from Romantic influence, reaches the climax of *The Cantos,* and some might argue his career, by falling back on Whitman and quoting him in the most celebrated section of *The Pisan Cantos.* Stevens, on the other hand, navigates a path through both Romanticism and Pound and "modernist expectations about the image," discovers a style of his own that pivots between Modernism and Romanticism, and finds himself (or his work) either shunned or occupying actually a strangely unique place in the Modernist canon.

An ethos is a recognition of the limits of human behavior. Among the oldest philosophical questions is the identity of the agency that imposes those limits. All the major religions have assigned the agency to a divine being; Rousseau's social contract was the Enlightenment's way of repealing that understanding. Yeats (and less specifically Emerson) went further, and identified that limit with "Fate": "Among subjective men (in all those, that is, who must spin a web out of their own bowels) the victory is an intellectual daily re-creation of all that exterior fate snatches away." The agnostic, the atheist, or the secularist will assume that such limits are nearly always the product of consensus. So must the lyric poet. Unlike those of the narrative or dramatic modes, the ethical border of the lyric is what Eliot called personality and Yeats called the self. After Wordsworth, the lyric stance implicitly claimed the whole of the "moral" realm to be inferior to the realm of the free human subject. Outside becomes inside, and the moral and the aesthetic are conjoint, avoiding exactly the contradiction that Nietzsche points out and then resolves by saying, no, there is no difference between the ethical and the aesthetic. The difficult moral position in which this puts the lyric poet rises to a whole different register in a century of two major global wars, economic depression, mass extermination, and the invention of the thermonuclear bomb. The context of composition, once revealed, becomes part of the work itself; it becomes for some a matter of moral urgency to know, for instance, not that Coleridge plagiarized or that Poe suffered from multiple addictions but that, from his idyllic depiction of Tintern Abbey, Wordsworth eliminated the homeless vagrants who slept on the sward that was "green to the door" of every cottage, and that he was likely spying for the Crown in the junket to France that produced *The Prelude.* For some, it becomes of more than passing interest that Hawthorne was a racist who held that urban white workers "are ten times worse off than the Southern negroes," that what had really got under Arnold's skin in "Dover Beach" were the tides of immigrants coming to England, or that few women of any race were allowed to rise to positions of solo dominance in the arts.

Among the earliest diagnosticians of the moral dilemma facing the lyric poet, the most theoretically sensitive and astute was Coleridge. Coleridge's poems constantly elude the Wordsworthian elevation of the self and solipsistic self-containment by retreating to the sentimental grounds whence all poems start—marriage, domestic responsibility, friendship, even the nursery. Years ago Gene Ruoff noted how Coleridge's poems "undermine claims for the self-sufficiency of either the individual poetic imagination or the monological lyric." Coleridge has never, as far as I know, been credited with having invented in the Conversation Poems a kind of pre-Confessional poetry, though perhaps he should. While this is not even distantly the subject of Altieri's book, the truth-value of metaphors and the epistemic content of the poems in which they appear is something that Stevens must, like Coleridge (and unlike Pound), have thought hard about. I sense that this is basically what "The Comedian as the Letter C" is all about (along with being, like *The Waste Land,* an anguished commentary on an unsatisfying marriage), and maybe why it disappoints.

In comparison, Pound's desire as a still youngish man, "to resurrect the art of the lyric," seems not only uninformed but overripe, maybe irresponsible. It includes no understanding of the existential complexity of the lyricist's situation for the simple reason that Pound, ever caught up in disputes over their technique and disinclined to honor "the personal element," refused to recognize the contribution of the Romantics to poetic theory. Eliot was no help, wary of the tendency to "corrupt our feelings with ideas" and resisting looking past the surface of a poem for something more, and famously dismissing *The Waste Land* as "the relief of a personal and wholly insignificant grouse against life." As Altieri says, the poetic "image also has to point to itself as the fulfilling of a chain of impressions and desires that produces an object now ultimately outside of ordinary time." He is obviously thinking here of Eliot's objective correlative, which is paradoxically an attempt to describe subjectivity and as unsatisfyingly far as Eliot own thinking got him, in which the "emotion" evoked "terminates," like a plug in a socket, in the physical object. It must in other words participate in and actively reflect the circumstances of its production. The particularly confining character of the lyric is one of its characteristics as a genre, and it hardly matters whether the lyric is Wordsworth's daffodil poem, Shelley's "Ode," Pound's "The Garden," or Percy Sledge's "When a Man Loves a Woman." "Pound's most glorious moments," Altieri says in an inspired footnote, "are when he joins fact with a commitment to participation in what beauty affords."

Stevens's philosophical situation is peculiar because he was nearly alone in confronting its complexity, and he does so mainly in the poems themselves. His approach to his own work positions him like the woman having the anxiety attack in "Sunday Morning" who needs to be scolded by the narrator, echoing Whitman, that "Death is the mother of beauty." Or appositely, he is like the Muse-like narrator of "The Idea of Order at Key West," who "Knew that there never was a world for her / Except the one she sang and, singing, made." Through her voice,

> . . . the glassy lights,
> The lights in the fishing boats at anchor there,

As the night descended, tilting in the air,
Mastered the night and portioned out the sea,
Fixing emblazoned zones and fiery poles,
Arranging, deepening, enchanting night.

"Poetry," Altieri nicely remarks, "must enchant within the parameters of a disen-
chanted world," but what precisely Stevens intends by *enchanting,* here at least,
is hard to tell. Yet *enchantment* must still somehow not be a self-justification
for high, self-jazzing rhetoric; it must do something in the world by enlarging,
not eliminating, feeling and passion. It must purify by refining, not negating.
It must see the nothing that is not there and the nothing that is. If nothing else,
it must entertain. The Key West Muse is troped into a figure of the lyric voice,
which occupies what it makes and in its isolation realizes that it has nothing
to teach the world and owes nothing to history, or culture. Or, as in "Reply to
Papini," a minor poem that Altieri associates specifically with "aspectual thinking," the powerful word *enchantment* recurs and is linked to the processes of
apprehending and *perceiving:*

These are hymns appropriate to
The complexities of the world, when apprehended,

The intricacies of appearance, when perceived.
They become our gradual possession. The poet

Increases the aspects of experience,
As in an enchantment, analyzed and fixed

And final.

It wouldn't be going too far to call such poems "hymns" since they celebrate
their own power to enchant, and when, as here, the proximity of *apprehended*
to *perceived* echoes Wordsworth on the creativity as well as the *limits* of all perception. The point is the intense—Yeats would say tragic—finality of all experience, when intensely felt. So it is that the Key West Muse suffers (in the literal
sense) both the pang of creativity and its moral outcome, why the elders who

glimpsed Susanna "felt / The *basses* of their beings throb / In witching chords," why the one who perceives the jar sitting on that hill in Tennessee can measure both its power over his perception and his own limitation as perceiver—why, in other words, one must have a mind of winter.

And it's interesting how "The Idea of Order of Key West" foregrounds the word *order:* the maker is the totality of what she orders, but also her own problematic. She is not quite the equivalent of the God that broods over Void—Stevens would never go that far in reverse—but a providential extension of her own sensuous agency, an Emersonian avatar, or a version of the Classical muse. Her song masters the chancy plasticity of what it orders, and for the Horatian formula (*doceat, moveat, delectat*), substituting its American version, *arrange, deepen,* and *enchant.* The Classical is only appropriate for Classical makers whose makings are works of art, beautiful things-in-the-world that have either severely limited or no apparent epistemic value, and no *moral* value at all outside of their particular place or specific representational meaning. They tell us nothing about how we must suffer our own knowing while only ever mirroring what we think we know. Primarily, her *mastery* is contingent on her participation in what she orders, on both "aboutness and participation." She is the Emersonian, a part of all that she has met, the personal muse—or what Stevens called the Interior Paramour—reconceived as a figure out of tragedy.

It may not have been obvious that Stevens's work silently turns away from the stance of Pound and Eliot, for whom the poem has no epistemic value beyond the historical facts it refers to or, as in the *Four Quartets,* a value based on a divine ideal; or for Moore, who called poems "imaginary gardens with real toads," or Williams, for whom they were "machines made out of words." But Stevens's poems lecture the reader (and their author) on their pained self-sufficiency, their irreconcilability with anything but their own struggle to *apprehend* what is real. Stevens, by this measure, is the High-Toned Christian Woman who must be reschooled: "Poetry is the supreme fiction, madame. / Take the moral law and make a nave of it / And from the nave build vaulted heaven." The wordplay, which Stevens often finds irresistible, puts an even finer point on the lesson that from the moral law anything can issue—innocence or knavery, seriousness or silliness, a basis for belief or the basses in a brass band. Or again, in "Reply to Papini," which Altieri describes as blending the highly rhetorical with the prosaic, Stevens adopts the persona of Pope Celestine VI (the pope

Dante put in Hell for having resigned the papacy). Stevens/Celestine makes a powerful claim: "The way through the world / Is more difficult than the way beyond it." The way through involves ethical principles that seem grounded, sadly, in an imaginary and wholly equivocal transcendence. Transcendence, even a saint might ask, of what, *from* what? The poem's epigraph tells you that Celestine himself had called poets "calligraphers of congealed daydreams." As Blake elsewhere says, "In up and down worlds, up and down are equivocal."

Crucial to Altieri is to succeed in showing "how intelligently and complexly the poetry of Wallace Stevens makes a distinctive contribution to the lineage of significant philosophical poets in the West." So he undertakes a brief survey of the background, starting with Wordsworth, with stops at Arnold and, finally, Pound. He begins by repeating the phrase associated with the crack-up of traditional humanist confidence in poetry, "the divorce between fact and value"— once a buzz phrase, now a cliché—and elaborates its consequences, beginning with Wordsworth, whose remembered ruins and daffodils are recuperated in imagined reverie. When "the world of fact" could still be recovered and reasserted as proof of the sublime, mind and world lived happily together. So Wordsworth could announce, in "spousal verse," "How exquisitely the individual Mind // . . . to the external World / Is fitted:—and how exquisitely, too— // The external World is fitted to the Mind." Altieri is not alone in noticing how often Wordsworth uses the word *fit,* here and elsewhere; in Wordsworth, the mind and the world represented the perfect marriage.

Altieri continues his survey with Matthew Arnold, who is the clearest if not the gloomiest messenger of Victorian dissatisfaction, and "Dover Beach," which Altieri claims is "the locus classicus for Victorian desperation" and "counts as substantial philosophical poetry." The antidote to Arnold according to Altieri's summary of the historical background is Imagism, introduced by an analysis of Pound's short lyric "April." Altieri spends time discussing the poem's sonic environment, moreover, which is refreshing given how the High Modernist lyric presented itself à la MacLeish, i.e., as "palpable and mute." But the poem's language is constitutive of the event and not really "descriptive":

Poems like "April" do not present the world as preexisting the language that rises to the challenge of representing it adequately. Instead, the poem makes it seem that we begin not with the world but with a certain condition of emotion that is inseparable from the language composed for the poem. . . . The object just is what language confers on the scene for the reader: the emotions and reflections language composes completely establish what spirits can see in April. And it is our task to learn to see and to feel as those spirits see and feel.

The trick, then, is for the Imagist poem to perform on the page in a manner that mimics, through a subtly varied technique assisted by Pound's wonderful ear, the changes one sees in nature. Its focus—to use a phrase from Altieri's rich section of endnotes—"is not on situations but on stances." And suddenly, his opening triangulation of Wordsworth, Arnold, and Pound seems a good idea, framing the rest of his argument and positioning Stevens on the margins of the highly circumscribed (more than one would have thought) community of work to which his poetry belongs and from which that work stands out. Where *is* Stevens in his poems? Which voice is "authentically" and not authorially his? The work has always had an autotelic if not autistic intensity that confused even editors like Harriet Monroe, who, to make "Sunday Morning" look sort of Modernist, rearranged five of the eight stanzas that she published—making matters worse. Stevens just didn't fit the available profile. Unlike Pound, who was essentially a satirist, or the pre–*Waste Land* Eliot and his pious preoccupation with what was always sexual alienation, if Stevens was making fun of something or in love with something, it was not always clear what it was. As often as his technique appears traditional or formalist, he surprises you with "Thirteen Ways" or "The Man with the Blue Guitar." He was and has been always difficult to match to a "type," which partly explains why he is a major poet.

And so he remains. Despite Altieri's ferocious attention to the poetry and admirable inventiveness, I wonder how useful a discovery tool the *aspectual* is, or how much closer it takes you to sensing the absolute weirdness of Stevens. A weirdness, that is, beyond the range of philosophical examination; it reminds you of the difference Kenner once pointed out between the great *writer* of poetry and the great poet, between, say, a Byron and a Shelley. Still, it's a difference difficult to assess except by indirection—especially by his impact on the work that succeeded him (for instance, the Ashbery of long meditations like "The Swimmers" or "Self-Portrait in a Convex Mirror," where the lyric and the narrative seem to smear together). I appreciated Altieri getting Nietzsche into the conversation because it showed what a strong reader Stevens was (unlike Pound, who at times seems to have read everything and understood nothing).

Altieri will have to ignore my annoyance at the (admittedly few) citations of the insufferable, generally unreadable, and always distracting Heidegger, whose obscurity may mask profounder defects, and for my skimming then skipping much of the Wittgenstein stuff. If this makes me the only concrete thinker in the room, so be it, but I have to agree with the late Helen Vendler, cited in a note by Altieri: "The cause of the setting [of imagination and reality] at odds is usually, in Stevens's case, passionate feeling, and not merely epistemological query." Thank you for landing the plane and reminding us that Stevens at heart was a great erotic poet.

Though the book busily demonstrates Stevens's complexity, what it cannot seem to engage is how passionately the work itself suffers, even wears that complexity, which can be so heated he might be compared to Donne, Dickinson, Keats of course, but especially to Shelley, the notorious disbeliever who wrote some of our greatest religious poetry. Poets who have the ability to think inside their lines deform all form; Stevens, like Shelley, whom critics for more than half a century never found the discipline or the patience to learn to read, treats each metaphor as the achieved or active potential of the one before or next; section 12 of "An Ordinary Evening in New Haven," with its sequence of cascading figurations of the same thing, for instance, seems a variation on the figurative logic of "Ode to the West Wind." Each poet was engaged in the creation of a psychomachia of the mind seeking sufficiency and never finding it. The lyric poet has to perform or endure perception without going off into mere reportage (a lot of Whitman, much of *The Cantos,* some of *Paterson,* much of *The Fall of America*), flaccid memoir (most of Langston Hughes, early Crane), sentimental or pious propaganda (Sandburg, Amy Lowell, parts of the *Four Quartets*), baroque opacities (portions of *The Bridge*), dressy anecdote (Williams at times, Stevens at times), or stultifying and humorless exercises in concretism or graphomania (L*A*N*G*U*A*G*E poetry, Oulipean poetry, Erasure poetry). The lyric poem—to borrow a hint from Sontag—is about the *erotics* of perception.

And yet Stevens may be far more "idealistic" than this credits him with being. I join Altieri in thinking that "At the core of Wallace Stevens's thinking, there is a metaphysical morality play. The positive figure bearing redemption is the imagination; the one bringing the threat of damnation is identified with 'the pressure of reality.'" Altieri's translation of Stevens's thinking sounds like a paraphrase of Shelley: "Imagination is as the Immortal God which should assume flesh for the redemption of mortal passion." As it well might: Romanticism has always seemed an aestheticization of religion (a secularized Anglican-ism), God replaced with the in-Godded self and the sensual life raised to the power of the divine. Like Yeats, Shelley, and Wordsworth before him, Stevens empties and then repopulates conventional theology with his own substitution terms, demonstrating the truth behind what Hulme meant by "spilt religion." He does the same thing in "Sunday Morning," where the dew on the feet of the wild men chanting at the sun (section 7) joins them to the "dreaming feet" that walk over water to Palestine (section 1), linking immortal to mortal and con-firming our pained doubleness. The structure of "An Ordinary Evening in New Haven," moreover, is a trellising of tercets, gathered in sections like Dantescan cantos, the form that Shelley learned from Dante and that is the fingerprint of the modern meditative poem from "Ode to the West Wind" through Am-mons's *Sphere*. Section 5, only part of which Altieri reproduces, like "The Final Soliloquy of the Interior Paramour" is addressed to an implied interlocutor. Here is the whole section 5:

> Inescapable romance, inescapable choice
> Of dreams, disillusion as the last illusion,
> Reality as a thing seen by the mind,
>
> Not that which is but that which is apprehended,
> A mirror, a lake of reflections in a room,
> A glassy ocean lying at the door,
>
> A great town hanging pendent in a shade,
> An enormous nation happy in a style,
> Everything as unreal as real can be,
>
> In the exquisite eye. Why, then, inquire
> Who had divided the world, what entrepreneur?
> No man. The self, the chrysalis of all men
>
> Became divided in the leisure of blue day
> And more, in branchings after day. One part
> Held fast tenaciously in common earth

And one from central earth to central sky
And in moonlit extensions of them in the mind
Searched out such majesty as it could find.

The whole poem is, again, launched on a wordplay, with, as Altieri notes, "the eye's, and *I*'s, version of the real caught in a flat objectification that cannot satisfy the questioning mind." Again, why not? The subject is poetry, which is after all about the language that makes it up, and its often clumsy, if hopelessly physical, engagement with the world. In section 5 the poem elaborates on its opening and makes it clear that the "eye's plain version" is an understatement. The eye is actually "exquisite," and vision is not just seeing but beholding, sight raised to the next power. What's more, "The point of vision and desire are the same" (3:1). Stevensian irony is situational (one might say Romantic); when it is not, like Crane's it can fall flat. Or, as here, the situation is staged as a phony syllogism. There is no such thing as an "ordinary" evening in New Haven, or anywhere else, at least if you know how to look.

To be human is to desire what we see, and to desire *is* to see. And what we see is neither "really" real nor "really" illusory, since from the point of view of imagination, there is nothing to guarantee the basis of fact in the first place. What we see is a series of loving displacements of "plain versions"—a mirrorful of reflections in a room that seems to float on a glassy ocean, New Haven upside-down in a window shade, the sky and the earth elaborated, extended and both fused and happily confused—enchantment achieved. This poem of thirty-one sections or mock *canzone* begins with a simple, even silly pun and yet ends up as a meditation on phenomenological extremes: the "common and the central earth," what is real and what is apprehended, "Naked Alpha" and "hierophant Omega" (6:2), "beginning and end," and so forth. What better way of staging the serio-comic human drama of apartness and division than by way of such a prelude, a lowly wordplay? We are divided by language because language divides us and our worlds are made of language. The happy capacity of Stevens's imagination is matched by the generosity—I nearly wrote magnanimity—of his moral imagination and erotic vision, either of which moots any final attempt to demonstrate how deeply and morally connected he was to the world.

—2014

Ammons

THEOLOGY FOR ATHEISTS

> ... take anything
> think about it, and it blows up in wonder.
>
> —A. R. AMMONS

If you came to A. R. Ammons's poetry in the mid-1970s, you instantly noticed what wasn't there. The confessional autobiographies that Plath, Sexton, and Lowell gave their audience were missing; and despite Plath's outraged feminism, it was really the same audience of mandarin taste and educated preference. Instead, what you saw in Ammons were serial observations of the natural world that disarmed you with their earthiness and openness. There was no outrage, no searing recollection of childhood, no show-stopping performance like "Daddy" or "Waking in the Blue," and little urban realism or political sentiment. At times he reminded or fooled you into thinking he was of the school of Olson via Pound because of an occasional habit of leaning on a vaguely mythical persona ("So I said I am Ezra") and a prosody that walked the eye down the page. But the poems contained elements un- (or rather anti-) Modernist in the extreme, such as a tendency to personify abstractions and to position the speaking "self" in a self-deprecating light on those occasions when (as in *Tape for the Turn of the Year*) Ammons centered the work on himself. It was either in the late 1970s or early 1980s that I ran across something by Harold Bloom that canceled the possibility that the Ezra of Ammons's "Ezra Poems" was either the prophet Ezra or Ezra Pound; it turned out to be a childhood friend.

Ammons now seems more a Romantic than ever. For one thing, he wrote "nature poetry" and always seemed closer to the Lake School than Black Mountain or Modernism's London or Paris. Ammons would never relent from taking the natural world as his only subject until the end of his life when personal details suddenly began to penetrate the poetry and to alter the narrative direction. In late lyrics like "Parting," the voice is so intimate it's nearly unrecognizable as Ammons's:

> She was already lean when
> a stroke or two slapped
> her face like drawn
> claw prints; akilter, she
> ate less and
>
> sat too much on the edge
> of beds looking a width too
> wide out of windows

Those last two lines make one almost wish he had done more of this kind of personal portraiture.*

After a career devoted to marginalizing the confessional "note" and avoiding all those signature gestures that marked American poetry from the Lowell–Plath moment in the 1950s, Ammons abruptly gets personal. A disruptive yet novel addition to his achievement, it gave a ninety-degree twist to your appreciation of how much work he had put into distancing the lyrical host of the poems from the cultural or professional self of Po-Biz. Reading "Parting," for

---

* In 2003 the *Paris Review* published the following short lyric, found among Ammons's papers:

You came one day and
as usual in such matters
significance filled everything—
your eyes, the things you
knew, the way you turned,
leaned, stood, or sat,
this way or that: when
you left, the area around here rose
a tilted tide, and everything that
offers desolation drained away.

It was followed by an editorial note: "This poem was found after the poet's death on the back of an envelope from Helen Vendler, November 28, 1981."

instance, the poet who comes to mind is William Carlos Williams (and the poem "The Widow's Lament in Springtime"). Yet even with the addition of the autobiographical elements, the superficial syntactic likeness, and the American-ness of the diction, the differences between Ammons and his apparent original are antagonistic. Williams's poem is a dramatic monologue and an elegy to his mother; Ammons's is a little horror movie about how the body often dies *after* the mind, told through no interrupting persona. Williams occasionally looked as closely at the world as Ammons does but did not have it in him to write a poem as harshly objective as this, in which the body is one more thing in the world. By comparison, Williams seems a comparative sentimentalist. To read Ammons's *The Selected Poems: Expanded Edition* convinces you that certain writers need a lifetime of looking at the natural order in order to measure the human world for what it is, to see it as a naturalist sees life anywhere, human or not, exposed in its tragic haplessness and as vulnerable as trees or rocks. Am-mons's naturalist pose, I suppose it must be added, never became an argument against humanism (or a derivative antihumanism) probably because his obses-sion, from start to finish, was remaining objective in the face of the very implau-sibility of "objectivity," or taking such a position. Such "objectivity" is or was neither Imagist nor Objectivist. It was centered on knowing at once what it is to be human and at the same time one more lonely thing-in-the-world. Wil-liams counseled "no ideas but in things"; Ammons's poetry is filled with ideas *and* things, along with a profound nostalgia for seeing things as they are or, more likely, as things would be if things could look and talk back. As for senti-mentality, he did not so much escape it as outrace it, or allow it to outrace him. This couldn't have been easy given how it was all around him in the poetry of the 1950s into the mid-1960s. Somehow he maintained a belief in the human without sentimentalizing his subject or relaxing his commitment to locating human concerns in a natural environment that he finds it difficult if not useless to "humanize" in any normative sense.

An early minor poem, "Bridge," is typical of how Ammons orients himself toward surroundings. It begins in a very muted Williamsesque way:

A tea garden shows you how:

      you sit in rhododendron shade
at table

on a pavilion-like lawn

    the sun midafternoon through the blooms
and you

watch lovers and single people
go over the steep moon bridge at the pond's narrows

where flies nip circles

    in the glass
and vanish in the widening sight except for an uncertain

    gauze memory of wings

The poem starts by echoing the famous proleptic opening of "The Red Wheel-barrow," where the answer ("So much depends upon") is given before the question is posed. There is also a hint of the self-conscious formality Williams brought to writing about the everyday, a habit that in Williams seems, now, nearly an old-fashioned mannerism. Common objects and common settings: so Ammons presents *a* tea garden, any tea garden, some random elision of similarly made-up settings where human and natural interests blur into an amalgam. The definite article might raise hairy possibilities and substitute or superimpose pompous importance—the garden as symbol, for instance—that the typical Ammons poem will not, from first to last, either sustain or abide.

Yet there is that other typical Ammons gesture: because the garden "shows you how," the poem openly personifies the amalgam, a psychological gesture—and nearly the fingerprint of the Romantic poet. This is no late Modernist, or Imagist, for whom the poem is a self-articulating vehicle of meaning or Objectivist who believes that things can be arranged to speak silently of a posthuman significance, and in which context ordinary objects have a kind of iconic (in the Platonic sense) weight. Nor is this somehow a version of twentieth-century pastoral, to be set alongside Pound's "The Garden" or Yeats's "Wild Swans at Coole." An American tourist is leading you somewhere actual and human; he is at the same time a lyric poet who is prepared to "make a statement" in the manner of the traditional lyric. The tea garden itself will therefore become a kind of classroom, a scene of instruction, and also whatever can lead us to such a place (whence the title, "Bridge"). I have quoted the poem's first dozen lines, but in the first line you get what is most typical of Ammons. That willingness, nearly an urgency, to surrender his own agency to the natural world and allow it to lead him to a place where decisions are made (a bridge); the graceful acceptance of *what is there,* the world's beloved thinginess, no matter how trivial or useless; the elemental love of stuff—details, trash, pebbles, water, garbage (the latter a title of one of his late collections)—for its sheer sensuous weight.

As this early poem proceeds, it lays out the central argument of all Ammons poetry. The drama—a lot, after all, can happen on a bridge—occurs in the mind. The poet as the "you" of the text goes on to "sip from the small thick cup" and to "watch / the people / rising on the bridge" and then "descend into the pond / where the bridge and mirrorbridge merge." With their ascent and their descent, the pedestrians' reflections disappear from and then reappear in the pond that the bridge spans. The description is striking: both the actual bridge and the one in the pond, the "mirrorbridge," "merge" and "[return] their images to" the figures moving past the poet's vision. It's an incredibly, absurdly *active* still-life. What's more, the human presence, denied its "image" as it goes up over the bridge, has it returned once it has crossed; the human has been permitted to "see itself" in nature. Crossing the bridge is therefore an exercise in loss and recovery of the self-image we carry into the social world and we look for the world to give expression to (here, in water), hence to give back to us.

In Ammons the physical world is an active agent in our coming to know who we are; in which the world of phenomena, or whatever we choose to call our "objectivity," is a limited partner in human perception, an active collaborator in coming to self-knowledge. Thus Ammons is and never could be the visionary reporting on physical impressions and stacking them against mental ones in a way that suggests mental bookkeeping. Nor is this the passive nature poet that the early Coleridge occasionally ridiculed—stretched out in the grass and drinking in "natural influxes" to reflect upon later. The lyric self of a typical Ammons lyric, early or late, actively measures and negotiates distances between poet and world, which is to say that for Ammons the lyric poem is *the* phenomenological experience, epitomizing the extraordinary character of the everyday. Maybe this is the unique distinction of the American lyric since Whitman: its fascination with overcoming lyrical distance, with taking the measure of the individual agent against all this American real estate—with "bridging," in other words, the gap between the Me Myself and what Emerson in a late diary entry called "the Abyss." A garden for such a poet in such a tradition is both a physical environment and the unfolding of an old psychological drama: after the Now of all this sublime physicality, what Then?

Ammons raises the question by wrenching his prosody through a queer and difficult turn, from the here-and-now to "farther things," defined in the poem as that moment when the spirit comes to the bridge of consciousness

> and climbs higher and higher
>   toward the peak no one reaches live
> but where ascension
>   and descension meet
> completing the idea of a bridge

The explicitness of the connection between the physical and the psychological "bridge" is self-conscious enough to make the ironist wince. "[T]hink," he continues, "where the body is, / that going too deep // it may lose touch, / wander a ghost in hell." This is about as wrenching and self-conscious a transition as can be imagined in a poem composed, as this was, in the shadow of American Modernism, Williams et al., where the natural object, as Pound counseled, was the "adequate symbol." The excursus transforms an encounter with a physical act (walking over a bridge) into something between allegory (a Puritan divine's "typological" reading of the world) and a highly abstract analogy between physical facts and a poetic expression of a spiritual reality.

The meaning is easily parsed: consciousness bridges fundamental "object" reality and the "higher and higher . . . peak no one reaches alone." That "peak" is unidentified—Mount Purgatory, possibly, though the critical thing is that Ammons does not seem to prefer one world to the other. He wants both, an amalgam of the physical (natural) and the spiritual (human), whose sign is the mingling of ascending and descending agencies in the water and the stage for which is the place that he occupied in his original setting out: a tea garden. To have one without the other is a kind of catastrophe. "Think," he says, "where the body is" if the spirit were to wander off. Hell here is not the site of Christian punishment; or rather it is not *simply* that. Ammons's Hell is Emerson's via

Blake—the world of the body distinct from the spirit, an Ulro of pure object relations, Milton's "universe of death." Hell is a *purer* physicality, space void of human agency and spiritual imagination, where we are lost because we, as beings doubled in nature, are reduced to only one. The spirit broken off from the body may, as he says later, suffer a different kind of Hell—may "go off weightless // body never to rise or spirit fall again to unity, / to lovers strolling through pepper-tree shade."

The poem's trickiest abstraction is that word "unity." It points to a unity both philosophical (mind-body) and everyday, the plain unity of "lovers strolling through" mundane human shade. This elision of the natural and supernatural, a comment on the pure paganism at the heart of Christianity, more importantly drives the poem's final movement or "turn" toward Dante: "paradise was when," Ammons says,

> Dante
> regathered from height and depth
>   came out onto the soft, green, level earth
>
> into the natural light, come, sweat, bloodblessings,
>   and thinning sheaf of days.

Dante, "regathered from height and depth," emerges from his journey unified (or *re*unified) and ready to return to the world. But for Dante, the motivating agency is intervening divinity, the kind that mythical poetry has been describing since Gilgamesh, "l'amor che move il sole e l'altre stelle." But not here. Ammons assigns the "regathering" and the motive behind it to an agency that is anything but divine despite the reference to *The Divine Comedy*. At best, it's indefinite: the self seems to "regather" through "finding itself" in the elemental, the here-and-now.

At the very start of his career Ammons gives you this, a robust, positively American reading of Dante, as he prepares to continue his own journey, his perusal of the "thinning sheaf of days." Dante is the great image of the spiritual quester, a Christian Orpheus, the lucky pedestrian who's guided by a complex spiritual love as well as by love for his lost beloved, Beatrice. It's tempting to dismiss Ammons's point as another expression of the need to see our life as a kind of spiritual journey, but *spiritual* here should be put in big scare quotes—it means both more and less than what it connotes. What the poem describes takes a lot less than a day to unfold and includes, as experimental by-products, sweat and possibly semen ("come"). Not just every day but at every moment in its "thinning sheaf of days," consciousness is gapping itself and the abyss, which is a habit with a lyric poet. He wants what Yeats called "Unity of Being," that fusion of higher and lower natures, of spirit and sense, and of the physical or natural and the spiritual or human. The result is a kind of natural theology for atheists, a stance toward phenomena that echoes the philosophical doubts of Greek skepticism but also stipulates that room has to be left for the traditional responses of the believing, at least the nondoubting or receptive post-Enlightenment poets.

Ammons's motto might be the three opening words of maybe his greatest single poem, "Gravelly Run," from 1960:

I don't know somehow it seems sufficient
to see and hear whatever coming and going is,
losing the self to the victory
    of stones and trees,
of bending sandpit lakes, crescent
round groves of dwarf pine:

"I don't know." Whatever its ecstatic affirmation of nature at the level of details and objects, the "I" that foregrounds all that he perceives is also a great doubter of its own agency, its power of knowing things, which we value as the self's most precious agency. Lyric poetry has always had to face this problem: how do you measure the distance between the self and the object it desires across the ontological space both subject and object occupy, and occupy exclusively as figments of language? It is the central problem in poetry for the past two hundred years: *what does poetry know?* Ammons begins by hoisting the standard of all Romantic lyric—the first-person singular pronoun—but ties it to a negative predicate in a way that disarms you. Coming to the rest of the line, the thought's completion in "sometimes it seems sufficient," the absence of internal punctuation seems a deliberate omission that forces you to rush from not-knowing to a highly qualified sense of what's *sufficient* (a word that in this context is still owned by Stevens's reflections on the "poem of the mind"). Ammons is saying that this is not only going to be about a place called Gravelly Run but about how we know things, anything, about how much knowledge is sufficient, and what finally will or can satisfy our *cravings* for knowledge of the world (the place, Gravelly Run) and the percipient (the *I* who does or does not know).

This will not be a process of simple keeps and discards. Line 1 gains its gently disruptive power partly as the result of an omitted punctuation mark that forces it to be read, or heard, as an artifact of casual conversation, a blunted or butchered colloquialism ("I don't know *but* somehow it seems sufficient"; "I don't know *if* somehow it seems sufficient"). We've wandered into an exchange between two voices representing the same being—a American Dialogue of Self and Soul, as it were, in a soft Southern accent. Line 2 continues the pattern, presenting an odd or apparent inversion of a common idiom ("what is coming and going"). To "see and hear what is coming and going" is the anticipated syntactic movement, the ordinary vernacular equation, for describing one way of satisfying curiosity. But note: in Ammons's poem the line reads "to see and hear what coming and going *is*" (my italics). This is the way ordinary folk talk to each other; it's a formulation that breaks with formal usage because it depends on the live delivery and the hammering of that tiny word *is*. Imagine how you might write this in a typical or appropriate expository setting ("to see and feel what [the essence of] coming and going [is]"). Plus, it echoes the skepticism of the very opening words. It is the difference between seeing and hearing in a world of stable, isolated objects, of little whats or quiddities striking attention like flies hitting a windshield, and seeing and hearing in terms of comings and goings *generally,* as processes, not outcomes of the process of things going from here to there but of things as they are. The poem seems to be calling attention to processes isolated from the very agencies that perform or produce them rather than to the agencies themselves (*L'Amor,* God). In the spatial language of High Modernism, it's as though Ammons wants to call attention to the space around the thing rather than the thing itself—a kind of inverted Imagism.

The next lines reveal the key to seeing and hearing "what coming or going is": it is in "losing the self to the victory of stones and trees" (3–4). Another disruption, and a fairly exacting one: by surrendering the self we find its weight, meaning, its reality among the natural elements which it seems both part of and apart from. Again, this is the lyric's question: what does the self—or the personality—contribute to what it knows about the world? While the poem attempts to point to the self's origin and to credit it with a limited transcendence, the overwhelming fact is that the world will always appear to be victorious because it will outlast us. Depressing news, or a reason for tragic laughter? The hardest lesson the lyric teaches is the one Ammons is always repeating, rehearsing, or reliving. The world is our ethical limit, our destiny—what Emerson calls Fate—and at the very summit of our spiritual ascent we will always be forced, like Dante climbing Mount Purgatory, to remember our death, to think of the world and its beauty as the ultimate limiter and as anything but a benign (Wordsworthian) nurse. The Emersonian understands his or her relationship to nature as a debtor's to a creditor's. Either you can never fully repay, or you can repay by never having been a debtor in the first place—never having been born.

Ammons's subject here and elsewhere is always the same: the self's helplessly creative and energetic nature. Like all his nature descriptions, this one is not a "simple" one of nature stripped of human commentary, as his syntax confesses. In "Gravelly Run," as it would be in any descriptive act, the adjective signals the observer's ambivalence in participating in a somehow ironic objectivity, one that it undermines even while declaring it to be objective. Beginning in lines 5 and 6 ("bending," "sandpit," "crescent round," "dwarf") the adjectives interrupt and subtly alter the poem's musical environment: the philosophical lyric abruptly begins to *sound* lyrical, the vowels being lengthened either by the nearly alliterative *n*-sounds (*bending, sandpit, crescent, round, pine*) or are by their very nature long (*lakes, round, graves, pine*). The effect is to slow the line down as if to stop us from moving too quickly, to force us to look and to listen closely and see and hear whatever is there—or "whatever coming and going is." Much of what is there, outside us, is meaningful because we "half create" what we perceive.

And the whole sestet concludes on one of the grace notes and minor prosodic signatures of Ammons's poetry, his use of the colon as his preferred mark of punctuation. Richard Howard's commentary from *Alone with America* (1971) is succinct, smart, and still a good place to begin:

> Ammons has found, or fetched out, besides a functioning arrangement of words on the page, the further device of the colon, which he henceforth wields in its widest application as almost his only mark of punctuation—a sign to indicate

not only equivalence, but the node or point of passage on each side of which an existence hangs in the balance.... [O]ne of the limitations of his method, of course, is that Ammons requires length in order to indulge his effects, lacking that compression of substance which amounts to a "received form."

Hardly, that is, a stylistic affection, the colon is a sign of equivalence that marks off discursive regions of equal importance and of shared meaning. What comes after the colon completes the sense of what precedes it. The colon is forward-pointing punctuation, a mark of prolepsis, and it's perfectly at home in the typical Ammons poem, where the motion is forward, pointing to a meaning not yet predicated, followed by a list or inventory of items whose expository value completes the sense of the opening proposition. His poems often remind me, with their piling up and piling on of detail, of the Chinese artist Song Dong, whose "portrait" of his deceased mother was the entire contents of her kitchen and bedroom spread out and covering a whole floor at MOMA: the objects tell the story, the things themselves *narrate* and attest to the life being lived. At the most schematic the structure can be understood as a series of precepts mated to corresponding examples, the exemplary demonstration of which is "Corson's Inlet."

As nearly the only terminal punctuation in the lyric environment of the Ammons poem, the colon is rare (if not unprecedented), perhaps philosophically out of place, even unnatural, in as much as it contains a suggestion of an unfolding sequence of explanations, of listings of parts, as in a rule book or tour guide. I bring this up for two reasons. Ammons's poetry is in Whitman's tradition of the inventory or catalogue organized according to no preemptive valuing of their importance in isolation. The difference is that the typical unit of an Ammons list is not a thing but a block or bunch of things—and again, the reader need only take note of how stingily he uses adjectives to demarcate the boundaries between seer and scene. That each *unit* of perception is thus marked off suggests that at the heart of his approach is a sense—given his skepticism, it's certainly not a *belief*—that the givens of perception do hang together organically, but that in the longest run we can never be sure of the principle of organization. Maybe that principle exists in some freestanding ontological sense, somehow outside of or extrinsic to our lives and desires. Or maybe our ordering of the world is an innate property (and perhaps handicap) of consciousness, what scientists call the anthropic principle, meaning that we arrive in the world imposing an order where there isn't any. "Gravelly Run" reraises, if more briefly, the phenomenological question that Shelley, for instance, in a poem like "Mont Blanc" tries to confront: does the physical world exist apart from me, or is my perception of it responsible for its being there?

The next stanza begins the poem's phase of self-conscious declaration that seems oddly formal in a "nature poem": the preposition "for," here, used as the subordinate conjunction *because,* announces that what comes after lines 5 and 6 will explain everything that came before. The reflective mind doubles back on itself, signals its turns with the colon. The content of the reflection, moreover, is critical to the poem's movement and contributes one of the most beautiful passages in all of American poetry:

> for it is not so much to know the self
> as to know it as it is known
>   by galaxy and cedar cone
> as if birth had never found it
> and death could never end it:

This is Ammons's variant on the American theophany, what Emerson experienced as he walked into Boston Commons, on Stevens's vision of the snowman and the one Crane invokes in "Voyages VI," where the Imaged Word confirms the lover's knowledge that no divinity exists apart from or other than ourselves, that the "God within" is the only God. It's a shock to realize that the passage hangs on a negative particle (*not*). All imaginative creation—this seems to be the point—involves an initial act of circumstantial negation, a decreation of everything that is objectively "there."

Something else about the passage marks it as like nearly nothing else in Ammons: its musicality. His work rarely (if ever) rhymes or seems designed around mnemonic strategies; it's not usually so vocable or memorable. Yet this formal quintet is both memorable and memorizable: the rhyming of *known* and *cone,* for instance, and the conclusions of lines 10 and 11 in the same pronoun (*it*). The poem's balancing of intellectually symmetrical elements (*birth* and *death, found* and *end, galaxy* and *cedar cone*) frames the larger correspondences the poem uses to plot the rising asymptote of perception—first and last (*birth/death*),

origin and destiny (*found/end*), large and small (*galaxy/cedar cone*)—and sup-
ports the larger objective of these five lines, or line 7 and the four that follow: to
teach us that the "control" of the self is possibly known by some entity outside
it, perhaps exists prior to birth's lovely "finding" of it, and that perhaps it may
survive its death. The claim, though, is tentative, and hedged by qualifiers (*not
so much, as to, as if*) because it is as close as the agnostic comes to advancing a
creed. It may be there and it may not; we can only hope or hold ourselves (and
our poems) open to what he calls, in "Corson's Inlet," the "possibilities" of an
"external" order.

What follows, the last three stanzas, or movements, of the poem, seem vastly
different in terms of time and direction. The poem reverts to elementals, to the
given physical environment: the swamp, its running water, the highway bridge,
the holly on the banks in the distance (the poem seems to have us panning
backward) and the cedars. All the details are filled with, haunted, or touched
by evidence of the mind and of human agency, and again the prosody slows us
down, reasserts the opening emphases:

> the swamp's slow water comes
> down Gravelly Run fanning the long
>   stone-held algal
> hair and narrowing roils between
> the shoulders of the highway bridge:

The string of long vocalics (*slow, comes down, long, stone-held, roils, shoulders*)
pile up into nearly alliterative consonantal groupings (sw*amp*'s slow, long stone-
held al*gal*). The description comes alluringly close to personification and to a
self-consciously reflective symbolism in stanza 4 when the "algal / hair" gives
way to the green rubbishy fungal threads "formed" by the water, threads that
run or are drawn out between the bridge's "shoulders." The cedar trees of the
next stanza look so much like church spires surrounded by holly that Ammons
simply states the obvious in not so obvious language, that the experience "could
make / green religion in winter bones."

The operative word is not *religion* but *green,* which has only an accidental
relationship to the contemporary environmentalist agenda. A "green religion"
is Wordsworth's in his earliest, most pantheistic poetry, where Nature is nurse,

guide, anchor, and soul of his mortal and moral being. But Ammons can't add his voice to Wordsworth or such a belief—to what Shelley mocked as Wordsworth's "mild faith" in a benign nature. "Green religion" is exactly where the poem has been going; it's what the mind cultivates, actively grows out of the whole spectacle the poem has been describing. Ammons interrupts that growth, that movement, and won't go where the Wordsworthian referents point, to the marriage of mind and world. Nature will never confirm our sense of transcendence or the desire for implicit immortality raised in the first stanza of "Gravelly Run." It cannot because it is we who personify, animate, bless, and call it benign, malign, or indifferent. The connectedness Ammons asserts is denied by his own deep suspicion of his own language

And so the poem's conclusion is a profound reflection on his own practice, where no amount of looking and reflecting ("as I look and reflect") can burst the "glass / jail"—the very being-in-it—that constitutes consciousness. The air, here, is only by a stretch a symbol (something Ammons won't allow since he is no more a Symbolist than a materialist). The important element is not the air but the "jail," which comes from nonhuman stuff and perhaps through nonhuman agencies. Think how different a poem this would be if the modifying word instead of "glass" were—as, say, in Yeats—*soul's* or *mind's* or *the flesh's*. The world is hermetically sealed against us: nothing lives in it except what sense memory or imagination puts there (gods, philosophers like Hegel, lyric poems). Because the "sunlight has never / heard of trees"—an idea taken right out of Emerson's "Nature"—the "surrendered self" finds itself alone among "unwelcoming forms," forms that may welcome our meanings, but not us. We are no part of nature in Ammons, or only insecurely so. It explains the temptation for the reader of Ammons to read the world as an allegory, as an abstraction, metaphysical or scientific, of physical experience; it is always blunted by his conviction that the best we can hope for is a correlation, not a connection.

For the English and American Romantics, the basic theoretical burden, the big lift, was how to explain—or justify—the elevation of the "solitary" thinking self to a place of importance occupied, in most theories of art, by the "world," howsoever we choose to understand it (as psychological, purely material, i.e., the plenum of phenomena, or as simply as "culture"). If you do not write poetry for an audience other than yourself, then there may be no need to feel agitated over the world's absence from or abandonment of the scene of interpretation. But no writer, and no poet especially, writes hoping he will never find a reader. So the inherited anxiety of every lyric poet since Wordsworth comes from the promotion of the lyric *I* to a status—absurd no matter how you think about it—where it is its own subject. The older sense of the lyric as the vehicle for "love" poetry went by the board with the Romantic sonnet. Whitman in *Song of Myself* demonstrated, with such raucous emphasis, that the lyrical self occupies so many chaotic poetic environments (plain narrative, autobiography, the speculative or "philosophical," even the dramatic) that following his lead has baffled results: we get the lyric as history (*The Cantos*), as celebratory national narrative (*The Bridge*), even as a Dantescan comedy of technique (Ammons's own *Tape for the Turn of the Year*). Each seems ground down by their authors' inconsistent sense of their audiences, an inconsistency, not incidentally, already apparent in *Song of Myself,* with its mixed points of view and juggling of the purely autobiographical (section 1) and, for instance, the dramatic (section 11). The lyric poem, at war with its own generic expectations (to use a phrase that once had a great deal of value), wants to extend itself past practice into new registers where the traditional lyric and the living lyrical host can coexist, with the writer and the audience happily keeping score. Nowadays, though the possibility or probability that the primary audience for a poem is the poet (usually, the one who wrote it) remains hugely troubling, so solipsistic an understanding of poetry (and especially of the lyric) seems the cost of decades of careerist impulse and, in America, the institutionalization and commodification of the art to an extent that we seem psychologically disabled by anything that fails to reflect our better selves.

To the major American poets after Emerson, such an understanding is unacceptable. Harold Bloom once argued that Ammons is the most successful descendant of Emerson, and in one respect at least he appears to be right: a purging or surrendering of self-consciousness is necessary to discover what (if any) external order exists, given that the mind is habitually imposing order on everything. Emerson, especially in such psychologically vital lyrics as "Each and All"—in a sense the poem that is the textual germ of this whole essay—insists that this spontaneously iterated intellectual creativity *is* our genius, our "godhood." The way out of the trap that the physical world sets for the ego, and out of whatever we call the agony that every consumer experiences once he realizes that the objects of desire, once possessed, are always somehow a letdown, is to re-create the desired object imaginatively. Ammons, though, is aware of his position as a writer with an educated appreciation of systems; he's looked at the calendar. So the self, positioned in the foreground of his poems, is one whose desire for self-denial and self-deletion compete and who is oriented toward the Emersonian conviction that the objective world must be decreated in order for its essential truth to appear. As Emerson himself details the drama in "Each and All," the individual spectator of the world, looking for his own importance there, has to come *on his own* to the conviction that the given world, because given, is useless and must be negated. Only then will his reader be able to say with Emerson's speaker in "Each and All," "I covet truth; / Beauty is unripe childhood's cheat; / I leave it behind with the games of youth," and thereby leave in the background the sensuous, Keatsian naturalism that for Emerson is the abyss against which the Self is perennially (self-) defined.

But there is a difference. Emerson never bought Keats's equation of beauty and truth; for him, truth is both human and godlike. For Ammons, however, the natural world seems to retain some objective, extrahuman value, a significance, not to say a *reality* independent of imagination. If we believe with Emerson that there is only the self and "the Abyss," then the solution to our disenchantment with the world, the question raised by the lyric stance itself, is a denunciation or denial of what's out there—whether it is "there" or not—followed by a re-creation of the world as something possessable only through the imagination. Stevens shares Emerson's conviction that the nothing that is not there is the "real" world, and that the imagination's one and only gift is the recognition of the self's majestic isolation as the chrysalis of the human. Yet the possibility that some objective reality corresponds to what we mean by and what we call nature, at the heart of twentieth-century positivism and early Modernism, also continues to nag at and motivate Ammons, good Emersonian that he is, whose final response is enthusiastic ambivalence. And not only enthusiastic: timely. I remember an essay from years ago that kept misinvoking Emerson and crediting him with the "idea" that the American lyric poem of-

fered not a virtual but a literal, textual "home" for the unaccommodated self—
the lyric as homeless shelter. Then I remembered the opening lines from "Gravelly Run" and realized that the way around much of the fakery of our poetry lay
in realizing the moral and philosophical importance of Ammons, whose work
is permanent and whose voice is irreplaceable.

—2004

John Finlay's *Hermetic Light*

RELIGION AND POETRY

One of Dante's first encounters in *Inferno* occurs in Limbo, the vestibule of Hell, where the ghosts of the "virtuous pagans"—Classical writers and thinkers whose spiritual life lacked only the perfection of Christian Baptism—sit out eternity undisturbed but barred from permanent communion with either the saved or the rest of the damned, condemned never to possess the beatific vision. The four "grand shades" of antiquity, Homer, Horace, Ovid, and Lucan, greet Virgil, a charter member, and then welcome Dante as, Dante notes proudly, "a sixth" in their great number. The moment of welcomed uplift is followed by a note of Dante's characteristic ontological realism: in the background Dante notices a castle with seven battlements and seven gates. The notes tell us it is the Castle of the Seven Liberal Arts, which is illuminated solely by the light of human reason. Its appearance so early in the narrative cheers us up only more successfully to bring us down to earth. It's a reminder: unaided by faith, or so the canto implies, our minds are a mid-world of half-lights situated on the border of Hell.

The lesson would not have been lost on John Finlay, who near the end of his life, in a poem titled "A Prayer to the Father," continued a lifelong, conscious meditation on the divine as freedom or release from thinking, or thought as a barrier to knowing God:

> O God of love and power, hold still my heart
> When death, that ancient, awful fact appears;
> Preserve my mind from all deranging fears,
> And let me offer up my reason free
> And where I thought, there see Thee perfectly.

All thought, David Hume claims, begins in the body, at the surface of sensation and sensible feeling. The poem is a measure of Finlay's disagreement with Hume and distrust of thought, not for what it contains but for whence it proceeds. In this collection of essays this distrust becomes an informing, powerful, and unifying thematic for what might otherwise be dismissed as a collection of incoherent metaphysical reveries.

That his mind would suffer an extinction before his body is the terror in the foreground of these essays, which are driven by a compulsion to explore one question: how can the mind really know God? The terror comes from a double recognition—that our personal terror gains little relief from nursing the compulsion, and that our situation is rooted in a tradition of speculative thought that, or so Finlay maintains, has been mismanaged to the point of irrecoverability. He insists that all thought since Locke had culminated, with Hume, in the intellect finally attacking and destroying its own ascendancy. *Hermetic Light* is therefore an implicitly complicated salvage operation, Finlay attempting to master the thought of some representative casualties of a failed tradition. When Finlay died in 1991, he left a large group of essays published and unpublished from which the six in this collection have been taken. David Middleton, the book's editor and executor of Finlay's literary estate, notes in a probing, pointedly elegiac afterword that "His essays are not merely secondary criticism but press toward primary forms in which a psychodrama is being played out and in which a theomachia involving the ultimate things is being almost desperately waged below the cool surfaces of the prose." Exactly right. Each is a meditation on what Finlay termed the "gnostic spirit of modern literature," which Finlay defined as "the idea of an ontological alienation of God from both the natural and the human world."

It is distasteful to have to round to a point these six moving reflections, much of whose power owes principally to their character as arguments without a distinctly enunciated thesis. It is the claims of a deeply learned and religious sensibility, not of journalistic intelligence or scholarly protocol, that give this book its center of gravity. Finlay found much that was dismaying, anguishing, or simply wrong in the modern "gnostic spirit"—the embrace of mystery over certainty, its religion of the mind against the ancient faith that he himself embraced as a convert to Roman Catholicism, and its agnostic compromise with a life of ironic uncertainty, prolonged to the point of final irresolution. Each error he identified with a larger one, "the alienation of God from the mind," it-self born of an intuition that "there is no analogy between [God's] pure essence and the gross matter of this world." His way out of this ancient dilemma was through Thomistic philosophy. The discovery of the will's dual nature as both elective and affective belongs to Aquinas, who taught that will was doubled in its capacity to act on both the spiritual and appetitive levels while remaining a unity. Luckily for Finlay, Aquinas, if a dualist, was no world-hater, no Pauline enemy of the sensuous life. Maybe this is why Finlay was having Aquinas read to him on his deathbed. While our nature is a unison, our everyday destiny is repeated encounters with the multiplicity and division of the material world.

Finlay sets out by examining the impact of this gnostic spirit on one rep-resentative personality after another, beginning with Flaubert and proceeding through a roster of mixed reputations: Newman, Hopkins (who was spiritually mentored by Newman), Valéry, Yvor Winters, Kafka, Freud, and Nietzsche. Some, like Newman and Valéry, are merely wounded; others, like Freud and Nietzsche, are fully handicapped; and only one, Winters, Finlay's LSU disserta-tion subject and clearly the wild card in this group, emerges intact. His handling of Hopkins indicates precisely how tortured Finlay was by this project as well as just how entirely idiosyncratic is the character of his approach.

In his analysis, Hopkins is a triply-intersected war zone where three partic-ular strains of thought—a native English puritanism, a nostalgic Romanticism, and doctrinaire Thomism—struggle to control and further confuse Hopkins's already neurotic sensibility. The puritanism compels Hopkins to view the world as a staging area for the battle between our higher and lower natures. More problematic is Hopkins's Romanticism, which advocates a unison of the war-ring natures through a renunciation of original sin. The final complication is Hopkins's Thomism because it seems, frankly, more like Finlay's: open to intel-lect and compassionate toward lower, fallen nature and human will, it might, if Hopkins were Finlay, have brought the Romantic and the puritan out of iso-lation and into the range of rational theism and something like traditional An-glicanism. But Hopkins embraced a thoroughly analytical, Thomistic under-standing of deity; at the same time, given his Romantic side's tendency to see in the good moral life the salvation of natural will, it was as impossible for him to accept it as it was hateful to his puritan side. Hopkins suffered from what might be called spiritual strabismus: his God, distributed across the divide that

separated the puritan from the Romantic, is a doubled figure either perfectly
dominating and immanent or just as perfectly Gnostic and absent. Occasionally, Finlay's prose seems mimetic in its desire to claim the things he loves. You
read, for instance, how Hopkins's concept of "selfbeing" is "reinterpreted in
the divine oneness to the destruction of its original life," which seems to be a
description of how the will, the "thisness" of our selfhood, is finally assimilated
to the divine antecedent and disappears. The encounter between two such idiosyncratic styles reveals their comparable need to own physically, in language,
the content of thought.

But these stylistic issues are ripples in the medium. At its most elegiac, Finlay's style is cool and controlled. On Hopkins: "He died at forty-five without
coming to a completely intellectual awareness of the exact harm that his two
wills had done his religious life and his psychological integrity as a man. Our
final impression of him is that of a nature close to insanity in its struggle against
both divine injunctions and human desire." That *our* is a signal flare of a writer's
assuming or imploring his audience to agree with him. Or again: "[Hopkins]
surrendered the craft of poetry to psychological compulsion. It became for him
a kind of neurotic symptom." Near the end of his essay on Valéry he offers this
startling formulation of the problematic nature of the mind's explanations of its
own contingency: "Even if the mind should obliterate the universe, stay within
itself and study only itself, it still must meet at every turn of its purest process
the same constricting [*sic*] that it shares with the contaminating universe at
large." The mind, that is, has to come to accept the possibility that solipsism is
just as chancy a refuge as religious faith. Yet again and again, behind the cool-
ness you get the sense of terrible disturbance, of intellectual distress pushed
nearly and knowingly to the point of a desperately regimented intellectualism
that comes close to intellectual violence. Sometimes, as in his essay on Valéry,
Finlay seems so overwrought by the spectacle that his account both describes
and, in its sensitivity to nuance, relives, his description suddenly verges on elegy:

> The European mind, by which Valéry meant the scientific instrument of the
> Enlightenment, had severed itself from any accountability to a theistic abso-
> lute. It pursued its investigations as if it had decided beforehand that the moral
> and metaphysical claims for human nature were all pieces of conceit. The wars
> unleashed a savagery that it did nothing to contain. Its "new science" perfected

those weapons that can kill on a scale only imaginable before this century. The inapprehensible impulse of this mind *in its purest state* is toward the disintegration of that relationship between subject and object, which had been at the heart of nearly all previous philosophy. . . . What else indeed but anguish can the human being experience in such a mind in which he and his world are obliterated?

With or without his italics, his rhetorical pitch breaks the surface of that concluding question.

The collection's most interesting piece, "The Dark Rooms of the Enlightenment," gathers Locke's remark, that the human mind is a dark room illuminated only by the "windows" of sensation, into Finlay's suspicion that the Enlightenment was actually anti-intellectual in its distrust of the mind and its powers and hostile to both theism and intellectualism. On its face the claim is hard to accept until one notices that it will lead, late in the essay, to a discussion of David Hume. It would be pointless to attempt a summary of Finlay's synopsis of two centuries of intellectual history or show how it takes Finlay right to John Henry Newman, to whom he is reluctant to concede much out of disappointment with Newman's Wordsworthian distrust of reason. Finlay depicts Newman as an accidental inheritor of the Enlightenment's anti-intellectualism, an unwilling shill for Romantic nostalgics whose longing for a redemptive irrationalism, what Keats called a "life of sensation rather than thought," makes them inheritors of the worst of both movements. As a result, Newman "saw the intellect by its very nature in fallen man as an agent for spiritual decadence." Finlay begins mastering Newman by working backward from the *Apologia pro vita sua,* which described his conversion from Anglicanism to Roman Catholicism. He concurs with Newman in thinking that the Enlightenment mind "has been and continues to be inimical to any form of religious certitude" but argues against Newman's characterization of it as "exuding that self-confidence that comes from the possession of unlimited power" and goes on to reproduce a lengthy passage where Newman is distinguishing between reason in scientific inquiry and "right" or common reason. Finlay claims that Newman thinks of intellect as wild and capricious, "as if the intellect contained the core of sin itself, and the irrationalisms of the will and blindness of psychological compulsion were nowhere involved. But is Newman historically accurate in this characterization?

Do we indeed find such a powerful and vigorous intellect informing and be-ing displayed in the thought of the Enlightenment?" Newman, that is, in a full retreat from skepticism, tried to "baptize" the intellect; but the attempt, de-scribed in his *Apologia,* foundered on what Finlay apparently believed was a confusion of the intellect with its contents—the contents of the fallen world, which starts out as the intellect's conscious preoccupation with the life of the senses and ends as a narcissistic obsession. Newman's elimination or ousting of reason thus leaves empty the dominant position it had occupied until later in the century, when first Nietzschean will and then the Freudian unconscious enter to claim its position.

The figure who most haunts these essays, and whom Finlay's impassioned sensibility does not fully domesticate, is David Hume, who comes in for par-ticularly hard interrogation. According to Finlay, "David Hume thought that reason should be the slave of passion, and, consequently, with him no com-pletely intellectual explanation is possible for a single act of the mind." The tricky modal "should" in that last sentence masks as a moral imperative what in Hume's prose is actually an empirical principle—all thought begins in the body, in sensuous experience: What Finlay calls "reason," then, has no choice but to draw its evidence from the senses in the first and last places. For Hume, the absence of aprioristic grounds for asserting the mind's claims of independence of matter—material being, physical phenomena—makes any determination of differences between "what thinks" and "what is being thought about" unlikely if not impossible. Hume, in other words, annihilates the "about" (and calls into question everything we think we know, including our very perception of cause-and-effect relationships, in which Hume finally concedes limited confidence). The master text here (apart from Hume's complex biography) is his "Enquiry Concerning Human Understanding," where the central insight is contained in the second section, which I think needs to be given in full:

> Every one will readily allow, that there is a considerable difference between the perceptions of the mind, when a man feels the pain of excessive heat, or the pleasure of moderate warmth, and when he afterwards recalls to his memory this sensation, or anticipates it by his imagination. These faculties may mimic or copy the perceptions of the senses; but they never can entirely reach the force and vivacity of the original sentiment. The utmost we say of them, even when

they operate with greatest vigour, is, that they represent their object in so lively a manner, that we could almost say we feel or see it: but, except the mind be disordered by disease or madness, they never can arrive at such a pitch of vivacity, as to render these perceptions altogether undistinguishable. All the colours of poetry, however splendid, can never paint natural objects in such a manner as to make the description be taken for a real landscape. The most lively thought is still inferior to the dullest sensation.

Hume has tried and has failed to bridge the distance between theology and rationalism; he sounds less like a man crowing over victory than someone mourning philosophy's failure to comprehend two lines of conjecture native to all human thought. Later in the essay, it is true, Hume's tone alters sharply and turns bellicose: he advises his readers to "commit . . . to the flames" any metaphysical speculation that fails to arrive experimentally and logically at its conclusions. But that conclusion is painful and hard-won and the inevitable product of Hume's method.

Finlay must have known this: his survey of Enlightenment thinkers is compressed, beginning in Locke, who "shrunk the proportions of the mind," and concluding in Mill. It's a survey, however, after all, a poet's hardly comprehensive summation of a broader field, and this is no place to quiz Finlay on matters referable to any competent graduate student's grasp of British Empiricism. What's impressive in this collection is not how thoroughly he did his homework or how energetically he could quibble but how tenaciously he could continue to nibble away at the same problem. The texture of his prose is meditative, not theoretical, and its accuracy is that of a sensibility panoptic and wounded, principled, and impassioned: "The mind requires the illusion of stability if no stability actually exists. . . . Philosophy and human nature, consequently, part company in David Hume's mind, which human nature must reject if it wishes to survive. Outside his philosophical study he lived according to principles that inside that study he rejected as non-existent." Life for Hume, in other words, would have been death for John Finlay. His distress over Hume's claiming the ideological high ground at the expense of his own humanity strikes me as accurate: Hume's biography bears out how much the discipline of philosophy crippled him psychologically and nearly drove him insane. Behind Finlay's distress is an aggrieved compassion for a great mind that confronted a nightmarish choice—to reject either immaterial mind or material creation—and whose failure of nerve somehow precipitated the "agnostic obscurity" of twentieth-century unbelief. "It is," Finlay says in his introduction, "the alienation of God from the mind, which we can see in *even* such a writer as Cardinal Newman, that I find most disturbing" (my italics).

There is a second unmastered personality: Nietzsche. In his essay on Yvor Winters, who is spared the full force of Finlay's withering disappointment, he concedes that Winters "would rather himself have done without God" but that Winters did in fact embrace God as a logical necessity, though sadly in much the same spirit that Aristotle (to put Winters in more esteemed company) surrenders to the theoretical need for an Unmoved Mover in his *Metaphysics:* things that end must have beginnings. The problem is that human understanding in Winters's account requires God to be *systematically* elegant. Finlay then goes on, correctly, to gently associate Winters with Nietzsche, and his final paragraph goes even further and anticipates the full-frontal assault on Nietzsche mounted in the collection's last essay, "Three Variations on the Killing of the Father: Nietzsche, Freud and Kafka": "Nietzsche, too, would rather do without God, and he does, without saying that God does not exist, but with saying that He is dead, a totally meaningless statement." And a reader would have to agree with Finlay that, so decontextualized, Nietzsche's "statement" is "totally meaningless," which sounds convincing until you realize that Finlay fails to mention that the "statement" is spoken in the persona of a madman in one of the parables in *The Gay Science.* And even though in the final essay Finlay attempts to recontextualize the remark, it seems odd he would have overlooked in Nietzsche exactly the element—irony—that makes him more Modernist poet than late Romantic philosopher. Even Nietzsche might have agreed that "Nietzsche found it impossible completely to rid himself of God" (which is, in Finlay's plain English, essentially the charge that Heidegger leveled, in typically mind-bending syntax, in "The Word of Nietzsche: 'God Is Dead'"). Agreeable or not, persuasive or "meaningless," Nietzsche's flight from determinate meaning was perfectly consonant with his larger project of a "revaluation of values" and of conventional habits of thought through interrogations of the language that embodied and the systems that inform them.

I have to register these objections merely to get them out of the way. They are not exactly quibbles, but at the same time they are hardly disabling objections if you are at home with the idiosyncrasy and informing religious passion behind Finlay's approach. His essays leave you impressed with the results of a mind driving its way through, in order fully to acquire, an entire philosophical inheritance, and assuming all the way that there can be no great understanding that is not simultaneously informed by faith and principled by experience. And the book left me with another impression: no alienation is as complex or as pained as that of a mind locked in self-examination and finding only more and more images of its own incompleteness, which, for a religious sensibility, may become the ground for an undermining, and ultimately exhausting scrupulosity. The world of fact, even after being confronted or "baptized" by faith, never really seems to go away even after it has been absorbed by the religious system—it merely finds another shape to dwell in. A sinful deed thus becomes a curable sickness in the *materials,* not the doer, and we're counseled to forgive the sinner but condemn the sin. Sin, consequently, becomes what Aquinas called a defection from the good, human evil a weakness, a crack in the will, and reason the lonely umpire assigned the job of separating sins from sinners, good from evil. Let Hawthorne be the secular theologian here: "It is to the credit of human nature, that, except where its selfishness is brought into play, it loves more readily than it hates." This is the argument of that routinely ignored masterpiece *The Scarlet Letter:* "the heart's native language" is love, after all, and that human beings should be credited for their essential if embattled goodness (so much for the Fall) inasmuch as we would sooner do good than evil. Everything is settled, then, until history confronts you with its own inevitable and stupefyingly problematic examples.

At length the final test of accuracy rests in how completely empirical fact has been mastered by the demands of the religious sensibility, and in Finlay's case, those demands must surely have been taxing. In 1982 he received an AIDS diagnosis; by the end of the decade he was dying and he knew it; he died early in 1991. In a posthumous essay of 1994 from the *Hudson Review,* "The Night of Alcibiades," which is not included in this collection, Finlay suggests that the source of Socrates's fortitude at the end was "his belief that he himself was not his body but his mind"; then he goes on to reconstruct the philosopher's last moments:

From his belief in this immortal and god-like intellectual principle in him Socrates derived his inner strength, his self-control, his courtesy of wholeness. It explains the actual meaning of his pregnant sentence that no evil can happen to a good man in this life or in the next. For how could it if the man is such a soul? And so the inexpert and tragically blind and misguided democracy could poison and kill his soul . . . but the executioners could not reach the man. Even as the hemlock was coursing through his blood, Socrates was already somewhere else in the indestructible cohesion of the undivided intellect.

We prepare ourselves for the worst by migrating into the personalities of the best to have suffered it. Finlay was in these essays preparing himself for the moment "When death, that ancient, awful fact appears," and doing so through that dangerous habit of transmigration that poets know and practice best.

Late in his singularly short career, Isidore Ducasse, Comte de Lautréamont, claimed that "Poetry cannot do without philosophy. Philosophy can do without poetry." It was 1869 and Ducasse was announcing not just the waning of Romanticism but probably the end of his own poetic powers. (He would die, at twenty-four, a year later.) Any poet reluctant to release his art from the requirement to satisfy truth, no matter its source or its impact on his art, says something valuable, reveals a stubborn skepticism about the value of poetry, and particularly whether it has any final cognitive weight, any truth-value. Keats may have put it best in his famous letter describing Negative Capability. Call it the Coleridge Stipulation: "Coleridge, for instance, would let go by a fine isolated verisimilitude caught from the Penetralium of mystery, from being incapable of remaining content with half-knowledge. This pursued through volumes would perhaps take us no further than this, that with a great poet the sense of Beauty overcomes every other consideration, *or rather obliterates all consideration.*" Emerson, of course, would later reject the idea that there is any competition, anything to consider, in "Each and All." So the question of the truth-value of poetry remains unsettled. No one writing so late in this damned century, and certainly no American poet, has been able to avoid the confrontation with this inheritance, or the difficulty of going on the record about it. If nothing else, Finlay's prose is a Pyrrhic victory over the temptation to avoid the encounter completely. When truth seduces the poet from seeking salvation through metaphor, what then? Where, Finlay asks, do we find the metaphysical optimism equal to saving not only our souls but our life's work?

—1999

The Reckless Nostalgia
of Gerald Stern

Years ago I was reviewing a half-dozen translations of the *Odyssey* and noticed something. The most important word in the invocation is *nostos,* or "home," which appears in line 5 and is the root of *nostalgia.* Two lines later, and as part of a connected construction, is the Greek word *atasthaliesin,* or "recklessness." Odysseus, in Fitzgerald's translation, is credited with trying "to bring his shipmates home," but "their own recklessness destroyed them all." Hardly surprising—they just spent ten years on the battlefield, and Odysseus, though the invocation unsurprisingly lets him off the hook, is among the most bloody-minded and reckless members of his crew. Item: the first thing he and his men do on leaving Troy is to raid tiny Ismaros, a small, neutral seaside town north of Troy and certainly not on the way home, which was southwest.

What is sort of surprising is that the poem makes their desire for home, their *nostalgia* and their *recklessness* neighbor words, as if nostalgia and recklessness were somehow symmetrical. Nostalgia is good, but theirs is human and thus impure—mixed with recklessness. Yet without recklessness there would be no rescue of Helen, no Kyklops or Scylla, no seven-year sabbatical with Kalypso, no Kirke, no visit to the Land of the Dead, no Tiresias, no reunion in Hell with bitter Achilles and betrayed Agamemnon, and most important, no poignant—and not quite "touching" because she is all fleshless spirit—goodbye to his mother, the dead Antikleia. In other words, no fun, and certainly no *Odyssey.* I don't think it's an accident that the poem situates these two words so closely: nostalgia and recklessness are twins of desire. One earns praise, one censure—Gilgamesh, Odysseus (in Homer and Dante), Jonah trying to skedaddle to Tarshish, and even the pious Aeneas are all reckless. Reckless, we leave; out of nostalgia, we return. One makes us long for home, the other for anything but. When nostalgia is productive, it's Joyce writing *Ulysses* about a place he can never go back to physically; if it's destructive, it's the young Hmong dying a kind of brutal, parodic crib-death once "safe" in America.

Autobiography probably has to begin in nostalgia, but nostalgia is never pure any more than autobiography is purely objective. Historically, nostalgia is not an "emotion" but a medical condition first diagnosed in the nineteenth century in British soldiers returning from the Boer War. Nostalgia was not only unproductive but destructive. This is among the lessons of *The Odyssey*. The impurities make it interesting and guard against surrender to sentimentality and the sentimental odysseys that fill bookstores. The antidote to sentiment is usually fact, but fact, like chemotherapy, can kill the patient. It can enervate life-writing. What can "fact" mean when you are writing about yourself, which is the literary equivalent of burglarizing your own house? The answer is the excluded middle of the saving lie. The past has to be retold slantwise because memory can be false and because fact polarizes. Now that autobiography has replaced the lusty and healthy fabrications of fiction as a way of getting closer to "reality," the memoir (or its anxiously rebranded twin, "creative nonfiction") has become so obnoxiously nostalgic that even adults can sound like fifteen-year-olds and their books like YA fiction. Nostalgia can be poisonous, can produce pious apologies or a pedantic dullness, as the greatest writers have known, and life-writing has never been about reciting facts but about distorting them. The tradition of semitruthful autobiography goes way back, well beyond poor Rousseau, who always gets the blame, through the wise Montaigne and Dante (*The Divine Comedy* presents itself as visionary autobiography) directly to St. Augustine. Garry Wills tells how, in book 2 of the *Confessions,* Augustine bemoans his foul youth, how he looked for love in all the wrong places and "stank" in the eyes of God. Yet one of the products of that foul past was a child named Adeodatus (God's Gift). Facts leave blank pages. No writer ever feels nostalgic about a blank page, or if he did, he would leave it blank.

Gerald Stern's poetry has always been autobiographical, and yet always a backhanding of nostalgia and the perils of memoir. His solution is and was to pitch the autobiographical lyric as an exercise in biography, which is always conjectural and wracked by guesswork and inexactitude. "Bio III," from *Divine Nothingness,* begins,

I will go down in history without a hotel
for I have been dispersed though what I wanted
was nothing, a box for my mail, a key,
an easy chair and a floor lamp with tufted string,
a coffee shop with access inside and outside
next to the lobby with a red-headed waitress.

This is about as close to nostalgia as this or any of the poems in the "Bio" series comes—a longing not exactly for "home" but for some temporary lodging, which is home for the permanently displaced, the career nomad. It is not quite homesickness but a recognition that the objects of longing are pretty ordinary. The mailbox and the key, the chair and the floor lamp that is remembered as having a "tufted string," are connected syntactically, by apposition, to the word "nothing," which is itself introduced as an afterthought ("though . . ."). This is no real hotel but some imagined corollary out of film noir—call it faux nostalgia. Real nostalgia, on the other hand, is a composite of objects we experience that never achieve total individuality in memory. Hawthorne says of Hester's Pearl, "in this one child there were many children," and in this one "floor lamp" are many floor lamps—the Platonic floor lamp, if you will. It's the sense in which we never sleep with just *one* person. The remembered stuff that populates his work is an expression of the sublime, though for Americans the sublime is not natural but manufactured. I am not talking about or invoking the sublime of theory, commerce, or psychology, though sublimation is part of the process. One of Stern's insights, which joins him to poets like Ammons and Dugan, is that junk—not just daffodils or the meanest flowers that blow—makes us nostalgic. Keys, stuffed chairs, floor lamps with *tufted* string—recklessly desired, impulsively bought, recklessly discarded. This is American nostalgia, because for American poets theirs is a "homemade world," which was the title of a book by Hugh Kenner. Nostalgia is dissolved back into its basis in the world of the discarded things that fill up the poems.

Discards are all over Stern's work—you would think all the poems contain is junk—and started to appear in poems like "Behaving Like a Jew" nearly fifty years ago. That poem still surprises me—a bitter memorial to a dead opossum that is also, and this is what so surprises me, a condemnation of "the spirit of

Lindberg over everything." Lindberg, American hero and later an infamous
Nazi sympathizer, makes an appearance in the poem, not as a synecdoche for
evil but for something more clownish, mundane, and insidious because so banal, in the sense that Hannah Arendt intended the word. He represents a rigorously disciplined recklessness that coins terms like "collateral damage" or
"best practices," of which the concentration camps were applications of the
latter to solving the problem of the former. Stern insists on memorializing
the dead opossum in order to remain human, to memorialize without moralizing over all that is evil, from roadkill to Nazis to the uninflated acronyms
of industry.

And it also means remembering the reckless innocence of the driver who
ran over the opossum and "the country, the bloodstained / bumpers, the stiff
hairs sticking out of the grilles, / the slimy highways" of America. Sentimental
fiction and autobiography tend to overparticularize, to skip self-indictments
and icky details—the blood, the stiff hairs, the beslimed highways, the Lind-
bergs, the mind-bending pathos of daily life—that spoil nostalgia. The poem is
(no pun intended) a Jeremiad—at heart Jerry Stern is a moralist—whose target
is Lindberg and nostalgia itself. Nothing is more selective than memory. Nostalgia is made impure by circumstance—my motto is: scratch a sentimentalist
and find a bully (both Hitler and Stalin were given to fits of nostalgia)—and
the impurity is part of the poetry. For the opossum or the voice that is raised in
mourning of it to mean anything at all, the impurity has to be acknowledged.
That impurity or circumstance is the ambience, which is this, our America: the
poem surrounds its subject without explicitly naming it. The process of remembering the opossum includes a whole history of public grief stretching back to
World War II and beyond. The title tells you this, but so does the syntax—line
after climactic line ("I am going to be unappeased . . . / I am going to behave
like a Jew . . . / I am not going . . .") laid out like tossed tally sticks, syntactically
disconnected yet pointing in the same direction.

Or maybe not *tossed*: "for I have been dispersed" is the second line of "Bio
III." To toss something implies a direction and intent, but a *dispersal* implies
neither. If you are dispersed you are scattered, leaving you in a situation that
may be entirely new. Or it might be a grim reprise of what you have known,
which is also, probably, what we will come to know and see all over, or so says
the remainder of the poem:

I was waylaid, given what I was, by
2,000 books and a Plymouth station wagon
thirty feet long and easily twelve years old
that I could carry a piano in and park
anywhere I wanted, given the year then.

And I had a bench where I could think it through
when there were two seconds of silence in between
the delivery trucks, before my coffee got cold
and the crumbs on my lip were gobbled up by sparrows
catty-corner from Saint Andrew's Episcopal
where there is opera music four times a year
and you put clothes on the porch to give to the poor
—if I could compare one life to another—
though what I loved always got in the way.

I will talk in a moment about how the presence of the simple conjunction "and" in these poems is a decisive technical move. The "and" that begins the last stanza tells you that there is more to "it," the dispersal and dispersions that are being thought about, the "thinking through" that complements recollection. The last line means that what we remember is supplemented by what "always got in the way." What got in the way was "what I loved," and to think of being in love as "dispersal" is disturbing but still beautiful in the way that disturbing truths often can be. Love makes going down in history *without* a hotel a triumph. No doubt there is a story behind the floor lamp, the redhead, the Plymouth wagon (were Plymouths ever thirty feet long?) and the "2000 books"—a context that clarifies and connects. But context in isolation is never narrative, and narrative is not always poetry any more than every perfectly symmetrical face is beautiful. Context in these poems yields to mystery, and the mystery has to be preserved because it's a sign of how chaotic memory can be as it scatters and disperses. Even if Stern were to tell me the name of the redhead and the titles of those two thousand books (and show me a picture of that thirty-foot Plymouth), it would make no difference. What is "reckless" in the person is the constant habit of falling in love, which you can only learn if you are dispersed and can feel only when you are no longer a one but a many.

On the other hand, if you are dispersed by constantly falling in love, your particular dispersal is a contraction of, say, the grander synonyms associated with the word—resettlement, removal, ex- or repatriation, or the now worn-out and casually misapplied term *diaspora*. A poet's diasporas are more intimate. They are mini-dispersals that embody the macro. Dispersal is ongoing and occurs every time he looks at the world, which is the same as looking at oneself, that thing that keeps expanding like gas in space. The style tells you this because style *is* perception in poetry, whether strong or weak.

Since *Lucky Life* (1977), a typical Stern poem does not so much ruminate like Lowell's or obsess like Berryman's or root around like Sexton's inside some personal precinct. It unravels, expands, swells and flattens, unpeels, dissolves in Whitmanesque jags and eddies. In some ways, this late style reminds me of the outrageous opening of "Out of the Cradle Endlessly Rocking"—an implosion of prepositions, *from* this and *out of* this and that and the other, twenty-some lines racing to earth at different speeds and from different directions and joining up at, or splashing down onto Whitman, our American ground zero. But Stern's work is really nothing like Whitman's. His instincts are more anaphorical than metaphorical, and insistently more declarative, even incantatory, than grand and magical and declamatory. His prosody has more in common with older traditions and with novelists like Hemingway—it relies on coordination and equivalences rather than subordination. It is chatty like great stand-up (which he reveres), jazzily discursive, and the twin not only of his vision but his physical breath; it is a way of talking that passes into writing, the ironed-flat lyrical mode of the American Sublime (Levine, Ammons, Dugan), a kind of majestic verbatimizing. In the "Bio" series each poem is given a Roman numeral like the poems of Catullus or Horace, but no title, because each is part of a continuing monologue:

> . . . And where your rabbi is buried
> and how you talked for hours about which cemetery
> *you'd* go to but she died first though decades younger
> and though her hill has a pine tree and even catches
> the wind, it is your voices that count the most,
> that salad of chopped-up lettuce engulfed in tuna

the two of you spent three hours over, the subject
death, and what the Hittite nose was like,
and how Jeremiah will sound when he comes back
and what would he do in Camden or East St. Louis
and could they hear him break another glass bottle
and could they bear his curses perish the day,
the noisy geese in formation too late maybe,
my own steps icy, Thelonious Monk playing
Duke Ellington in the small living room
and underneath that the Unaccompanied Cello,
consideration in the green kitchen and almost
kindness on the dedicated shelf,
entwined pigs and a rooster, if you can stand it.

This is the conclusion of "Bio V," which I produce deliberately out of context
to demonstrate a point about style. Style is perception: it follows the contours,
takes the shape not of one freestanding object but the subjective experience
or remembering of some one *thing*. We remember all the things that surround
and confine some particular other thing; we can no more easily think of one
isolated thing than we can visualize one object without the space surrounding
it. Memory is a mess, and these poems describe the messiness (but only "if you
can stand it"). Why must my memory of a girl I loved include a hairy neck and
a naked plain of back acne one blanket over from ours? Or of a false friend,
suddenly looking up and about to say something profound at lunch, with his
mouth open and a single spot of pesto on his tongue? Or of someone I loved
and deeply miss lying dead on a gurney, jaundiced, his mouth open like a yellow door somebody forgot to close? Syntax is an EEG. It follows the contour of
memory, but memory, like the spider in the Whitman poem that keeps throwing out "filament after filament," usually snatches and grabs everything in the
neighborhood. Whitman is a joiner: he constantly seeks to combine elements.
Stern wants to keep things distinct because, given his lyric sense, the lyrical
memory is solitary confinement. Out of that confinement comes the need to
grab and snatch. Stern will have none of it. He wants the mess, the intense par-
ticularity that makes our experience ironically hang together.

The technical tradition behind the "Bio" series is more narrative than lyr-ical, closer to prose and oral storytelling. The narrator, excitable, inspired, lets the elements shape the narrative rather than stacking them in an artsy formal series that attracts densely figured metaphors—metaphors that slow you down. Artifice retards. The tension between the written sign, which anchors memory, and the outward-bound tug of desire against that anchorage, is exposed. In a way Stern's practice is the final exhaustion of Romantic practice, and the Ro-mantic poem. James MacFarland, who coined the term *diasparactive,* "broken in pieces," to describe Coleridge's work, argued that the height of Romantic poetic achievement was the fragment, and that the Romantic lyric is a self-unraveling, a self-dispersal: the poet tracks the breaking up, the ejecta, including himself as both the source and a piece of the eruption, and the poem (depending on which critic you read) either fails or achieves greatness. Stern's approach is a mingling of visionary temperaments, as much Romantic as it is Talmudic, but the dias-paractive dominates, and its stylistic marker is the successions of *and*s. Line by line, each is like a boundary stone marking a threshold of nostalgia:

> and how Jeremiah will sound when he comes back
> and what would he do in Camden or East St. Louis
> and could they hear him break another glass bottle
> and could they bear his curses perish the day

To view this as babble—I get a kick out of imagining how somebody like Lea-vis or his New Critical progeny would have viewed this—misses the point: it is *supposed to sound* like babble. So, for that matter, is Pound's

> And the days are not full enough
> And the nights are not full enough
> And life slips by like a field mouse
>   Not shaking the grass.

The technical term for such syntax is *polysyndetonic*—an ordering that accu-mulates without measuring, coordinates without evaluating the members of the whole, growing heap. Is this not how human memory works? The question is not why but *where does it lead?* Working backward—though backward and forward are, like up and down in outer space, meaningless here—this is the opening of "Bio V":

> Keep in mind how callow I was and how
> sarcastic walking down that dirt road
> with no room in any of my outside pockets
> for your left-over straw or the gold leaf you gave me
> for high achievement in the art of ridicule

This is the source of nostalgia, "if you can stand it," that is, if you can avoid being *merely* nostalgic and remember everything else. The first three words ask you to "Keep in mind" everything that follows; it is a clever opening mainly because it's a toss-up how much the writer actually remembers and how much he's making up. It assumes that you and he are in the middle of a conversation or at least that you're overhearing an ongoing monologue. "Keep in mind," in other words, the other poems in this group, remember that one of us must keep talking. The end completes but does not explain the beginning. And this exuberance over what is discarded is expressed as the desire, as he says in a poem from *Rejoicings* (1973), "to close the whole world in my grip," to surround the whole world with a poem. You cannot do this, however, without an understated technical intelligence, and in this case it is usually overlooked. I am reminded that one of Stern's strengths is that he writes *books* of poems rather than just the "good poems" that win Pushcarts and get picked off by anthologies.

There are poems that do not ask you to do this, that demystify themselves, shift the load from the inside to the outside, poems that don't ask you to keep anything in mind or end all guesswork by sending you to footnotes, the library, or Google. "Dover Beach" is still grace before meals in intro-to-lit courses and it justly has been celebrated for its pathos and its interesting prosody, but I've always believed that the reason is because it explains itself. The amplitude of the pronoun (*we*) that the poem deploys to expand the size of the narrative host and allow you to share Arnold's despair is too easily assumed, even presumptuous, even slightly odd: isn't this a love poem? So is the preposterous comparison of

the English Channel with "The Sea of Faith," a bit of learned self-indulgence
that nowadays comes off as a bit silly. The poem, yes, has internal harmony and
ironic balance and leaves nothing unglossed. The poem seems fairly self-assured,
if not self-aroused, by the invocation of Classical authority and learning and the
conviction that Sophocles and Homer are in agreement with Matthew Arnold
and his gloomy views on High Culture and Victorian England's cultural and
political situation, which is the problem. It all proceeds from his conviction that
there is, or was *once,* a clear line of sight connecting the cultures of fifth-century
Athens and late nineteenth-century London, the former irrigating the latter.
But this was so only in the minds of pedants, politicians, and the nineteenth
century's prophets of empire.

Another scholar-friendly poem is Yeats's "The Sorrows of Love," which exists in two versions. He revised it at least once and, in doing so, ruined it. Here
is the first, unrevised version:

> The quarrel of the sparrows in the eaves,
> The full round moon and the star-laden sky,
> And the loud song of the ever-singing leaves,
> Had hid away earth's old and weary cry.

> And then you came with those red mournful lips,
> And with you came the whole of the world's tears,
> And all the trouble of her labouring ships,
> And all the trouble of her myriad years.

> And now the sparrows warring in the eaves,
> The curd-pale moon, the white stars in the sky,
> And the loud chaunting of the unquiet leaves,
> Are shaken with earth's old and weary cry.

All those *and*s, in stanza 2, must have struck Yeats, who by this time in his career
had grown suspicious of Whitman, as blemishes. So he revised it and turned
out the version that exists below. Critical apologists for the so-called "Middle
Yeats" dismissed the poetry of "Late Yeats" and cringed at how his prosody was
swamped by emotion—his grief over Maud Gonne's umpteen rejections (ac-

tually, six) of his marriage proposals—instead of being informed by fact and
sturdy classical myth. Consequently, anthologizers often pick the revised version, version two:

> The brawling of a sparrow in the eaves,
> The brilliant moon and all the milky sky,
> And all that famous harmony of leaves,
> Had blotted out man's image and his cry.

> A girl arose that had red mournful lips
> And seemed the greatness of the world in tears,
> Doomed like Odysseus and the labouring ships
> And proud as Priam murdered with his peers;

> Arose, and on the instant clamorous eaves,
> A climbing moon upon an empty sky,
> And all that lamentation of the leaves,
> Could but compose man's image and his cry.

Lots of info! But shame on you if you voted for version two. The cost of
revision was a lot of overthinking, and (to me) dullness and overwrought syntax. Yeats, in touch with his inner explainer, purged the poem of the simple
coordinates, the *ands* that begin all four lines of quatrain 2 and that swell the
total number of coordinate conjunctions to seven. Greater catastrophe then
beckoned: he changes the point of view (from second to third). The result is
a stiff, mummified cadence and wooden sentence structure that dead-ends at
the semicolon in line 8 and, because it needs to make consecutive, discursive
sense, throws up the white flag of "Arose," the word that opens the last stanza,
which quickly sinks under its own triumphalist diction. All this just to include
the endearingly nonsensical references to Odysseus, Helen, and Priam, which
can then be reexplained in a user-friendly footnote. Version two, corrected for
academic consumption, comes with its own tutor. It demystifies itself, which
is bad for poems and deadly in life in general but beloved of the editors who
work for W. W. Norton et al. I am not sure, even, that the second version is really about the *same* Maud Gonne, since it demotes her from "you" to "a girl."

The Maud Gonne who was a sexy brunette and even in her photographs comes through as a force of nature circa 1891 was probably better off than the Maud Gonne who, twenty years later, is rhetorically miscast, hardly a girl, then re-masked, stuffed in a gown, and made a proxy for the perennial symbol of hapless beauty, Helen of Troy.

Many years ago I was standing in Stern's kitchen and he asked me to write down the name of a particular book in one of his notepads, a 5″ × 8″ theme book with white unlined pages. I noticed that on the facing pages was a handwritten draft of a new poem, and that he had turned the pad *sideways* to write it down landscape-wise—he had big squiggly handwriting. And—the memorable thing—each line was preceded by a number in a circle. Intriguing. I asked him about the numbers. They were to guide his typist, of course, to ensure that these lines be broken not just anywhere but at *these* points, in these places. These were *formal* decisions that had nothing to do with "form" as it is usually understood. Reading Stern's work may give you the impression that he is simply verbatimiz-ing and that you are reading a transcription, concatenated talk chained into lines, chunks, fragments that went straight from voice to typescript to print. He is loquacious, but not chatty: even if the syntax is simple (lots of coordinate clauses) the thought-scape is not. For a few pages let me pursue the way Stern uses *and* in his later work. It is rare to see any reader of Stern talking about the work's technique because the poems themselves feel so underwrought.

Whether or not anybody has ever charged his work with being inaccessi-ble, it is amusing to see how so much of it since 1980 seems never to come to rest on a particular subject, or state it with precision. For a contemporary poet, this is real audacity, and its culmination is *American Sonnets* (2002), the book that followed *Last Blue* (2000). The title asserts that Stern is joining the most venerated formal tradition in the history of Western Lyric, but in the book's fifty-nine poems there is no trace of meter or rhyme or octave-sestet divisions or obedience to the fourteen-line limit (the lengths vary); they are not even all *love* poems, at least not on first reading. The only trace of the twelfth-century form is conjectural: the sonneteer stages a conversation or argument with himself—which you would expect in a form invented by a thirteenth-century Italian lawyer—its back-and-forthness codified in the traditional Q and A division between the octave and sestet. The regimented internal dialogue between, let's say, self and soul, is still present, only reckless and uncontrolled.

Here is "Winter Thirst," by far one of the more successful poems in this book, and one that comes nearest to feeling if not looking like a sonnet:

I grew up with bituminous in my mouth
and sulfur smelling like rotten eggs and I
first started to cough because my lungs were like cardboard;
and what we called snow was gray with black flecks
that were like glue when it came to snowballs and made
them hard and crusty, though we still ate the snow
anyhow, and as for filth, well, start with
smoke, I carried it with me I know everywhere
and someone sitting beside me in New York or Paris
would know where I came from, we would go in for dinner—red
meat loaf or brown *choucroute*—and he would
guess my hill, and we would talk about soot
and what a dirty neck was like and how
the white collar made a fine line;
and I told him how we pulled heavy wagons
and loaded boxcars every day from five
to one A.M. and how good it was walking
empty-handed to the no. 69 streetcar
and how I dreamed of my bath and how the water
was black and soapy then and what the void
was like and how a candle instructed me.

More self-dispersal. The way the poem spills out from that initial detail is nearly comical—coal, sulfur, rotten eggs—and when it runs into that semicolon in line 3 it feels almost as if it were taking a mental breath. Then it pivots, restarts and/or reboots with the mentions of snow, filth, smoke. It is possible, by the way, to object to the pattern of pure association, the way the poem gets to where it goes next, to the air of strained innocence and constant indirection, and to how far, how distractedly it moves from where it began. It does not stick exclusively to its own opening logic and circle back to *bituminous* to report what "actually" happened. The only thing we might all agree on is that it's not about "mining," at least not the mining of coal. If you can get that far, then you can go farther, as things get woolier, even more annoying with the reported or invented conversation between the speaker "and someone sitting beside me in New York or Paris," through the tenuous connection between *filth* and the *smoke* he carries in his lungs, which leads to the mention of which "hill" in the hilly city of Pittsburgh the speaker comes from:

> . . . and he would
> guess my hill, and we would talk about soot
> and what a dirty neck was like and how
> the white collar made a fine line;
> and I told him how we pulled heavy wagons
> and loaded boxcars every day from five
> to one A.M. and how good it was walking
> empty-handed to the no. 69 streetcar
> and how I dreamed of my bath and how the water
> was black and soapy then and what the void
> was like and how a candle instructed me.

And this *and* that *and* the other: playful, excitable, flexible. The subject is not coal or smoke or snow or food (or mining) but coal *and* smoke *and* snow *and* food: the subject is the process of finding what is homey, *heimlich* but not "at home." It is a kind of detective work, only you don't always know what you're looking for, and the scene keeps changing. The prosody works hard to get you to the observation about the white collar (notice that the memory is not necessarily the speaker's: it might be his interlocutor's) and halts at a second semicolon (there are two end-stopped lines out of twenty-one total), so that all that prefatory seminarrative, all that chitchat around disconnected details, is silenced: ". . . and we would talk about soot / and what a dirty neck was like and how / the white collar made a fine line." These are pauses in the conversation between two people who suddenly realize they like each other, maybe have something in common. It is as if a judge were bringing the gavel down four times, with four bangs (*white, collar, fine, line*). If I were a conductor and this were a musical score,

I would tell the players not to rush through the lines that follow the second semicolon. The semicolon is as it were a musical *rest,* the *and*s like dotted notes.

The poem then ends by resolving a whole range of dissonance into a closure that offers no closure: "and how I dreamed of my bath and how the water / was black and soapy then and what the void / was like and how a candle instructed me." The isolation of the lyric is complete. The candle, the one stuck to the miner's hat—if you insist on bringing all your reading and expensive education to it— might point to Stevens's "highest candle" in "The Final Soliloquy of the Interior Paramour," which itself points to Prophets 20:27 ("The spirit of man is the candle of the Lord"). Or maybe it's just a miner's candle. It hardly matters because the closing, like the opening, is conditional and discloses as much as it hides. The nonphysicality of the "physical" once it enters memory is what the poem is about. A detail in a poem is simply one more pointer to some external and distracting external thing, at least until it is sublimated in imagination; a fact, as Keats said, is not a truth until you love it. In a way, Stern is reminding you of the long fight twentieth-century poetry waged against, and mostly lost to, the Romantics. The Romantic knew that things do not need poetry to be things, that a poem engulfed in its own thinghood is not a poem but something else. The physicality of the world is guaranteed to end the poet if the poet ends at the world. Whatever the poet understands, then, his poem understands that the mine is a "void" and the miner's "candle" is what enlightens it.

Williams declared that there should be "no ideas but in things," but *Paterson* demonstrates that he could not master the tricky demands his mandate lays on the lyric poet; there is too much random freight for the vehicle to support. The great cautionary examples of the Romantics, and Keats and Shelley in particular, insist that the lyric must court the physical world but never move in with it, and *Paterson,* like *The Cantos,* enters an up-and-down relationship with objectivity and often mistakes facts for realities, or factoids for facts. Pound's *Cantos,* especially, after the first thirty (and with the exception of the *Pisan* group), is one long ellipsis, stymied at times by unassimilated fact, constipated by ideology, too often barely readable, and in the end doomed by a reading of history so idiosyncratic it seems at times diseased. "Stupidity and ignorance all the way through," as Pound himself described them to Ginsberg. But Crane, Stevens, and the great but perpetually overlooked D. H. Lawrence never forgot that the lyric poet romances the given world but steps out with the imagined one, that "the world imagined is the only good." *Paterson* has always reminded me of a hoarder's bedroom or backyard; its incoherence is not the incoherence of, say, *The Bridge,* whose incoherence is more profound, rarely boring, and erotically far more intense. Even with the dominating persona of Paterson as a giant "who lies in the valley under the Passaic Falls," Williams's gatherings of letters and transcribed notes remain just that, and Pound's inventories of half- or misremembered facts do not always rise to the higher wisdom, never become sublime because sublimation and the investment of intimate feeling is what both set out to avoid and what Williams rediscovered, along with some of his earlier greatness, in the late, lovely "Asphodel" poems.

Stern is reschooling a particular technique—the conventional "catalogue" or litany, a version of the "show don't tell" approach—in some derivative of the Romantic sublime, where beauty and terror, the homely and the unknown, our love of beauty and our need to deface it, intersect. My sense is he is doing this consciously. "I created an unassailable Utopia amidst Max Factor the powder" is how he begins his "Bio IV," to me a commentary on his work over the past fifteen years:

> and sang such that I entertained a small living room
> full mostly of berouged women in the days of Bobbie Breen,
> and played for money nine-ball instead of reading my Kant
> offering my substance to suffer by inattention and suffer
> again by the final wiping out of the cosmic mirror.

Plato at length concedes that the ideal city of the *Republic* "is a pattern laid up in Heaven," and by *heaven* is also meant the soul, or what nowadays we have to call, to evade messianic or evangelical lunacy, "mind" or solipsistic memory. Stern's "unassailable" utopia has room for everybody—including Bobby Breen ("Canadian-born actor and singer of the 1930s": *Wikipedia*) and pool hustlers. The only "unassailable" Utopia is subjective, self-organized out of personality, which is a clutter of small rooms, women who come and go in makeup, unread philosophers, and given that last line, which is an uncanny impersonation of the cadences of the Ginsberg of "Wales Visitation," other poems. His "Utopia" is the isolating lyric. Our self-organizations end only at death, the one limit the poet must recognize, only not in his poems. When he says near the end, "I am

/ occult, though you'd never know it," he is admitting that his, like every other utopia, is a saving lie. The occult is his area of study; but also, as a thinking subject, he is always *occult,* always "hidden"—in the poem, in worn clothes, or in the body:

> and we do the motion of arms and legs as with a thread-bare
>
> tire the left hand fitting it into place the right hand
> holding the bumper-jack a shoulder even
> keeping the car upright the smell of dead birds
> escaping from the woods my good luck to find
> two bricks to keep the car from rolling
> violets for beauty a gust of wind for love.

"And," again. The word ends the last line of the penultimate stanza and kick-starts the first line of the last, and then goes away, having set in motion a prosody that shifts from the simple to the complex—from coordinated statements to a piling on of gerunds (or are they present participles?) that crawl like a Slinky down the page to conclude in the poem's most beautiful line. The poem has to keep saying *and,* else it will end. It must continue saying it even at the cost of coherence or comprehensibility. Some of the lines, I mean, hardly make practical sense: "the smell of dead birds / escaping from the woods" is, like the thirty-foot Plymouth, not a fact but an extravagance, or a truth of the imagination. (A dead bird in the woods is effectively deodorized by the surroundings; my 1960 three-on-a-tree Plymouth Fury was around a mere eighteen feet long.) Is it the impression you get whenever you're changing a tire and steadying or holding the wheel up, like Atlas, with your shoulder, that you're smelling dead birds when what you're actually smelling is burnt rubber? But you are not really doing that either—the tire-changing is also remembered, i.e., imagined, just like the "smell." The question like the answer is a philistine's; the point is the swiftness of thought as it sucks up individual details and maybe damages them as it does.

You can construct a narrative, a storyline, around the details and write your own ending—the poet finds a couple of bricks on the shoulder of the road by a wood and smells something, then sees a dead bird, chocks the tires to keep the car from rolling, then notices a couple of violets and feels a gust of wind . . . but probably not, and anyway, so what? The details are there not to educate nostalgia but to confuse it, to stimulate the habit of reimagination, which is what memory really is. The nostalgic violets anchor you to what is real, physical, and beautiful, whereas the wind, which is not only Shelley's wind of prophecy but of reckless desire, unmoors you, sends you on to the next thing, and makes you other than what you are.

We were having lunch at a place just up the road, a slow ride from Lambertville with Stern at the wheel. We had lunched there several times and loved every meal. He was asking questions—he is a close questioner and meticulous listener—about our backgrounds and talking about his own, and he interrupted himself to launch into a related anecdote about Ukrainians and the Eastern European "bloodlands," about Baltic Nazis and the slaughter in Belarus during World War II, when he suddenly shifted from what we call history into reminiscence. And then he stopped. "I hate nostalgia," he said.

It was the last time we ate there. The owner soon sold the place. The name may be the same, but the original restaurant no longer exists.

—2016

The Poetry of John Prine

The first and only time I saw John Prine live was on my thirtieth birthday. It was a present from an old friend who showed up in Philadelphia with his new girl-friend and took me and my new girlfriend to the Schubert Theatre. The sound was concert class, with no coffeehouse brick walls to ping it back, no damping drapery or chatty crowd to interrupt with a cough or a request. John Prine in a concert hall was, to paraphrase one of George Gobel's best lines, a bit like wear-ing a pair of brown shoes with a tuxedo. This was precisely his appeal.

He did all the songs he's remembered for—"Hello in There," "Sam Stone"—but the one that lit me up was his masterpiece, "Angel from Montgomery." The song is like nothing else in the American song book or contemporary American lyric poetry, set to music or not, but these lines in particular sat me up straight:

There's flies in the kitchen
I can hear 'em they're buzzin'
And I ain't done nothin' since I woke up today

How the hell can a person
Go to work in the morning
Come home in the evening
And have nothing to say—

How many times had I heard some version of the same rhetorical question raised over a family dinner, from a booth at the corner bar, or from a porch across the street? How many of my buddies would arrive on the corner at noon rubbing their eyes or having come directly from collecting their workers' comp check, proudly repeating some version of that third line? These seven lines don't sound or look like much—they don't even rhyme in any consecutive, which is to say conventional order—but their plainspoken beauty took my breath away. Bonnie Raitt covered "Angel" on a live album years ago and turned it into an aria, because she is, after all, Bonnie Raitt; but it came nowhere near to the way Prine pitched it himself. Some approximation, say, to and in the same dramatic mode as Lear's final outburst, when he repeats the word *never* across a line of pentameter and you hope it ends there. It doesn't look like much until one gives the vernacular context a ninety-degree twist and exposes the polarizing punch of the question-that-isn't-quite-just-that and the devastating off-handedness of it all. Many years ago a book titled *The Poetry of Rock* appeared, and recognizing, knowing by heart, and having sung many of the entries at dozens of weddings and frat parties, graduations and mixers, I dismissed the book and its thesis. But Prine's work gave me cause to reconsider. This wasn't rock, but it *was* poetry.

It's also what sets Prine (and Joni Mitchell notably, who deserves her own Nobel if the Swedes ever get around to it) apart from their contemporaries. There are very few in their company—Lennon and McCartney by cultural fiat, Dylan by Nobel fiat, Cole Porter and Sondheim, Paul Simon, Holland–Dozier–Holland and (for pure musicianship) Brian Wilson; and the pure "folk singers" like Guthrie and Seeger. But Prine was more than just a folk singer. His lyrics were always scrubbed of politics and the usual up-front formalities—strict cadence and rhyme and those choruses that arrived like the 7:10. He gravitated to conversational rhythms he was used to or picked up while delivering mail in Chicago, and he grabbed rhymes where he found them, but they weren't mandatory. He was a writer who, like my teenage crush Thomas Hardy, wrote compressed novels in verse, like Housman impersonated his various characters and rarely intruded, and like Pound throve on gossip, anecdote, and direct lifts from remembered speech. If all poetry aspires to the condition of music, American poetry's aspiration is to the bump of the street, to the uniquely self-owned sound of American English, which to the King's is what a wraparound windshield is to a windscreen, especially once isolated within the particular endtime of its utterance. This is hard to describe unless and until you've listened closely to your neighbors ordering pizza over the phone, dealing with their wayward kin or their kids, or listened closely to yourself. It helps to have read Whitman and particularly Dickinson, but also outliers like Bukowski and Amiri Baraka—*aloud,* I mean.

Prine wrote "Angel" as he walked around Chicago making deliveries. His compositional praxis, in other words, was close to Whitman's, walking along

Market Street in Philadelphia, or Dickinson's, who scribbled lines or whole poems between straightening the beds or pruning her roses, or Stevens's, who composed in his head as he walked to the Hartford Insurance Company every morning, or even William Carlos Williams's, who pulled his car to the side of the street on the way to work to describe a young housewife in a housedress getting the newspaper from her step. You grab the moment as it flies by. When asked about "Angel," Prine claimed that something like what the ancients called—he never would have called it this—"divine afflatus" brought him the song by way of the voice of "the character." It was, he said, "dictated" to him, and I believe him; lots of good writers have said the same thing. A poet takes his or her muses wherever they can be found. Plus, it's a bad idea and a pedestrian way of thinking not to believe a genius when he or she tells me how lightning strikes and produces a masterpiece. If Dante says he actually lived the *Comedia,* if Blake says he sees in a sunrise not a gold guinea but choirs of angels around the throne of the Almighty, let it be so. To demand more would be at the very least rude, and in all events irrelevant.

All of which leads me to wonder what the new puritans will allow a poet to say, or whether a writer like Prine is anymore possible within the precincts policed by the cultural Stasi. "Angel's" opening lines—"I am an old woman / Named after my mother . . ."—might, alas, strike some as effrontery or insensitivity, coming as the lines do from the son of two white Kentucky natives who moved to just outside Chicago, where Prine was raised and grew up with a Chicago accent. His Southern one is therefore merely Southern-ish and as phonied up as Dylan's, the great Ronstadt's, or the dozens of Brits (Jagger, Joe Cocker, Clapton, Rod Stewart) whose come-and-go Southern or Blackish accents were pure fakery. The character's gender came with the voice, which makes perfect sense. Prine was actually asked about the woman's voice once. I love his reply: "I got asked years later lots of times how I felt I could get away with writing a woman's song first-person. And that never occurred to me, because I already considered myself a writer. And writers are any gender you want." Yes: *writers are any gender you want.* Coming from an American folk singer, this suddenly much-contested claim, which has never been met by the intellectual equivalent of a real argument, stripped of any and all theoretical regalia and melodramatic pomp other than my italics, sounds as simple as the song itself: "writers are any gender you want." It is a freedom that every writer worthy of the name and worth remembering has claimed since *Gilgamesh.* Why relinquish it now? Says who?

Louis Menand a while back, writing over the competing claims of artists and the identity cops, wrote that we have arrived at the stage where, to para-phrase, unless you are born it, you cannot perform it. If you answer *yes, I agree,* you can stop reading now. Because it's suddenly impossible to know what to say to Pound when he pretends to be the river merchant's wife—a Chinese woman around sixteen years old, at that—or Stevie Smith when she impersonates an older man married to a younger woman during the Blitz—or to Milton, when he puts words in the mouth of the world's First Lady, or to for that matter Meryl Streep, who so successfully impersonates a rabbi in the opening scenes of *Angels in America* you may not have known it until this very moment. This is not really news, is it? The culture is presently being irrigated by an often-poisonous cultural narcissism, which has turned personal identity into another commodity, though with the best will in the world we pretend not to notice, and we wait, terrified, for the inevitable vulgarian backlash, and celebrate the fluidity of the flesh and identity while condemning the fluid imagination. The sources seem obvious—the American addiction to extremes, especially extreme non-solutions, to tech that automates unnecessary tasks, to our willingness to believe that equality and equity are the same things and to cave in to whatever Big Tech underwrites, to "reality" this and that, and to politicians who know how to win but not to govern. Our overseers' antidote is *more* memoir and born-to-the-manner or -manor accounts of lives, many of which are better left unexamined, whether they were worth living or not.

Again: John Prine. The husband who leaves in the morning and comes home and sits silently over dinner, maybe reading the paper, maybe staring out the window, is as much a victim as the angel he married. The difference is that she has the words, the language that matters, and you might imagine her voice rising when you again listen to "Angel," which after all is her soliloquy. Note how he inflects the third and fourth lines of the quatrain I began this with—

> How the hell can a person
> Go to work in the mornin'
> And come home in the evenin'
> And have nothin' to say

and how he runs the syntax of the line 3 runs into line 4. As blues singers have always known and have taught several generations of white crooners, not all songs are *lieder;* some copy the registers of unscripted speech and try to approximate as closely as possible speech as it is spoken, living and ungrammatical, uncensored and nasty. The earliest performers of Homer or of *Gilgamesh* performed their songs from memory. They must certainly have known or discovered the natural power of enjambment when intoning those long lines of the *Iliad* when Andromache mourns the dead Hector, or when Gilgamesh cries over the dead Enkidu. They were not just singing but *acting* the parts, like Judy Garland doing "Born in a Trunk," for instance, or Merry Clayton's backup on "Gimme Shelter." The volume is lower, but Prine's run-on identifies this as the climactic moment, when the old woman's voice is either rising or falling—in rage or out of frustration, derision, or despair, who can say? And, by the way, how old is she? Social security age or still middle-aged, maybe even younger, and yet totally burnt out?

My ears hear a woman too worn down and worn out to yell at a husband who won't have a ready reply anyway, and writing this I already see her biotype from when I grew up, shaking her head in voluble disgust or sadness while brooming leaves from the stoop, then bursting into soft laughter at the silliness of their shared life, his and hers together. They've been married not long but already it seems like a life sentence. Or maybe so long it might as well be forever. Yet she still picks up his filthy drawers and socks and makes dinner and thanks him when he gives her a new bowling ball for her birthday, when she doesn't bowl. She still grieves when he dies on the job, or climbing the steps to the bed he never reaches.

Moral or not, politically with it or not, it does what art does. It allows whoever is listening to migrate for a moment into an alien or alienated consciousness, spend some time there, and maybe rise to that level of "compassion" generally unavailable (we're all pretty busy) and yet constantly bellowed about as the very condition of cultural health, moral strength, and national sanity.

—2021

On Translation and Translators

Translation Is/As Play

In the mid-1990s I was invited to join a group of poets who had been invited
to render the corpus of Greek drama into English "versions," or "translations,"
or "adaptations"—none of the participants was entirely sure what to call them
except that they would not be "exact equivalents"—to be published by the University of Pennsylvania Press. By the time of my involvement, many of the volumes were out for sale and review. Among the participants were writers with
national reputations or with backgrounds in Greek like me; but in that latter
category I was in the minority, and anyway my Greek was barely post–prep
school and very rusty. With Greek, to stay fresh you must constantly return to
it, and I hadn't. Many had no background in the Greek language at all, and a
couple had little, borrowed, or faded interest in Classical culture or in the play
he or she was assigned. Some did have a Classical education like me—beginning
in tenth grade, we memorized the first ten lines of *The Odyssey* and sang it back
to the tune of *The Stars and Stripes Forever* with a priest conducting the chorale
with a stick of chalk as a baton. None of this mattered, though, to the series editors. In every case, we were encouraged to ignore precedent since a reliance on
it might discourage the range of skills, talents, and hands involved.

The unifying element was that each of us was a poet who came to the project
with a poet's needs and expectations. When I first spoke to the series editor, I asked
if I'd need anything beyond my copy of Liddell and Scott's *Greek-English Lex-
icon* and my old and very beat-up copy of *Tutti i verbi Graeci*. No, not really; I
wouldn't need even those books. Would I be paired with a Classicist the way
Oxford had married a Classicist and a poet back in the 1970s, to ensure minimal accuracy, and accountability? No, because this would not be a translation
project in the traditional sense. We were poets charged with responding as poets
to earlier poetry. The result would be work of critical interpretation as much as
anything else. We were urged to build our own translations out of whatever am-

bient versions were still in print. We were not told what to call them—homages, versions, adaptations, even "translations," which strictly speaking they weren't. Nobody would be reading over my shoulder and checking me for literal or historical accuracy, my rendering of the aorist or the subtleties of conjugation. Make it new, in other words, and so we mostly did. Even before the final volume appeared, however, the whole series was torpedoed by a professional Classicist in a major review. By the time my *Children of Herakles* appeared in the late summer of 1999, after several pained and painful revisions, sales were dead and the series effectively stillborn. My play got one review, buried in the *Bryn Mawr Classical Review.* ("Despite the liberties Barbarese has taken with vocabulary and line structure, his translation reads well . . . is vivid and fast-paced." Mission, or so I thought, accomplished.)

Since then I have occasionally wondered what the whole point of literary translation is, at least now. Later I got emails from another writer, a poet, who said the series was shot down because classicists, now occupying one-person departments where they teach the Classics in Translation, were acting spitefully, as obstructionists, and that some had personal agendas beyond keeping their jobs secure, which is hardly a minor consideration. Well, OK, I thought, but their agendas aren't the point, nor are they surprising. They're simply political applications of the disciplinary goals of any academic department, especially one as threatened as the Classics. Mid-meditation, I realized that the point had suddenly shifted from *why* translate to *how* translate, in any traditional sense of the term, or to the very meaning of translation in an ugly epoch when education was being hawked as a "product," traditional educational goals being sacrificed to consumer desires, noble old disciplines being coerced into reshaping themselves into user-friendly commodities, and everything, including college degrees, seemed headed online. To make things trickier, I had had to deal with a "problem play," where the lacunae were both ample and critical and better ignored than confronted if only to get the job done. Either blocked or compromised therefore were two highly traditional goals: fidelity to an esteemed original and fidelity to one's audience—though in this case the audience was a modern one, with virtually no knowledge or experience of fifth-century Athenian drama.

So each took a slightly different route: for reasons I spelled out in the introduction to the play, I decided to work in rhymed couplets. Why "translate" when the traditional curricular rationale is no longer supported even by the institutions where well-trained translators seek harbor? Why worry about adhering to Classical form, hendecasyllabics and all that, when T. S. Eliot's most celebrated poetic work, much beloved by the American public, was now a personal diversion called *Cats,* which my mother, who never heard of *The Waste Land,* had by 1999 already seen twice and which was already entering its nineteenth year on Broadway? The argument seemed to be: better watered-down classics than no classics at all. (It paralleled the controversy over the then super-popular Potter books: better kids read crap than nothing at all.)

Translation has for writers always been a means of self-preservation. It is not a problem in or of philology so much as psychology—it is a personal, and not a public service. For writers with no direct "training" as creative writers and uncredentialed—I am speaking of myself, who led many workshops but attended only one in his life, and then accidentally—one's credentialing can come through passionate intimacies with the models that appeal to you, often well after your first encounter with them in their native languages. My own personal MFA "workshop" was a circle of empathies I found pretty much circumstantially, by haunting the bookrack of the local Rexall Drugs and the public library, paging through school anthologies and accidental encounters with the like-minded: on my own Hardy and Housman, in school Eliot, then later Pound, Dickinson, Crane, Stevens, Auden, and Whitman; then on street corners or in diners with other souls trying to find their voices, and later comparisons of our earliest (bad) poems and stories on the same corners and in the same diners. These went along with the high school enthusiasms I learned by reading the original—"dirty" Catullus, handed to us by a canny Jesuit, Homer's *Odyssey,* and that school-imposed enthusiasm Virgil, rendering ten lines a night while listening to WIBG on a transistor radio. After a year of sophomore French there followed Villon, Verlaine, the often-impenetrable Mallarmé, Prévert, and Apollinaire, and much later Wace and Chrétien and Ronsard, all independent discoveries. These became my first writing teachers, and some (Ronsard, and Villon especially) taught me what it meant to be untranslatable. There is such a thing as selfless, artful translation; but the contribution of the artist's self to the act of translating has always to me seemed paramount, in contrast with one's commitment to translation as an *art,* or an extension of the profession of teaching. A writer who translates is not always a translator and the art he serves is not, though there are obvious exceptions, the art of translation. He is never out to "teach" anybody but himself, and the lesson is how to bilocate, how to get from where you are to where you want to be or, just as likely, where you need to be.

Translation in the traditional sense is or aspired to a form of psychic or cultural migration, an idea and a phrase that is not mine but William Arrowsmith's. Call it channeling, or, to exaggerate wildly, an attempt at past-life regression, only the life was not yours. An attractive idea: the translator is a mere point of departure, and the original is the destination. While there is reciprocity in the exchange, it is always somehow unequal, at least equivocal, though the usual image that can come to mind is cargo being handed laterally across the banks of a river. Or it is like double-entry bookkeeping, where all the debts are on the side of the translator, who always owes something to the original. The translator's engagement is with a critical *difference* of which his native language is the current measure. But that measure is more like a slide rule than the ruler in my desk, and the difference is always an approximation of the amount of time that's elapsed between the creation of some original and the translator's present. One result is that the original is always reconceived as a historical entity to which the present work owes not only respect but its life; you rarely hear of a translation "surpassing" the original in quite the way I might say that the novel is not nearly as good as the film version of, for instance, *The Godfather.* Plus, given occasional etymological relationships between the new and the old and of course scholarly interventions, whether commentaries or other translations, any such "distance" is an illusion.

Translation in that older sense, then, is the ultimate application of Eliot's argument in "Tradition and the Individual Talent" and of the whole of New Criticism: a matter of recovering literary conventions understood as the coalescence of the cultural, the historical, and the social, all brought together and taught to behave in more or less perfect consonance with learned expectations and, in the case of plays especially, with audience taste. As William Arrowsmith said, one moves "from the original's conventions into a different but analogous convention of your own language." Except for the French Structuralist term *conventions,* Arrowsmith's formulation is implicit in the New Critical idiom and still as close to perfectly accurate as such a thing might be.

There are also the obvious and time-honored distinctions among translators, adapters, and writers of what Dryden called "imitations." Translation proper attempts to "migrate" into the body of the original by tracing its literal shapes back to some significant, in-dwelling meaning. It is work that merges the historical and the aesthetic at once: its fidelity is to an originality the translator recognizes as simultaneously prior to and insistently and problematically greater than his own. That priority belongs to what predated the translator, who embraces his lack of originality and elected inferiority either with gusto or a measure of anxiety. It is the Voice that supersedes his voice, the voice that is greater than any within any one of us because so much grander, more beautiful, or "universal." This is an agony that has probably plagued most translators down through time, beginning with the learned scribes moving *Gilgamesh* from the original Akkadian into Sumerian.

To me, the exemplary if unintended description of this paradigm comes, surprisingly, in the eleventh chapter of *Survival in Auschwitz*, where Primo Levi describes trying to scramble together from memory what he remembers of Dante's Canto 26, the Canto of Ulysses, as he and a young Frenchman named Jean are carrying a vat filled with the morning ration of soup across the camp as it sloshes between them. Levi himself says he doesn't know why it had suddenly sprung to mind, and yet it did; and as they labor to carry the big cauldron of soup between them without spilling a drop, it becomes of pressing importance for Levi to remember all of it and to translate it into his limited French for Jean, who has no Italian. But Levi can remember only pieces, and as he remembers, he translates each fragment into French for Jean. At length he comes to a triplet that he remembers completely; I give it here in the original, followed by Longfellow's translation. The speaker, of course, is Ulysses, urging on his companions:

Considerate la vostre semenza
fatti non foste a viver com bruti,
ma per seguir virtute e canoscenza.

Consider ye the seed from which ye sprang;
Ye were not made to live like unto brutes,
But for pursuit of virtue and of knowledge!

It was like "hearing it for the first time," Levi writes, "like the blast of a trumpet, like the voice of God. For a moment I forget who I am and where I am." The recollection lights up their own shared and thoroughly miserable situation and reminds Levi of the reach of great poetry. So much so that he can go on to feel that day "unhappy in the way of normal men."

To me, this is as accurate if accidental a conventional exemplification one can find of what the translator usually does: the translator is the servant who humbles himself before the original, and the great original chastens and reminds him not quite of who he is as much as of where he comes from. He knows the original language, but his sense of his audience is weak or uncertain or missing entirely. The original is the grand imperative that reaches providentially into the world of ordinary language, a human version of transcendence but one alienated by any attempt to bring it closer. Like the god of the Old Testament, it speaks invisibly from behind and through history. The original gives substance and body to the isolated, otherwise meaningless self of the present.

The arc of Levi's chapter (titled "The Canto of Ulysses") rises toward and settles upon the same point: the *Lager* represented perfected brutality, the peak of horror because so perfectly adapted to the demands of modern industry, and a perfection worse than Dante's Hell because Dante's—where guilt is perfected—is only poetry, and the camps were real, and a travesty, the apotheosis of the Ford assembly line. What irony: the camps existed to eradicate the individual will—of the both the troops and the prisoners—and in the process exposed the individual will to its critical role in human survival. So if there is something greater than the self—we should call it culture but probably not "civilization," given, as Ellison's *Invisible Man* reminds us, the vexed nature of what it now means to be "civilized"—it must be reconstituted as art and out of the savagery and selfishness that are also, sadly, the bases of human expression. Levi's account suspends subjectivity over history and there lets it dangle, perhaps for pedagogical reasons, though he was clearly too much the realist, as both a Jew and an Italian, for such simplicity, for so romanced an understanding of the writer's job. It is the American disease to find it easy and sentimentally appealing to assume that pain always comes with a compensating pedagogy and a printable syllabus, that painful experience is a "learning opportunity," or that, to quote Harry Truman's perverse maxim, "the reward of suffering is experience." Yet is this not what any translator as such will inevitably do? Surrender the self and personal vision to a tradition that is embodied in a language and an originality greater than one's own?

The answer is contained in history and is one of the grander ironies of twentieth-century verbal art. The Modernist enterprise, for all its enthusiasm for the past, altered the translator's traditional role and seduced the translator into regarding the original as an engine with a certain amount of "play" in it—to use the word the way my father did when he was winding motors or installing brakes in his umpteenth used car. The degree of "play" seems to have expanded between marvelous frauds like *Songs of Bilitis* (1894) and Pound's intentionally naughty *Homage to Sextus Propertius* (1917), and still further expanded to include Zukofsky's gruesomely unfunny and unentertaining experiments with Catullus in the late 1960s, which still finds its defenders and possibly direct imitators within academia (and nowhere else if it ever did). No need to take a position on the perils of experimentation, or conduct cultural inquests into the success or failure of the experiments or experimenters. Experimentation, like all ambition, is what it does, and outside of the academy it is noteworthy only when it succeeds in gaining a wider audience, which it does rarely. Poets have always "played" with the text until it came out their way.

But how surprising that Modernism itself shifted the emphasis from translation as a disinterested act of cultural appropriation and of critical disinterestedness—"seeing the object as in itself it really is"—to something quite different, and oddly somehow closer to what Pater meant. And naturally there was Pound, as usual, present at the creation. Not everyone, of course, agreed, then or recently, on the value of that creation. It is one of history's tastiest and nastiest of facts that Pound is buried in the same graveyard—"twenty feet from"—Joseph Brodsky, who called Pound, whom he already despised for his anti-Semitism, a fraud as a translator, who misled an entire generation of readers and poets. His 1993 verdict on Pound's *Homage to Sextus Propertius* is withering: "Propertius' . . . standing with the American public is either nonexistent or incomprehensibly low. This may in part have to do with a singular disservice done him by Ezra Pound's 'Homage to Sextus Propertius'—the moronic pastiche of our eternal sophomore"—Pound, of course—"enamored of foreign name-dropping." In one swipe Brodsky annihilates not only Pound but the American public that always troubled Pound himself.

But why this "shift in emphasis"? "Modernism" was really a species of neo-

Neoclassicism, an aesthetic neoconservatism cultivated by an almost uniformly well-heeled and well-educated (indeed, Ivy League) elite.* Yet it was also Modernism that was behind the "creative adaptation," as it is now called, and that exposed the "play" in the translator's machine. What is more, as a subgenre of twentieth-century art, playful translation, creative adaptation, or "moronic pastiche" comprehends a good deal, beginning with Pound (from his Canto 1 to the *Cathay* sequence through the "Seafarer" and the breathtakingly beautiful "The River-Merchant's Wife: A Letter"), through Williams's not entirely successful *Kora in Hell,* right up to and including Robert Lowell's *Imitations* and, I would argue, wilder spinoffs, such as translations not from another language but of an achieved form, like Gerald Stern's *American Sonnets,* on the face of it not "sonnets" in any normative sense and, unusually for Stern, vaguely recognizable as sonnets only to the generous minded or an audience of experts. Perhaps it is due to the way creative adaptation takes a fascinating stance toward authority: on the one hand, it respects the past as a repository of works of genius; on the other, its respect is that of a parasite for its host, a relationship that is almost by definition transactional, or hegemonical. The adaptor is struggling in a highly conscious and even obnoxious way with the meaning of authenticity. And why not? He or she is always primarily *a poet,* which is to say that originality and authenticity are the primary goals, and every visit to the past is either a raid or a burglary.

The translator (in the old sense of the term) undertook the same struggle but settled, as it were, out of court: the translator compromised personal originality in order to serve or preserve the original's beauty along with what it had to teach the present of morals or behavior. This compromise is reflected in traditional descriptions of the translator, where translation is described as a kind of treasure hunt, a salvage or rescue operation (with culture as the gold that, to quote Pound, "gathers the light against it"), or where the translator admits to his status as willing captive to the past. So Cowley, in the mid-seventeenth century, said that translators should seek "to supply the lost Excellencies of another Language with the new ones in their own." Dryden divided the translator's activity,

* Cummings, Eliot, Stevens, and Frost (briefly): Harvard; Pound and Williams: Penn; H.D.: Penn, then Bryn Mawr; Moore, Bryn Mawr. Only Yeats, arguably the greatest writer of poetry in English in the twentieth century, escaped the warping influence of an elite and really expensive education.

like Caesar's Gaul, into three parts: *metaphrase* (word-by-word rendition), *paraphrase* ("translation with latitude"), and *imitation*. Dryden's claim that translators are "bound to" the sense of the original is couched in a powerful metaphor: "[I]f the soil be sometimes barren, then we are sure of being scourged; if it be fruitful, and our care succeeds, we are not thanked; for the proud reader will say, the poor drudge has done his duty . . . slaves we are, and labor on another man's plantation; we dress the vineyard, but the wine is the owner's." Dryden hardly needs either an apology or an adjustment to present needs; but from his point of view, as the plowman is to the soil or slave is to master, so are translators to their originals, and no correction or improvement of his or her status is possible, or even thinkable. A translator is a drudge. Dryden's whole approach is relentlessly submissive, implicitly theologized, and as a theorist (though not practitioner) as lost to our own present as the ancients were to him.

How does it come to be that so damnably conservative an aesthetic movement as Modernism stimulated such violent departures from "traditional" practice? Isn't this snubbing of tradition what got under Eliot's skin and that chapped the behinds of Neo-Formalists in the 1980s? Yet the "break" is the one generally associated with Pound, and historical ground zero is that same *Homage to Sextus Propertius,* so despised by Brodsky:

> My cellar does not date from Numa Pompilius,
> Nor bristle with wine jars,
> Nor is it equipped with a frigidaire patent

This is even more delicious in the era of Microsoft's obnoxious spell-check routine, which refuses to allow the word *Frigidaire* to appear as Pound wrote it, with a lowercase *f.* The exuberance and panache of Pound's *Propertius* was so outrageous when it appeared that some conservative critics were left outraged, confused, or both, and uniformly irritated. Pound not only provoked their irritation, he embraced and mocked it. When he smuggled the adjective *Wordsworthian* into one of these "translations" as a replacement for a passage in the Latin original, William Gardner Hale, head of the Classics department at the University of Chicago, called Pound a fool for thinking he had actually found a reference to Wordsworth in the poetry of a contemporary of Julius Caesar. In a letter written to A. R. Orage in April 1919, Pound says, "As a Prof. of Latin and example of why Latin poets are not read, as example of why one would like to deliver poets of philologers, Hale should be impeccable and without error. He has no claim to refrain from suicide if he errs in any point."*

Along with Propertius there was, for me, *Cathay,* an amazement of creative adaptation and the source of at least two permanent contributions to our poetry, "The River-Merchant's Wife" and "Exile's Letter." The motives behind *Propertius* and *Cathay* are lost in the outcomes for which both of these tiny books, experimental or not, could take the blame. *Propertius* was silent preparation, in dealing with tonal registers and irony especially, for *Hugh Selwyn Mauberley,* a work of extended social satire and literary parody that is Propertian in diction and tone (though Pound's prosody is an imitation of the rigid formalism of Gautier's *Émaux et camées*). Pound looked opportunistically at Propertius's situation, that of a writer surrounded by literary hotshots who had grown fat off their mastery of literary politics, their sucking up to authority, and their habit of writing about war instead of women (the "new Iliads" of poets like Virgil, for instance). That's just the content, however. Some of Pound's later technical discoveries were stimulated by his monkeying around with Propertius, exploiting the latter's gift for metonymy and the polite insult. Without *Propertius* there would probably have been no *Mauberley,* and without *Mauberley*—though nowadays the concern is exclusively that of scholars—there would likely not have been *The Waste Land* as we presently have it, constructed according to Pound's editorial instincts.

What Pound produced is not Propertius for readers of Propertius but Propertius for readers of Pound, which is probably what Brodsky was getting at in calling Pound sophomoric. Not even the Pound of 1918, that is, but the Pound-in-progress toward what came later. The example is so decisive that I have always wondered whether Pound—obsessed as he claimed to be by the thought of a classically educated America—realized exactly how revolutionary and meta-Classical it was. To be clear, there is some truth to Brodsky's claim that the "real" Propertius had "a singular disservice done him by Ezra Pound," but only if you had no Latin, like most of America, or had no taste for poetry, ancient or mod-

---

* Pound's improvisation was suggested by a couplet from *Propertius* bk. 2:XXXIVb: "tu canis Ascraei veteris praecepta poetae, / quo seges in campo, quo viret uva iugo." The Loeb Library translates this as, "You sing the precepts of the old bard of Ascra, in what soil flourishes the corn, on what hill the grape." The "old bard" is Hesiod, though the allusion in the original is not mocking.

ern, or by way of a different register of critical interest in Pound's politics, if you couldn't separate Pound's literary practice from his anti-Semitism. Pound, by the way, claimed years later, in 1931, that "My *Homage to Sextus Propertius* is *not* a translation." But by 1931, the point was moot, *Mauberley* in print for nearly a decade and Pound routinely celebrated as a major American poet. Yet Pound could only get away with this "pastiche" because, as Brodsky says, correctly, "as regards the literature of antiquity, we are the barbarians." And like barbarians, we sack and pillage for personal gain.

If Pound did realize the barbaric energy of his *Propertius,* did he care? Probably not, given the evidence of the poetry that he wrote and published from around 1920 on. Not only *Mauberley* but his Canto I, which is mostly an adaptation of a Latin translation of *Odyssey* II. His example was followed by others, most far more conservative. Eliot's translation of Saint-John Perse's *Anabasis* is formal practice for the conventionally orthodox and occasionally lifeless *Four Quartets.* Even though its energies derived from Eliot's sexual and religious anxieties, Eliot's translation mostly behaves itself; there are no surprises. Marianne Moore's translations of La Fontaine came later and offer a more charming example of a poet who is most at home when visiting others; she takes no real liberties because she doesn't have to, her tone and the original's being so oddly harmonized, so courtly, even coquettish. Her embrace of rhyme and meter (long predicted by her own youthful practice) suggests that years of counting syllables and laying out rigorous syllabic gridirons earned her a kind of coming-out. The habitual exception to this, or the perennial anomalous example, is Yeats—anomalous because he was deaf to all music other than his own. (He at one point had Pound read him parts of Wordsworth because, when Yeats read to himself, it came out sounding like Yeats.) The beautiful "When you are old and grey" quickly tires of Ronsard's original after one quatrain and then abandons it so completely that it leaves Ronsard in the dust.

This list of the thus liberated includes many others and brings me closer to the present. Bly's versions of Thomas Transtromer, which came out in the 1970s, caused a small furor when it was revealed that Bly had apparently used a Fulbright to do the work without knowing a word of the original Swedish, so making Bly the Jack Gladney of the Po-Biz. Yet Bly's translations, however good or bad as such, were mostly valuable for whatever they inspired in and from Bly. Another exception, rarely noted, is James Wright, who was actively translating

both German and Spanish poets nearly up to his death in 1980. An exception
of a different kind, though, is Zukofsky's transliterated or "homophonic" Catullus, which made a small splash in the mid-1960s and are pure razzle-dazzle,
examples of a translator truly at "play," but joyless play, for academic insiders and
students of the artistic fringes of the last century. Zukofsky changes the rules in
order to straddle the divide separating "straight" translation and an improvisation based purely on phonic elements:

> Multos home es, Naso neque tecum multus homost
> qui descendit: Naso, multus es et pathicus

> Much a man you are, Naso, and that you much a man it is who
> comes down: Naso, much you are and pathetic/lascivious.

Having fun yet? The translator sure is. Zukofsky's earnestly disciplined versions
turn out to be anarchic *reversions* to a version of transliteration that seems a
dead end. Homophonic translation, the contemporary name for this, steps back
from the subjective brink (pure adaptation) only to fall into the seductive arms
of translation as a kind of sorcery—the poem as Ouija board. Zukofsky began
as an Objectivist and did manage to produce some small and refined and lovely
domestic lyrics as well as his long poem *A*. The general complaint against the
contemporary variants or progeny of Zukofsky and the Objectivist experiment
is that it sought to replace self-consciousness with language-consciousness and
makes a virtue of the very act (or fact) of writing as a kind of gleeful playing
with blocks, replacing self-consciousness with self-indulgence; it is the point
where the improvisational becomes pointless and joyless and memorable for
the wrong reasons.

A poet's obsession is originality, so it makes sense to poets who translate to
translate their source into their own idiom, and not the reverse. Yet it's hardly
possible to find in the history of aesthetics—certainly not in the body of
Victorian-Georgian criticism—a theoretical sanction for such a view of originality, or for the approach to the art that emerges from it. In the red-light
district of psychoanalytic criticism, maybe, or the precincts of Bloom's *The
Anxiety of Influence,* which will always be more useful for poets than for critics
and ought to be required reading in MFA programs, partly as a corrective to

their institutionalization of careerism. All theory is moreover parenthetical to the obvious truth: creative intelligences have always translated and often have equated translation with theft—stealing from a parent's wallet and not from the poor box. Again, examples other than the above are everywhere. Wyatt lifted Petrarch into English and launched the English sonnet; Sidney looked in his heart and found an English version of the French alexandrine; Pope's Homer sounds as if Homer had read Pope, Chapman's as if he had read Spenser. The English Romantics we can generally skip except for the best translator among them, Shelley: Blake was no polyglot, Wordsworth didn't translate, Keats had no Latin or Greek, and Coleridge simply plagiarized. The one great creative linguist was Shelley, whose versions of Plato and Sophocles still hold up—his translation of *Symposium* is permanent—but, more important, helped him write *Prometheus Unbound* and his "Defense of Poetry." If there ever was a line separating an original whose priority was established and unshakable from a "translation" that was the inferior product, that line has been abolished or is at least a good deal more blurred than it was before.

The change is probably beneficial. Shelley spent most of his last two living (and Italian) years reading *The Comedia* and instead of a translation produced the closest we have to an English model of *terza rima* in "Ode to the West Wind" and the powerful if unfinished "The Triumph of Life," poems that in turn engendered Stevens and Ammons. It makes you wonder if the old view of the translator as a curator or cultural straight man was ever true or anything more than pious nostalgia. How much have writers ever depended on what we've come to call, under pressure from declining literacy rates and shrinking readerships, their "sense of audience"? Was the audience of Chapman or Pope as savvy as we suppose, and how extensive was it? Those famous lines from Pound's *Mauberley* involving a multilingual pun, for instance, depend wholly on the ability of the reader to get the Greek, at least know the Greek alphabet. But before a reader can, the Greek itself must be correctly spelled by the compositor. The point of Pound's serious joke in *Mauberley*, where he rhymes the Greek particle τιν' with the English homophone *tin*, is totally lost, even in English, if or when the Greek word τιν' is miscomposed, as it often is, into an upsilon (υ), which kills the rhyme, botches the joke, and introduces a Greek word that never existed.

Of Hart Crane, Rexroth wrote, "Hart Crane never learned to speak French and at the time he wrote … *Voyages* he could not read it at all," and yet "*Voyages* is by far the best transmission of Rimbaud into English that exists—the purest distillation of the boyish hallucinations of [*Le*] *Bateau Ivre*." Crane lacked fluency in French, but he had enough of it in high school to follow the Eliot craze right back to the now forgotten Jules Laforgue, whom Crane translated when he was in his early twenties. The result was his three "Locutions des Pierrots," a tidy, faithful blue book exercise, but one that gets only half of the Laforgian irony—the lower half in the self-deprecating, sarcastic registers. This only makes Rexroth's intuition of a Rimbaud–Crane crypto-connection seem more accurate. Rimbaud's poem is a vision of judgment filled with rhetorical echoes of Revelations—"Je sais … J'ai vu … J'ai rêvé … J'ai suivi … ," a seventeen-year-old's version of John's Apocalypse. Crane in his own way was a religious poet—like Shelley, like Rimbaud—without the institutional chevrons. Moreover, we know he read Rimbaud, and in a sense his "Voyages II" is the best American version of Rimbaud we may ever have. And it doesn't end there. Here are the opening quatrains of the sequence's conclusion, "Voyages VI":

> Where icy and bright dungeons lift
> Of swimmers their lost morning eyes,
> And ocean rivers, churning, shift
> Green borders under stranger skies,
>
> Steadily as a shell secretes
> Its beating leagues of monotone,
> Or as many waters trough the sun's
> Red kelson past the cape's wet stone;
>
> O rivers mingling toward the sky
> And harbor of the phoenix' breast
> My eyes pressed black against the prow,
> -Thy derelict and blinded guest
>
> Waiting, afire, what name, unspoken
> I cannot claim: let thy waves rear

> More savage than the death of kings,
> Some splintered garland for the seer.

In his appendix to *The Complete Poems of Hart Crane* (1957), Waldo Frank wrote that Crane was reading, along with the outlaw Rimbaud, Donne and Laforgue, the latter two on Eliot's approved reading list. He was also reading other writers not on the list—along with Rimbaud the usual suspects, Whitman, Emerson, and Melville. His departures apparently helped him to get beyond the usual models and mannerisms, sparked his own idiom and got him to the strong work that became *White Buildings*. "When Rilke became convinced that Valéry was the greatest living poet," wrote Palmer Bovie, "he dropped everything else and proceeded to translate [Valéry]"—and, or so he implies, in the process he became Rilke, though what is important is that "he dropped everything else." Crane had a similar sensibility: thoroughly syncretic, incapacitated by analysis, instinctively elliptical in expression. His work therefore instantly "translates" his influences into something too rich and strange to be called anything but his, yet occasionally a sharp eye (like Rexroth's, another poet's) can see the fingerprints, hear the harmonies.

The personal stake is the decisive one—more so than accuracy or fidelity to an original. This is true of any and all work that profoundly influences writers, and is truest of poets especially. Nothing is more compelling than your own work; you read to find the element in another that liberates or illuminates what you're doing at the time. As Seamus Heaney said of his experience of translating *Beowulf*, "The translation should have some accountability. On the other hand, there are occasions when you see something in the jeweler's window of the other language and say, By God, I'd love to get my hands on that—the smash and grab approach where you rip off the original." What, then, exactly does "fidelity to the original" mean? To the original text of the author composing in a different language? To the conventions of usage of the language into which something is translated? To the formal elements that can be more or less easily described but usually reproduced with great difficulty? To a public that nowadays can get its translations through Google? Again, there are dozens of translations of Homer out there, yet has anybody produced anything as wild—or as darkly Homeric— as Christopher Logue's relatively "faithless" *War Music*? Has anyone made *Gilgamesh* or Genesis more accessible than Steven Mitchell?

Writers misconceive their pasts in order to reconceive their present. If they translate, they translate to find or lose themselves in an original that may be better than what they are but not better than what they hope to be. Maybe it's going too far to say that translation for poets comes down to half-remembered originals and the possibility that you must forget the other half for a good, if not a better reason. Wordsworth's counsel was to let Nature be your teacher, but that means that your memory is owned by nature, which has no memory, no ghosts. To poets, translation is dining with ghosts who no longer intimidate you. It is digging the pit and filling it with the barley, wine, and honey of instinct, experience and a good deal of reading, much of it done without discipline but with great passion. It is finding your destiny, getting directions home—but rarely a way of determining the direction of the culture to which you happen to belong. For that, we have politicians.

—2010

Ted Hughes Does Aeschylus

For over two thousand years the biggest news in Western culture was the Trojan War. Paris steals Helen; Agamemnon's forces lay siege for ten years; Troy falls, Helen is rescued, and the heroes return home, some sooner or, like Odysseus, much later. If the central players are still known to all of us, to the ancients the fate of Agamemnon was the darkest and most durable cautionary tale taught by the Trojan calamity, and possibly bigger news than Troy's fall or Odysseus's return. And it was a calamity: the fall of a city meant the end of a civilization. It may well have also supplied the material for the highest achievement of Aeschylus's dramatic art, the trilogy of the *Oresteia,* now translated by the late Ted Hughes.

Hughes, once poet laureate of England, his reputation at times eclipsed by his marriage to Sylvia Plath, wrote a dozen books of verse, including 1998's *Birthday Letters,* a collection of recollective lyrics about his marriage to Plath. *The Oresteia* is not his first translation, but it may be his best. He has accomplished this, moreover, without dumbing down the characters (nobody sounds like a television detective) or flattening out the formulaic elements of Greek tragedy that still remind us of its origins in religious ritual. Greek actors wore masks, stood in big shoes called buskins, wore huge-shouldered costumes like David Byrne in *Stop Making Sense.* Their voices were amplified by speakers built into probably heavy masks. The spectators were not there to identify with the characters—they couldn't in our sense because they were masked—but, in tragedy, to pity them in their fall. The language of tragic drama is a constant and rigorous measure of this spectatorial distance, a distance that Hughes respects. Yet it never becomes a stiff viewing experience to a modern audience in what are generally thoroughly performable translations of all three plays; the speakability of his versions is a real triumph of the poet's and the translator's art.

Orestes, eponymous protagonist, was the son of King Agamemnon and the one to whom Apollo assigns the grim task of avenging his father's murder at the hands of Agamemnon's wife and his own mother, Clytemnestra, half-sister of Helen of Troy, and her lover, the back-door man Aigisthus. Ten years after leaving home to battle the Trojans, Agamemnon returns, the city of Troy razed, Helen back with her husband, Agamemnon's brother Menelaos, and with Agamemnon smugly satisfied with the results. But things are never that easy for the royal line from which Agamemnon has sprung, the line of Atreus. Ten years earlier he, as commanding general of the Greek forces en route to Troy, had been persuaded by an oracle to sacrifice his daughter Iphigenia to Neptune. Her death becomes part of the lingering, unpaid price of the Greek victory. And Clytemnestra, who has taken Aigisthus as her lover in her husband's long absence, has never forgiven her husband the death of their daughter.

Though it may be difficult to blame her, Clytemnestra is hardly a sympathetic character, a woman who, if possible, is even less charismatic than Euripides's bloody Medea. In *Agamemnon,* the first play in the trilogy, from which Orestes is absent, she greets her husband's arrival and then murders him (offstage, of course) as he gets out of his bath. Then she and Aigisthus seize control of the kingdom and crow over their success, the play ending on her boast, "At last, the throne of Argos is ours." Things don't get much better in the sequel, *Choephoroi* (aka the "libation bearers" or mourners). Orestes sneaks back home from something like protective custody overseas and exacts vengeance, killing his mother and her lover with the help of his sister Electra and a fairly disaffected Cretan population. The *Eumenides,* named after the "furies" or demons who pursue and punish the guilty, completes the trilogy and takes the audience along on Orestes's flight from Agamemnon's kingdom in Crete all the way to Athens. The play ends there in a trial overseen by Athena and in which the god Apollo, of all figures, is the main defense witness.

Innocent readers expecting a literal translation won't find one here. Hughes takes wide liberties, but in every instance they are justified by the demands of the stage, if not what's on the page. Occasionally he opens up a passage and expands or extends it, or out of a habit of brooding attention familiar to readers of his poetry, he draws out the implications of physical details and plays a variation on the original meaning. Excepting one or two clinkers, the result is not only conscionable but enjoyable.

His most notable successes are small wonders of compression, when whole lines are telescoped into a phrase or a word. Usually he condenses into half as many short lines what several other translators will render in more elegant but inevitably flabby pentameters what the Greek has compressed in one or two phrases. In *The Choephoroi,* for instance, the Chorus describes with punishing accuracy how Clytemnestra first killed her husband and then mutilated the body: "She made a pile, on his torso / Of everything that could be hacked off it— / A bundled trophy, a display / To squat in your memories, / To rot your lives." Later in the same play, Cilissa, the nanny of the now grown-up Orestes, is suddenly overcome by memories of having nursed him. Hughes's version has her saying, "He was my life. / And I was his life. / A baby is helpless at both ends." By comparison, the good, competing and far more literal translation of Robert Fagles has "You have to nurse it, don't you? Read its mind, / little devil's got no words, it's still swaddled." A reader can judge which translation has got hold of the real Cilissa—Fagles's, who sounds like she's wandered in off the set of *Mary Poppins,* or Hughes's, whose eloquence is believably confined to one vulgar yet poignant axiom ("A baby is helpless at both ends"). It reminds you that Cilissa was almost certainly a household slave, as most such helpmates were, for whom it takes only a half-dozen blunt words to describe what it means to nurse an infant.

A professional Classicist might find Hughes (and other poets that preceded him) playing loose with his source and dealing disrespectfully with scholarship and scholarly tradition. Yet the fact is that this play succeeds as a script far more effectively than most and is in a class of translation (we really need a new word for this genre) that would include the series published by Oxford in the 1970s and the ill-fated Penn Greek Drama Series of the 1990s, in which I participated, that was torpedoed by professional Classicists. What both Hughes now and Oxford then have given us is not a text to teach but to act. There are good and obvious reasons to celebrate the event.

—1999

The Contemporaneity
of Homer's *Odyssey*

No matter how we read *The Iliad,* it is always a tragedy. Paris sins against civility and violates the divinely protected guest-host relationship, and his single act of moral incompetence produces a case study in misery that was nearly the *only* theme in Western literature for 2,500 years. The result is a continuing moral darkness broken by eruptions of pathos (Astyanax's outcry at his father's warrior headpiece), poetic virtuosity (the description of Achilles's shield), or occasional playfulness (Hermes's teasing of Priam in book 24). But the fantasy only worsens the bleakness, and even the comedy—reserved for Helen, who, pampered celebrity that she is, is always talking about herself no matter whom she is talking about, or to—is dark and gets darker the more you read. *The Iliad* is an unrelenting analytical demonstration of the impermanence of human life and the imperfection of all human designs; the best description of its tonal relationship to its "sequel," *The Odyssey,* is what the Old Testament's is to the New. We have no idea, of course, when the poems were composed or in which order; the name "Homer" itself most likely references no actual single poet but a whole tradition of oral composition, and means "the blind one," further testimony of scholars' helpless ignorance when it comes to the poems' origins.

The Odyssey is so different a poem that it is difficult for us to measure that difference. Our prolonged cultural acquaintance with it, no more so than in this century, has charmed us into accepting its measure of human character as our own, and its deviation from *The Iliad* as a given. When Samuel Butler argued in the late 1890s that Homer may well have been a woman, he voiced, and with an eloquence and panache that outperformed mere scholarship, a general sense that no one sensibility could have produced two such different poems. Scholars and readers, and many translators, have sensed for centuries a different compositional hand behind each poem. Even the differences, however, tend to mislead us. Robert Fitzgerald pointed out decades ago how the poem's actual ending so confused and irritated the ancients that both Archilochus and Aristophanes "are said to have called line 296 of XXIII the 'goal' or 'end' of *The Odyssey*," and so cut everything after Odysseus and Penelope's reunion in bed. This eliminates that troubling final book with its threats of a small civil war breaking out on Ithaka—more war, following one that lasted ten years and cost the island its whole population of able-bodied men? Unthinkable. And it tells us something important when we find two ancient critics registering the same unsatisfied longing for a happy ending that we still experience when we skip the "dull" parts (books 1 and 3 of the *Telemakhia,* the endless Eumaios chapters, and the second *Nekuia* of book 24) for the really hot stuff—Odysseus's four-book résumé delivered to Alkinöos and the three books leading to the flashy slaughter in the Great Hall of Odysseus's palace. This longing for a Disneyfied, romanced outcome persists into the near present, with, for instance, the 1997 three-hour *Odyssey* telemovie, the only watchable adaptation up to that time. Subtracting its overt weaknesses, which came from Coppola's approaching Homer the way he had approached Mario Puzo (and one of which is not Armand Assante, the first and only truly Mediterranean Odysseus to appear on film), Coppola's achieves the conventional understanding of the poem as an adventure story that ends with the nuclear family giddily and simply reconciled.* Nobody, in other words, really likes Homer's ending or is crazy about the gods having to intervene yet again in human affairs. The ending returns us with a thud to the real world. Athena steps in, imposes a "sworn pact" on all the disputants, a kind of bronze age Magna Carta, and restores a balanced but depressing moral realism to the poem that a few hundred lines earlier was about to end in erotic euphoria.

For all its fantasy, *The Odyssey* is a surprisingly skeptical and occasionally caustic domestic epic. Readers have long recognized and read it, perhaps too

---

* Uberto Pasolini's 2024 *The Return* is a retelling of the story from around book 12 of Odysseus's arrival in Ithaka but eliminates completely the gods and all of the fairy-tale elements. The result is a successful restoration of all the complications other versions avoid, such as the more probable outcome of an aged soldier's returning home with none of the hundreds of men he led into battle—a rough count is around six hundred—and trying to make peace not only with their kin but with an angry Telemachus and a justifiably confused, love-starved Penelope, more than a little aggrieved by her own struggle to remain faithful to him.

easily, as a critique of *The Iliad* and of that older heroic paradigm, which proposed that Fate, which answers none of our questions, may bring us heroes whose lives answer some but not all of those questions. But *The Odyssey* argues that reality is both darker and more complex, that there will always be unanswerable questions, and that the hard questions make up whatever is tragic or glorious in our lives, or so tragic that the best we can do is salvage some sense of our having "gloriously" survived. According to the poem, all human values—home, family, children, peace—depend on how successfully we recognize this. Odysseus's humanity matters to him for reasons the half-god Achilles never understood: because the gods do not know death, they are not only to be envied but to be feared. The ancient gods are (to use Pavese's word) *harmful* through and through; only the gods can afford a life of irresponsible recklessness, a life of fantasy. *The Odyssey* argues that our lives are to be prized because they are *not* fantastic.

It also foregrounds the essential character of the female as humanity's primary caregiver and curator of culture and the domestic arts, without whom there would be no civilized life; it is a poem in which a hero must count on a woman's intervention, again and again, to stay alive. This explains the poem's continuous emphasis on the hero's basic, bone-on-bone humanity, and why it is that, whenever he makes landfall, it is a woman or a girl who greets and saves him. Led by Nausikaa, the king's daughter, to the court of Alkinöos, that least warlike of hosts, Odysseus, the least peaceful of guests, is asked if he is a god. "Body and birth, a most unlikely god / am I," he says, "being all of earth and mortal nature." In our first glimpse of him, postponed until book 5, Calypso finds him "sitting, still / weeping, his eyes never dry," dying of homesickness; and again and again the Homeric similes measure him by way of a sliding scale of figuration (from women to children to dying coals). But it makes sense: *The Odyssey*, to the best of our reckoning, marks the first time in the history of the epic—which for its audience *was* history—where a mortal hero's blood is unmixed with a god's. Which is the whole point. If Odysseus's goal is to get home, his didactic function, which we must accept for the poem to make any moral sense, is to illustrate that mortality is as baffling to the gods as immortality is to men. If the gods live forever, they also feel little and know that much less than the women and men they harass. Their understanding of human life is purely intellectual, we might even say *virtual*. This is one way of understanding the true destructiveness of war. It seduces decent men into forgetting that they are not immortal; it damages societies, reducing them to the order of mindlessness parodied in the Cyclops episode, where civilized existence disappears and instead shrinks into a pastiche of brutal, gluttonous isolation ("the Cyclops have no meeting and no muster," in Fitzgerald's translation). War turned an Achilles into a cannibalistic, bloodthirsty psychopath, and his bad example survived his own death as a legacy of what can happen when men recklessly disregard the rational limits we need to obey if we are to live together.

And war did nothing for Odysseus either. Troy was still burning when Odysseus and his men, on a kind of joyride, headed north and sacked, pillaged, and burned tiny, unsuspecting Ismaros—the equivalent of, say, Zürich—before being forced back to their ships by a repulsing force. Instead of heading right home (as did Nestor, Menelaos, and Agamemnon), they went on a meaningless raid, caused bloody havoc, and gained nothing—"Six benches were left empty in every ship," as Fitzgerald has it, maybe a tenth of the total company lost, for nothing. These weren't civilized men, men prepared to take up again the peaceful roles of husbands and fathers; at least not yet. It will take him nearly a decade and the loss of his entire force to get home because his native brilliance, the resourceful domestic wisdom that would save Penelope from a forced marriage to one of the suitors, is smothered by the arrogance of a seasoned warrior. The cost in blood will be immense. After all, if we bother to estimate the number of ships and men lost in the first decade, then add in the 108 dead suitors in the second, the only difference between the respective depiction of carnage is that *The Odyssey* comes closer to supplying an actual body count and is, in my reading, if not a bloodier poem than *The Iliad,* then one in which blood is shed as stupidly, but more *recklessly*—a key Homeric term of abuse in *The Odyssey*. Had he only kept his mouth shut and not recklessly mocked the stupid son of Poseidon, Polyphemos, Odysseus could have quit Cyclops Island with minimal damage to himself and to his crew; had they not recklessly ignored their leader by eating the Cattle of the Sun, what remained of his crew might have lived to see home. That neither he nor his men could reform their behavior reveals how far the Man of Troubles has brought the troubles on himself. For we tend to believe that there is a preexisting threshold the hero must cross in order to enter the adventure; but the poem argues that when Odysseus crosses that threshold and pushes off from still-burning Troy, he actively collaborates in defining and even creating that very threshold, just as Milton's Satan, plummeting from Heaven, creates the Hell he comes to rule. And given its actual ending, Odysseus will need the gods' help to complete the crossing and restore domestic peace and the heaven-ordained orderliness that the poem is convinced is our *true* heroism. Even our noblest actions, if unassisted by external wisdom, can produce hideous consequences that are more so because totally unforeseen.

For the translator the task is maintaining these concerns in equilibrium and avoiding the extremes—a cheery, Bronze Age novel of sensibility (Rieu) or a plainspoken, frontier version (Rouse). If I am suggesting that *The Odyssey* is a harder poem to translate than *The Iliad,* then it is to the credit of Robert Fagles that he has attempted to strike this balance while at the same time, and consciously, taking into account competing versions—competing, that is, for academic praise and commercial shelf life. His accomplishment is to have made a translation that can seriously complement either Fitzgerald or Lattimore.

Fagles has given us a Virgilian *Odyssey* and an Odysseus closer in temperament to Aeneas than what we may be used to—in my case, the Odysseus of Robert Fitzgerald's version, first published in the 1960s. Odysseus's polytropic genius, for all its legendary power, produces as well as resolves all his problems: it is exactly because he is so resourceful that sooner or later he will run afoul of some god or other. A successful translation must therefore give equivocal emphasis to his resourcefulness and his recklessness. Fagles is remarkably consistent in returning Odysseus occasionally to the crowd of players from which he normally emerges and in grounding his behavior in his fatal genius; it's as though Sophocles had continued to identify Oedipus with the chorus after the opening scene and the king's coming down the steps to meet, literally to condescend to, his people. And it is the result of an aesthetic decision that registers in every line of Fagles's graceful and uniformly rhythmic rendition. Consequently, those elements of Odysseus's character that Fitzgerald is consistent in emphasizing—resourcefulness and recklessness—Fagles regards with an awareness more intellectual than enthusiastic. His Odysseus is presented with refined, unhurried, curatorial, nearly Nabokovian appreciation.

I am taken by the little things—the fact that in book 9 what Fitzgerald represents as Odysseus's decision to explore Cyclops Island and take the goatskin of unmixed wine along with him appears in Fagles as a subsequent and "sudden foreboding" that befalls the hero *after* he has already made his decision, which is now more the product of luck than design. Here is Fitzgerald:

> ... A wineskin full
> I brought along, and victuals in a bag
> for in my bones I knew some towering brute
> would be upon us soon—all outward power,
> a wild man, ignorant of civility.

Here is Fagles:

> ... I took this wine
> provisions too in a leather sack. A sudden foreboding
> told my fighting spirit I'd soon come up against
> some giant clad in power like iron plate—
> a savage deaf to justice, blind to law.

Here, for further comparison, is the recent Emily Wilson:

> I filled a big skin up with [wine], and packed
> provisions in a bag—my heart suspected
> that I might meet a man of courage, wild,
> and lacking knowledge of the normal customs.

And last, Stephen Mitchell:

> I filled a large goatskin with this, and I also took
> some food in a leather bag, since I had from the start
> a premonition that we would run into a creature
> of gigantic strength and savagery, who had no
> knowledge of law or justice. ...

Rather than experiencing a "sudden foreboding," Fitzgerald's Odysseus, with his punchier but smaller vocabulary, says flatly that he feels something "in his bones." He is more of a roughneck, and closer to the killer who mowed down

Trojans than Fagles's reflective Odysseus, who is, if not quite Hamlet, a bit indecisive, considerate, more destiny's pawn. This kind of elliptical thinking occasionally introduces a note of urbanity (or suburbanity) that I miss in Fitzgerald, who preserves, as here, the count-and-connect-the-dots approach of a hero rather more rustic than refined, more cagey than calculating, a leader that knows that all he really needs is a good loud voice. The urbanity makes a return in Wilson's straight-to-pentameter transcription of Odysseus as he contemplates what's to come. While I love her clear rendering of Odysseus's recipe for preparing unmixed wine that precedes this—"he poured / a single shot into a cup, and added / twenty of water," which clarifies that the wine, drunk straight, had a kick like brandy—I miss the note of urgency struck in Fitzgerald ("some towering brute / would be upon us soon") and Fagles's choice of "sudden foreboding" rather than Wilson's generally flatter diction ("my heart suspected") and tendency toward wry understatement ("lacking knowledge of the normal customs"), defining features of her version. Mitchell's, as accurate as the rest, is the one that presents the least impressive Odysseus, who totes "some food in a leather bag"—I'm imagining a pricey Yukon backpack filled with catered sandwiches—rather than Fitzgerald's choice ("wineskin"), Wilson's ("big bag") or even Fagles's ("leather sack"). This Odysseus is precisely the kind of guy who would have "a premonition," moreover, too sure of himself ever simply to feel something "in his bones."

This is not to suggest that one of these translators is the more accurate or even more "conservative" (whatever that may mean in this age of great translations and dying Classics departments). Compare their respective handling of one of the poem's climactic linguistic moments, nearly a pass-fail test for translators. Whenever Penelope mentions Troy, she puns on the name; in Homer's original she says κακιλιον (kakilion), a conflation of κακοσ (kakos, the source of our "kaka"), or "bad," and Ιλιον (Ilium). Fitzgerald renders the original pun (which appears three times in the poem) as "that ill wind / to Ilion" in his translation of its occurrence at 23:20–21 and leaves it at that, barely remarking its prior appearances twice in book 19 and raising no questions (or hopes) about Penelope's wit or sharp tongue. But compare Fagles: "Not once have I slept soundly since the day / Odysseus sailed away to see that cursed city . . . / Destroy, I call it—I hate to say its name!" A fairly laid-back solution, and since it's a formula in the original, one pressed into formulaic service all three times, so there's no missing the point either about the character (she's clever) or about the nature of the composition (formulaic, paratactic). And after all, why shouldn't the woman who comes up with that uncanny business of the shawl, and who is the poem's structural answer to all those evil temptresses, lovestruck goddesses, and lousy wives, add to her domestic resourcefulness the verbal resourcefulness of a good witch? Wilson's solution is shrewd but maybe a bit too coy: "that cursed town—Evilium!" in her translation of book 23 and in an earlier mention in book 19, adding, "the town I will not name." Mitchell more or less throws in the towel and declines to come up with anything better than "that city whose evil name I can't bear to mention," which he repeats verbatim on all three occasions it appears and so adheres to the poem's more formulaic moments when, according to the ancients, "Homer nods."

Such subtle but pervasive tonal shadings accumulate. In the Cyclops scene, for instance, Fitzgerald renders the poem's ultimate wisecrack as "My name is Nohbdy"; Fagles has him say "Nobody—that's my name." The inflection in Fagles is that of *pius Aeneas,* of a patriotic boy scout or prep-school sophomore pounding his hairless chest. Wilson and Mitchell both settle for the more conventional "Noman," the form taught in high school for the Greek ουτισ (outis). Later in the same episode, in Odysseus's description of the combined weight of man and wool on the ram he rides to safety, Fitzgerald's Odysseus, in the best of the four renderings, says that his ram was "weighted by wool and me with my meditations," whereas Fagles, leaning more heavily on the pentameter, gives "weighed down with his dense wool and my deep plots," drawing out the implicit link between the density of physical and mental materials in that series of long terminal vowels. Wilson's version, true to form, settles back into the pentameter: "Last of them all, the big ram went outside, / heavy with wool and me—the clever trickster," the last three words maybe too fussily filling out the meter. Though I have to add that her attempt is, for all its terse, eye-on-the-object immediacy, a lot more successful than Mitchell's wordier and frankly unconvincing description of how Odysseus "grabbed [the ram] / and swung myself under its shaggy belly and clung there / face upward, my fingers tightly gripping its wool / and as patient as I could be." There's no mention of cleverness, plots, or meditations, only the vague suggestion that patience and wiliness go together; the lines are slack, and further flab is added with the gratuitous description of the fingers "gripping the wool," which is obvious in context.

Generally, where we find in Fitzgerald a punchy, welcomed roughness of texture, Fagles gives us elegance and Virgilian suavity, Wilson a soldierly directness that borders on the laconic, and Mitchell a prosier, far less prosodically interesting compromise between the Greek original and your typical Hollywood action hero: where Fitzgerald has "we slept till morning," Fagles has "we fell asleep, awaiting Dawn's first light." Fitzgerald's Polyphemos is "a shaggy mountain reared in solitude"; Fagles's is "like a shaggy peak, I'd say—a man-mountain / rearing head and shoulders over the world"; Mitchell gives the wordier "like some cliff / that stands out against the sky at the top of a mountain"; and Wilson's has a fairy-tale grace and rustic precision that is endearing once you get used to the lines' iambic ticktock:

> . . . There lived a massive man
> who shepherded his flocks all by himself.
> He did not go to visit other people
> but kept apart, and did not know the ways
> of custom.

The diction might be straight out of an early translation of Grimm before they jazzed up the tales for an adult audience—the succession of simple sentences, the relaxed, down-to-earth diction ("he did not go to visit other people"), and the consistently disciplined refusal to elaborate when simple clarity suggests that there's no need. (In her introduction Wilson says, "My version is the same length as the original, with exactly the same number of lines," which I find mildly impressive.) Finally, there is the matter of spelling: Fitzgerald is faithful to the Greek's lack of the letter *c* and gives *Kyklops, Kalypso,* and *Telémakhos,* whereas Fagles, Wilson, and Mitchell adopt conventional spellings (Fagles omits most diacritical marks; Mitchell includes them here and there).

And then there is Helen, one of the three or four towering human presences in the *Telemachia.* Her exchange with Menelaos in book 4 is one of those master scenes in Homer, when every detail counts. Floods of memories trigger tear-floods among the men, so Helen drugs the wine to render them senseless to their pain and proposes that they "cheer the time" (Fitzgerald) with stories celebrating the genius of Odysseus. She begins, Menelaos follows. But in Helen's resolutely pre-Copernican universe, everything revolves around Helen, and as usual she reveals herself as a foolish and, in Fagles's version, a "shameless whore" misled by Aphrodite. The translations present her in vastly different lights. In Fagles, her every word is cadenced, balanced against her husband's and her reputation, and wounded by an experience that left her no less beautiful but still no wiser, either. She seems to retreat, like Claudius in *Hamlet,* into sonority to distance herself from shame:

> ... my heart had changed by now—I yearned
> to sail back home again! I grieved too late for the madness
> Aphrodite sent me, luring me there, far from my dear land,
> forsaking my own child, my bridal bed, my husband too,
> a man who lacked for neither brains or beauty.

What we have is a still gorgeous but fading ingénue whose biggest worry is picking out the right caterer. Reminiscent of *Hamlet*'s Gertrude, her cadences are not only measured but squared off, even rehearsed, and the pained naturalness that Fitzgerald achieves by breaking up the queen's lines is traded for an insinuating near-hexameter, aristocratic smarminess. I think Fitzgerald must have fallen a little in love with the character precisely because she has failed to evolve completely beyond the cluelessness that got her kidnapped in the first place:

> ... I had come round, long before,
> to dreams of sailing home, and I repented
> the mad day Aphrodite
> drew me away from my dear fatherland,
> forsaking all—child, bridal bed, and husband—
> a man without defect in form or mind.

Though still immature, and never "good," this Helen is never aloof; she is much more likable, and her phrasings ("come round") far more companionable to an American ear. Of the four, Wilson's, however, comes closest to something like "real American speech":

> The Trojan women keened in grief, but I
> was glad—by then I wanted to go home.

> I wished that Aphrodite had not made me
> go crazy, when she took me from my country,
> and made me leave my daughter and the bed
> I shared with my fine, handsome, clever husband.

This Helen is loveable for entirely different reasons. With her self-image clearly wounded in the retelling, it's so like her to separate herself cleanly from her ambience ("The Trojan women"), as if Priam had never treated her as a daughter or Andromache a sister-in-law. Still, she won't sugar the bitter truth; she is so thoroughly at home with herself you can't imagine her having the aristocratic education enjoyed by Fagles's Helen, with her enlarged vocabulary ("I grieved too late for the madness / Aphrodite sent me") or Fitzgerald's, with all her earthiness and brazen sex appeal. These differences naturally inform the different presentations of Menelaos's response.

In Fitzgerald, Menelaos is amused by what he's just heard and gently corrects her version of how the Trojan Horse was delivered into Troy and how mischievously Helen tried to trick the hidden Greeks:

> Three times you [Helen] walked around it, patting it everywhere,
> and called by name the flower of our fighters,
> making your voice sound like their wives, calling.

But in Fagles's version Menelaos all but comes out and calls her a liar, as his punctuation reflects:

> Three times you sauntered round our hollow ambush,
> feeling, stroking its flanks,
> challenging all our fighters, calling each by name—
> yours was the voice of all our long-lost wives!

Mitchell opts for flat description and leaves out all reference to Helen imitating the wives left at home:

> . . . Three times you walked
> Around our hiding place, patting it as you circled,
> Calling the names of each one of our commanders.

And in Wilson, if the temperamental note is gone, the dig is more subtle:

> Three times you went around the hollow belly,
> touching the hiding place, and calling on
> us Greeks by name; you put on different voices
> for each man's wife.

Fitzgerald's and Mitchell's Helen "walked around" (περιστειζασ), Wilson's simply "went around," but Fagles's Helen *sauntered*. And instead of the king's vague collective reference to "our fighters" in both Fagles and Fitzgerald and "commanders" in Mitchell, Wilson opts for the plain military concision of "Us Greeks," which seems somehow closer to the sense of the original (Δαναῶν ὀνόμαζες ἀρίστους), minus the qualifying "most noble" (aristous: Mitchell seems to bundle this into "commanders"), then adds the lovely "put on different voices." Menelaos then describes how Odysseus kept his head and maintained order. In Fagles, "Odysseus damped our ardor"; in Fitzgerald, "Odysseus fought us down"; in Wilson, the predictably pentametric "Odysseus prevented us from going." In each, the concern is not "closeness to the original" but wholeness of vision as well as the uniqueness of the translator's choices, along with interpretive integrity. The scene remains in our memory as an essential moment in the instruction of Telemachus, who has just seen one of history's greatest military stratagems reduced to human scale, and comic ambiguity.*

Then, naturally (or supernaturally), come the gods. Zeus's interest in human affairs is revealed in his initial speech to the Olympians, a meditation on the assassination of Agamemnon, for whom Zeus seems to harbor the sympathy of a fellow chief executive. Which makes sense, of course. When the issue is the human race, the attention span of the father of the gods is limited to lovely women and the harried aristocrats they marry or murder. Moreover, because Agamemnon was no ordinary general but essentially the leader of his world's surviving superpower, the expanding shock wave of his assassination seems to bounce off Olympus (book 1) and return to earth, touching first the home of Odysseus, his smartest counselor (Ithaka), then his older advisors (Nestor on Pylos, book 3), and lastly his own family (book 4, his brother Menelaos and

---

* T. E. Lawrence, in the strongest prose translation of the poem, renders it this way: "Three times you circled our packed lair, stroking it with your hands and calling by name the leaders of the Greeks. Your voice was the voice of all our absent wives."

sister-in-law Helen, in Sparta). No matter how often you read the poem, examples of such insinuating structural intelligence continue to impress—the echo of a past disaster shaping a distant one and entering human and divine conversations a total of five times in the four books of the *Telemachia*. Fitzgerald's Zeus, like any CEO or gangster kingpin, is a thoroughly informed but altogether removed button-pusher, who comes close to saying *it's their own damned fault*. He is especially worked up that another supreme commander should fall victim to "greed and folly." In Fagles, however, Zeus is slightly less dismissive: "Ah how shameless—the way these mortals blame the gods. / From us alone, they say, come all their miseries, yes, / but they themselves, with their own reckless ways / compound their pains beyond their proper share." The nice distinction in Zeus's use of the active voice, and the reflexive pronoun (*they themselves*) is effective in discriminating the mortal from the immortal share in human grief; he thinks narrowly, like every dictator, in black and white, and likes to keep things tidy. I'm personally impressed that Fagles imports with admirable near literalness the Greek word ατασθαλιασιν (*recklessness,* Fitzgerald's "Greed and folly"), for "reckless ways," which appears twice in the first thirty-four lines and whose didactic burden is so important to the poem. Fitzgerald's Zeus's introduction is a bit more bumptious: "My word, how mortals take the gods to task! All their afflictions come from us, we hear." The opening interjection is a handy solution to the original's ὦ πόποι (*o popoi*), which is a fairly mild exclamation, not quite a profanity; our closest equivalents range from "oh, crap" to "for crying out loud." But "My word" is too idiomatically British, more so even than Fagles's "how shameless," and once again Wilson ("This is absurd / that mortals blame the gods!") strikes a healthy balance and seems the most natural to an American ear. Mitchell, to complete the foursome, punts as usual ("How ready these mortals are to accuse the gods!").

Since every translator must test the original's flex points, no choices are more revealing than in where translators take liberties. The Cyclops's pathetic, lonely speech to the leader ram gives Fitzgerald the opportunity to explore how pathetic a figure the Cyclops is: "Sweet cousin ram," says one brute to the other, which may have influenced Wilson's own choice of "Sweet ram" in the same passage. Fagles's "Dear old ram" and Mitchell's "Dear ram" are closer to Homer but subtract the powerful interpretive grace note ("sweet *cousin*") that Fitzgerald interjects and that closes the distance between Polyphemos and the beasts whose sensibility his more precisely resembles. Fitzgerald also introduces another surprising nuance: he *rhymes* every message that Hermes brings to a human recipient so that each is an old-fashioned Western Union singing telegram, delivered by the god of swift communication and commercial fortune. Fitzgerald also cleverly preserves the distinction in singular and plural second-person addresses in the remarkably tender conclusion of book 4, when the good news of Odysseus's incipient arrival comes in a dream to Penelope in the image of her sister. The shift is not demanded by the context but powerfully effective. Fagles's Telemachus in book 1 is "the boy [Odysseus] left a babe in arms at home" where Fitzgerald, closer to the original, has "Telemachus, whom he left as a new born child"; and when Menelaos addresses Helen (4:148), Fagles has "My dear, my dear," twice repeating the endearment to soften his stiff-necked wife, whereas Fitzgerald and Wilson (and Homer) have him address her once.

In constructing this I went back to the suddenly many *Odysseys* that appeared in advance (and in the wake) of Coppola's film version of 1997. Along with Fagles and Fitzgerald, I looked at the still sturdy Lattimore, the indispensable T. E. Lawrence, the unkillable Butler (republished as a reprint with the film and with Armand Assante on the cover), and others—the competent but undistinguished Mitchell, the Rouse that I grew up with, the Rieu that the unenlightened still insist on imposing on seventh-graders, the fairly recent and totally forgettable Mandelbaum, and the awfully reliable Norton Critical Edition, with Albert Cook's smart and speakable verse translation. Eliminating the inelegant (Mandelbaum) and the respectable but dull (Rieu) is easy; but recommending the stylish Fagles over the rugged Fitzgerald, Fitzgerald over the ever-reliable Lattimore, the plainspoken Wilson over any one of the others is as useless as it is impossible, and so I surrender the bow and won't even try. Perhaps nobody should. Some forty years ago I read a sentence in Kenner's *The Pound Era* that has stuck with me: if we were to discover *The Odyssey* tomorrow morning, we would not know what to do with it, so thoroughly has it shaped our imagination of literary and cultural values. It is as though certain texts are as eternally here as oceans and hills; this is their *facticity,* their historicity. Certain classics not only clarify but make possible in the first place what we perceive as values. For that reason, and especially in an area of disappearing competence and confidence in a wider culture, we need all the *Odysseys* we can get.

—1999–2018

Four Translations of Dante's *Inferno*

When John Ciardi translated *The Inferno* well over fifty years ago, he approached it through a poet's sensitivity to the limits of translation and an amateur Dante scholar's sense of the scholarly headaches; and there are many. The total bulk of theological, political, and historical information is a problem for either Italian or English readers. Ciardi's solution was to produce endnotes that are not only lucid but so appealingly down-to-earth that the notes might alone justify the translation. The larger problem, though, is represented by the formal demands of *terza rima,* which you cannot just ignore and the likes of which exist nowhere in our English narrative verse outside of Shelley's last great lyrics, a feat of technical isometrics carried out against the example of his great original. This is no place to re-argue the inextricable dependence of form to idea, or how form in poetry really is ideology. Had Shelley finished *The Triumph of Life,* he might have left an English *terza rima* suited to the prosodic demands of verse narrative in our rhyme-poor and uninflected language. As it is, the form comes down to us intact in wonders like *Ode to the West Wind* or in more distant homages to its tensile strength, such as Stevens's *Auroras of Autumn.*

It's hard to approach Elio Zappulla's elegant, dignified, and altogether faithful version of *Inferno* without finding it already in the shadow of Ciardi. Zappulla's scholarship is satisfying, and his notes, from the vantage of amateur Dantescans, probably better—less interpretive, maybe a richer source of cultural detail. Take, for instance, Ciardi's note to the heroic political figure whom Dante only calls the "Greyhound" in Canto 1. As he often does, Dante refuses to demystify his readers; that's part of the spiritual test. Ciardi tells you only that the reference is almost certainly to the wealthy and powerful Veronese nobleman Can Grande della Scala, Dante's patron; Zappulla, however, reminds you that Can Grande—Big Dog—was not just Dante's literary godfather but a powerful and popular political boss. Zappulla's scholarship seems sturdier, less chatty, and on the whole more dependable, with an inevitability that is satisfying if you read the notes only for information.

Still, one can easily warm up to Ciardi's way of buttonholing you in those bibliographic alleyways that scholarship reserves for data that is useful but often makes indifferent impact on your understanding. Take this one example (among dozens) that occurs in a note to Canto 21, dealing with Dante's "coarseness . . . [which] has offended certain delicate readers":

> It is worth pointing out that the mention of bodily function is likely to be more shocking in a Protestant than in a Catholic culture. It has often seemed to me that the offensive language of Protestantism is profanity or blasphemy: one offends on a scale of unmentionable words for bodily function, the other on a scale of disrespect for the sacred.

"The difference"—Ciardi's note runs for two full paragraphs—"is not national, but religious," and to illustrate this Ciardi refers to Chaucer's *Pardoner's Tale.* If there were such a thing as a Footnote Hall of Fame, for sheer breeziness and as an example of how to launch a conjecture—he must have been great in the classroom—this one certainly belongs. In something as small as a note to a single Canto, Ciardi is ranging around, pulling all the ends together, organizing out of all the data, even seeming incidentals, the stuff of a worldview. It's what contributes to the lasting charm of Ciardi's translation, and what makes the Norton company's dumping of Ciardi's for Mandelbaum's relatively lifeless translation (in a recent edition of Norton's *World Masterpieces*) difficult to justify and frankly astonishingly stupid.

Yet Zappulla's choice of the English blank verse line may have been a mistake. Blank verse comes to readers of English smeared with the fingerprints of Shakespeare, who found it, along with straight prose, a more natural vehicle than rhymed pentameters for dramatic speeches. But it was Milton who decided that no supernatural character, hence no figure of epic stature, would ever speak in rhyme. In the tonalities of *Paradise Lost,* the highest dramatic poetry in the Western tradition and of all elevated rhetorical psychodrama, we hear the Miltonic rhythms that blindness and English politics had banished from the real stage to the theater of the mind. Milton invented a tradition of verse narration that departs so completely from formal precedent and natural speech that nobody has ever successfully followed it or imitated it; even attempts to circumvent Milton's prosody have ended in disaster (viz., the Puritan divine Michael Wigglesworth's *The Day of Doom*). Over the distance of three-quarters of a century, Pound's famous bellyaching about Milton now sounds like sour grapes at having found in the only English poet to have written a sustained poetic narrative no instruction manual for doing it again. "Milton ruined his work by not understanding that the genius of English is not the genius of Latin," he complained in a letter of 1912, "and that one can not write an uninflected language in the same way, using the same word-order that serves in an inflected language." Clearly, this objection, part of Pound's larger technical program excluding the use of inversions and archaisms, never occurred to Milton. Dismissive of rhyme and the organizational energies of lyric (stanzaic groupings like quatrains), Milton, perhaps because the English theaters had been closed by Cromwell, accomplished for extended poetic narrative what Shakespeare did for drama—advancing the claims of character over those of plot, of personality over the concept- and event-driven storytelling horizons that Homer discovered and Aristotle more or less mapped. Without Milton's permanent deformations of blank verse, there is no *Prelude,* no *Alastor,* no "Fra Lippo Lippi," and none of its scattered Modernist issue, accredited or not. The dramatic monologue, essentially a formal recognition of our greater interest in character than in plot, about the who and not the what, needed the examples of both Shakespeare and Milton.

But *The Divine Comedy* is really not about character, at least not in the Shakespearean or Miltonic sense. *Hamlet*'s drama is all internal and tracks a single character's evolution over five acts; whenever he's offstage we're in a different play.* But Satan never really changes: he is revealed to be as surprisingly multi-aspected—talented, intelligent, a gifted orator with a sharp sense of irony—and so (to the horror of C. S. Lewis et al.) surprisingly human. Yet Dante's charac-

---

* Or when he dies. It's always discombobulating to hear Horatio, the most conventional intellectual figure in all the tragedies, pray that choirs of angels bear to rest the man whose dying declaration only seconds before was that "the rest is silence," choirs and chorales be damned. Hamlet is the ur-contrarian, the archetypal liberal; he often resists agreeing even with himself.

ters will never evolve or grow. They do nothing to surprise us. They come to us literally from the end of time—as all commentators point out, from personal end-times—and speak to us through the personal apocalypse whose hero is also its narrator. These characters have made their decisions and entered them in the book of time, each mini-teleology there to recall the macronarrative that God is still busily writing. Hamlet can change his mind, and because it takes him at least four acts to decide what to do, *Hamlet* is for some three acts too long (as Eliot, missing the point, childishly complained). But the Ulysses of Canto 26, for instance, cannot change or be changed; he boasts that he would do it all over, the same way, given the chance. All Dante's characters have perfected their destinies; their personalities have matured, have accomplished what Aristotle termed their entelechies, the accomplishment according to Aquinas of potential as it becomes act. This goes for saints as well as sinners. When Saint Peter rages about the popes who have usurped *his* place on earth, though a heavenly being he can still sputter like a cheated landlord, apparently stomping on the floor of Heaven three times for emphasis: "Quelli ch'usurpa in terra il luogo mio, / il luogo mio, il luogo mio, . . ." (*Paradiso* 27:22–23). Dante's verse forces you to overhear the ranting of a saint who suddenly sounds unabashedly human: that's *my job, my job, my job.* Hayden Carruth's inspired term for this element in Dante was its "singing but simple tension," the tension between the mind and body reenacted in formal measures. Divine authority penetrates human language; the result is a persistent, oddly compelling, robust mix of the sacred and the profane. This is the source of the *Comedy*'s weird, unsettling matter-of-factness; it's as if human language had actually been elevated to the level of the divine.

Shakespeare's great discovery was that all great art begins in the raw, two-dimensional stereotypes that solitary freelancing genius transforms into full-blooded characters. Their changes of heart, whether instigated by themselves or inspired by the gods, destiny, or all those occasions that do inform against us, are never inarguably predetermined. There is no maturing of a preexisting telos and no automatic satisfying of generic expectations, the fact that so disturbed Eliot: *Hamlet* blows up generic expectations; *Lear* ends in a godless universe with Cordelia hanged and the country a mess and thus effectively redefines tragedy; *Coriolanus* leaves us asking what we mean by a tragic hero, *The Merchant of Venice* with what we mean by a "happy" ending. What shocks us in Shakespeare—and inspired Keats's notion of *Negative Capability*—was his agility at getting out of the way of his creations once the drama was in motion. The process of characterization in Shakespeare seems so self-sustaining, so unforced, that even in his early botches (like *Titus Andronicus*) the "real" Shakespeare seems never to have mattered.

And Dante is in that exact sense Shakespeare's precise opposite. The only way into Dante's characters is through Dante, whose outrageousness is his having compressed and then removed the tradition of heroic narrative into the domain that traditionally had been the precinct of the *lyric* singer. Dante introduces autobiography into epic and changes both forever. His very ubiquity is probably the poem's most outrageous innovation. You can never forget, once you have read it, the thrilling moment in *Purgatorio* 30 when Virgil disappears and Dante hears his name called by Beatrice: "Dante, do not weep, though Vergil goes." For the first time in history an author *names himself* by having one of his characters address him directly, and makes himself the protagonist—and why not say it?—the *hero* of his own epic. What chutzpah! The form of this poem, though, keeps reminding you that Dante's roots were in lyric, the radical grounds of the rootless self and the staging area of the earliest autobiographical impulses, which might take you as far back as Gilgamesh's lament for Enkidu, or Phemios's defense of the minstrel's job in *Odyssey* 22. There is no way to get around the lyric form and its isolating energies as what propels this extended, reflective song of the higher or reformed, prodigal self.

A comparison of Ciardi's, Zappulla's, and Robert Pinsky's translations of the episode of Paolo and Francesca in *Inferno* 5 may make the point. Circle II, its location, is the circle of carnality, a relatively minor offense in Hell's schedule of crimes. Ciardi has the sinners there confined being constantly blown around by "a war of winds," a clear representation of the power of blind passion, and Zappulla, by "storms that know no pity and no rest." Dante's transfiguration of the damned into cranes, birds helpless in a windstorm, is not arbitrary: the sin of these two teenage lovers stemmed from a voluntary loss of control, opening the descent to what Dante, at times the harshest of judges, aligns with bestiality. This is what makes every infernal punishment so nasty: each is the *logical* consequence of a particular misbehavior. The circumstances of the punishment reproduce the initial offense and heighten the anguish of the punished. The real punishment of transgression is the constant revelation of its real meaning, and how terribly *logical*, lawyerly it is. Having "betrayed reason to their appetite"

(Ciardi)—Zappulla commits a cliché and renders the line, "Permitted reason to be passion's slave"—they have obliterated the threshold between will and reason, and nature in them is all bodily intelligence, pure instinct—again, the logical outcome.

But despite his love of the logic behind their punishment, Dante takes no pleasure in their pain, and his conversation with the damned lovers yields to a subtle shift in emphasis. They are not like cranes, he says, but "mating doves," and when Francesca speaks, the verse modulates. Here is Zappulla:

> Love, the swift conqueror of gentle hearts,
> Inflamed my lover with a carnal lust
> For my fair form, of which I was deprived
>
> In such a way as to offend me still.
> Love, who makes the beloved love in turn,
> Enchanted me and sealed our common doom.
>
> In Hell we are as one, as once on earth.

Now Ciardi:

> "Love, which in gentlest hearts will soonest bloom,
> seized my lover with passion for that sweet body
> from which I was torn unshriven to my doom.
>
> Love, which permits no loved one not to love,
> took me so strongly with delight in him
> that we are one in Hell, as we were above.
>
> Love led us to one death. In the depths of Hell
> Cai'na waits for him who took our lives."
> This was the piteous tale they stopped to tell.

And finally, here is Pinsky:

> . . . My birthplace is a city that lies

Where the Po finds peace with all its followers.
Love, which in gentle hearts is quickly born,
Seized him for my fair body—which, in a fierce

Manner that still torments my soul, was torn
Untimely away from me. Love, which absolves
None who are loved from loving, made my heart burn

With joy so strong that as you see it cleaves
Still to him, here. Love gave us both one death.
Caina awaits the one who took our lives.

This is not a question of comparative accuracy. All three capture the sting of
Francesca's agony, and all three modulate into the lyric mode of *stil novisti* that
Dante and Cavalcanti learned (or stole) from the troubadours. But Ciardi uses
four words (*unshriven to my doom*) where Zappulla needs a line and a half and Pinsky nearly two; Zappulla does not reproduce the intricate rhyme scheme, which,
here especially, is not only effective but arguably demanded by the change in lyric
mode; to his credit, Pinsky does, though the result is that our rhyme-poor native tongue forces him into grabbing at approximates. To be fair, one measure of
the difficulty of strict adherence to Dante's example is glimpsed in Dorothy Sayers's now nearly eighty-year-old and still impressive version of the same passage:

"Love, that so soon takes hold in the gentle breast
    Took this lad with the lovely body they tore
    From me; the way of it leaves me still distrest.

Love, that to no loved heart remits love's score,
    Took me with such great joy of him, that see!
    It holds me yet and never shall leave me more.

Love to a single death brought him and me;
    Cain's place lies waiting for our murderer now."
    These words came wafted to us plaintively.

The tone is of a startled, spoiled debutante—Scarlett O'Hara in Hell. Clearly, the cost of a strict adoption of *terza rima* to English prosody is high—"love's score," the gratuitous and utterly out of character dissonance of the phrase "that see!"—no matter the gains for the reader, which are few.

In the long run it's a matter of taste: do you prefer emotional concision and fidelity to the source or something approaching the rhythms of contemporary speech and technical habits we are more used to? Zappulla's blank verse captures Francesca's dignified despair and the inescapability of their situation; Pinsky's translation of the near-incantatory, triple celebration of "Love" has moments of plainspoken beauty, but for some odd reason is introduced with the bombastic "Where the Po finds peace with all its followers," and includes moments of clunky syntax that break the spell ("Love . . . Seized him for my fair body"). This in Ciardi is more elegant and a lot clearer ("where the Po descends into its ocean rest / with its attendant streams"). But Ciardi has also, consciously and right down to the inversions, retained the very contours of the very *stil novisti* that Francesca goes on to condemn when she tells Dante what they were reading at the time, the story of Lancelot and Guinevere, along with the description of carnal desire which was its seductive subject. Their modern analogy is two teenagers left alone, who start by watching a steamy love story on their iPhones and end up making out in the basement. Only these two teens are royals and related through a no doubt arranged marriage, doubly damned by circumstances that heighten the pathos and the stakes. Ciardi's repetition of the word *Love* in three successive tercets exactly reproduces the shape and lyrical force of Dante's original, which ironically foregrounds the lovers' problem by casting it in the very form that reminds you of what probably got them in trouble in the first place:

Amor, ch'al cor gentil ratto s'apprende,
    prese costui de la bella persona
    che mi fu tolta; e 'l modo ancor m'offende.

Amor, ch'a nullo amato amar perdona,
    mi prese del costui placer sì forte,
    che, come vedi, ancor non m'abbandona.

Amor condusse noi ad una morte:
    Caina attende chi a vita ci spense.

The closest analogy I can think of in English is *Romeo and Juliet,* where the prologues for acts 1 and 2 and the exchange of sweet nothings between the lovers in 1:5 are cast in sonnet form. Romeo and Juliet are eternal teens, a Tony and Maria for all the ages—forever falling in or out of love and wishing the night will have no morning star. Since the sonnet once upon a time was *the* poetic vehicle for the expression of erotic feeling, how else might two gorgeous, aristocratic, bratty, doomed adolescents talk to each other except this preposterously, in the way their reading and upbringing trained them to talk? Similarly with Dante, who here prefigures Shakespeare, with this stinging difference: just as the sinners' punishments are infernal parodies of their crimes, the *shape* of their speech is a devilish, formal parody of their situation. The way we speak to each other exposes the fullness of our character. Our words x-ray us, indict us, and not just the words but the discursive vehicles that we choose to deliver them.

For Dante, a style is the embodiment of a philosophical or moral principle, the incarnation of vision, and an *absolute* way of looking at things: no wonder he was so idolized by the Modernists. What Zappulla gives you is what is so off-putting to us: the estranging banality of Hell, the likeness in unlikeness, the sense of suffering made all the more unacceptable by its near-perfect explicability and similarity to the suffering of the living. This sense of proximity to ourselves (and our own suffering) is behind the depictions of Hell in films as raunchy as Clive Barker's *Hellbound* or as relatively refined as Vincent Ward's *What Dreams May Come,* or in Birk and Sanders's surprisingly effective 2004 graphic novel adaptation, which never pretends to be a translation. But those are tamed simulacra of the great original: Dante's Hell is on the ridge that separates the sublime from the sentimental. What Ciardi gets, right down to the scene's stylistic grace notes—decisively beginning each line of Francesca's monologue with the word *Love*—is how alienated we are from that past, from the tragedy of heroic desire and the fact that tragedy by its very nature is inevitable. The language in which it is expressed will always in its beauty surpass tragedy's bleak and banal fulfillment. We are always ourselves, right down to the words that speak us into being, that move human potential into human acts. Dante is never so convincing, in fact, than when he lets the doomed bear witness to their crimes through the cold penal logic of which Hell is the final reduction. The logical or abstract clarity of the diagnosis is, as it were, more interesting to Zappulla than the aesthetic philosophy—it can hardly be called orthodox theology—that Dante conceived to bring it to life. I can see why; Dante's understanding of justice is so rigorously puritanical we might forget that it is nearly identical with the one that operates when a judge delivers a sentence or when—to take a more trivial example—a school administers a test like the SAT. You might be a fine person, but Princeton quality you're not. In that sense, it's just business, it's nothing personal. The most crushing fact about Hell is that there is nothing exactly "personal" about it.

The poem's formal demands are so formidable that the trickiest move for a translator who departs from them is to capture something of the original's nobility, its steadiness that is never stiffness, and its estranging beauty; and not all succeed. It begins at the level of prosody, and Allen Mandelbaum's version gives you a sense of the rigor of those demands and what happens when you disappoint them:

> When I had journeyed half of our life's way
> I found myself within a shadowed forest
> for I had lost the path that does not stray.
>
> Ah, hard it is to speak of what it was,
> that savage forest, dense and difficult,
> which even in recall renews my fear.

To accomplish even this much Mandelbaum is forced to adopt a version of barely idiomatic English ("paths" do not stray, people do) and drop in a lame inversion ("Ah, hard it is") to make the meter keep tick-tocking along. The prosody from the outset is a lifeless, unpropulsive pentameter. Now compare Ciardi:

> Midway in our life's journey, I went astray
> from the straight road and woke to find myself
> alone in a dark wood. How shall I say

what wood that was! I never saw so drear,
so rank, so arduous a wilderness!
Its very memory gives a shape to fear.

While neither Mandelbaum nor Ciardi has a convincing way with Dante's knotty sixth line (*che nel pensier rinova la paura,* with its hint of the conditional), Ciardi at least has Dante doing the "straying," and from the simply but perfectly phrased "straight road," which is echoed on the other side of the caesura in the word *woke.* I can't imagine hearing the phrase "in recall"—instead of "in recollection of"—outside of an ESL classroom or unless you're stuck for three syllables to fit the meter. And if *selva oscura* is "shadowed forest," there's nothing special about it; most forests are shadowy anyway. It is so only literally, and perhaps only in a translator's labored, literal first draft. Ciardi's "dark wood" and Pinsky's "dark woods," on the other hand, if less "poetic" capture the connotative reach of the phrase, which demands being taken extra-literally, and instantly announce what American readers generally don't want to have to bother with—the presence of allegory. Line 5, in Mandelbaum's rendering of *selva selvaggia e aspra e forte* as "savage forest, dense and difficult," merely fats up the syntax while hardly raising expectations, whereas "so rank, so arduous a wilderness" not only iterates the initial rotacisms and takes great Longfellowish metrical gulps in doing so, but neatly (for anybody who cares to remember) reminds you how America's greatest allegorist describes Hester as entering not just any forest in Massachusetts but a "moral *wilderness."* Nor do Mandelbaum's easygoing, tum-te-tumty rhythms communicate anything of the regimented dignity and shocking let's-get-on-with-it rhythm of Dante's simple *Nel mezzo del camin;* Dante's rhythms are flexible but anything but casual. Mandelbaum gets none of the scratchiness, the giddy-up, the ruggedness of the source, some ghost of which Ciardi (with its serial *n*'s, *r*'s and *m*'s) manages to capture.

Dante's poetry is so powerfully direct that its sheer muscularity can make you forget how preposterously abstract was the Afterlife prior to *Inferno,* when writers had only book 6 of the *Aeneid* to go on, or improvise from. Mandelbaum's version is admittedly direct and accessible, but it retains none of the original's fricative power. It comes across as a hopelessly confused attempt to copy the embarrassed reflexiveness, the predictive blah-blah-blah of much contemporary poetic diction, with its deliberate, self-consciously flat delivery (see Louise Glück) and moments of strained eloquence that it either ironizes or apologies for:

> Love, that can quickly seize the gentle heart,
> Took hold of him because of the fair body
> Taken from me—how that was done still wounds me.

This is Mandelbaum's rendering of Francesca's lament. Lots of ballast here: that "quickly" in the first line, that clumsy undergraduate "because of," even the dash in line 3 that introduces the stagey caesural pause. Read out of metrical context, the result sort of works, but as mediocre romcom dialogue. Here, it sounds pretentious, embarrassed, as if someone who knows better is trying to sound as if he doesn't. Even those familiar with the poem may be stopped by the emphatic vagueness of the pronoun *him*. It belongs to Paolo, of course, along with the "fair body," but Paolo is never directly named in Canto 5 (they *both* had "fair" bodies); he didn't need to be named since scandal ensured that everyone knew who he was anyway, hyper-identifiable as a member of the powerful Malatesta clan and through his well-publicized connection with his sister-in-law, to whom Dante assigns their story. Mandelbaum supplies a note that discloses the full backstory and the three major antecedents, but it's either a puzzling oversight or a tacit dismissal of the reader's situation not to anticipate the mental breaths you have to take before you can get on with it. Over the course of the translation the cost of such oversights, of all this democratizing and dumbing-down, is inestimable and unforgivable.

Here and there Mandelbaum coughs up rhetorical fur balls, no more so than when he comes to cruxes in the original that test the resourcefulness of the translator. Thus, "I think that he was thinking that I thought," is how he ping-pongs through Dante's mulling over Virgil's prolepses into his questions (*Inferno* 13:25). The original reads *Cred' io ch'ei credette ch'io credesse*. Mandelbaum may have been looking anxiously over his shoulder and trying to avoid plagiarizing from Ciardi, who gives us, "I think perhaps he thought that I was thinking," a nearly literal and skillful aping of the original's baffled goofiness that Ciardi declines to clean up—and nobody really has, or should, because it's deliberate. Dante's confusion is at times as vast as Hell and is reflected—here, refracted—in his syntax.* Ciardi's rhythms, especially ending the line on an un-stressed syllable, help him navigate the textual chop, whereas Mandelbaum's doinkettyy-doink rhythm is inseparable from the rest of the metrical environ-ment. Mandelbaum's major precaesural stress gives you the past progressive "was thinking," where Ciardi's simple past tense ("I thought") is more accurate and lands more decisively. Zappulla, trying to make Dante sound a bit more re-spectable or at least less like Lou Costello, has "I am convinced he thought that I believed," choosing three synonyms that do not exactly convey the character's awkwardness and pathetic confusion at this stage of the narrative, where when he is not fainting, he is trembling—Dante's avatar is something of a wuss—at what he is witnessing. The burden of the translator is to render the narrator's implicit helplessness and the slight absurdity of his mental position, but to do so gently, without turning description into an *SNL* sketch.

At other points Mandelbaum pushes the *Comedia's* comic possibilities to the point of slapstick. In 12:80–82, when Chiron the Centaur expresses amaze-ment that Dante, unlike the other ghosts in Hell, affects the environment phys-ically, Mandelbaum has, "Have you noticed / how he who walks behind moves what he touches? / Dead soles are not accustomed to do that." A pun worthy of a Quaker, or *Reader's Digest,* but nowhere in the original Italian, which has only *i pie de' morti,* with no pedestrian double-takes on *souls* and *soles;* Dante gives you no reason to suggest that Chiron has a middle-schooler's sense of humor or finds something funny in what he sees. Compare Ciardi's version, the first three words of which Mandelbaum silently pickpockets: "Have you noticed / how the one who walks behind moves what he touches? / That is not how the dead go." And Pinsky to his credit is even better:

Chiron drew an arrow's notch back through the tangle

---

* Longfellow: "I think he thought that I perhaps might think"; Sayers: "I think he must have thought that I was thinking"; Mark Musa (1984): "I think perhaps he thought I might be thinking"; Ciaran Carson (2002): "I think he thought I thought they might have come," the antecedent of *they* being the "voices" from the surrounding trees; and one of my personal favorites, the Birk and Sanders (and highly recommended) graphic version (2004): "I think / old Virgil saw me looking around and assumed that I / thought someone was hiding in the shadows, or something."

Of beard along his jaw to clear a space
For his large mouth, and to the others he said:
"Have you observed how that one's steps displace

Objects his body touches? Feet of the dead
Are not accustomed to behave like that."

Pinsky, with his sharper ear, at least takes a thrust at preserving the rhyme scheme while adding the charming detail of the great Chiron tossing his long beard back over his shoulder; his delivery, moreover, is what you'd expect of a minor divinity. The choice of *space / displace* and *said / dead* is smart and leads to the plain trochaic opening of the last line, where Pinsky loosens the rhythm and lets it lapse back into regular iambs; this is someone clearly listening to how his translation sounds. Chiron the Centaur still comes off sounding a bit like a museum docent instead of the suddenly amused, born killer who tutored Achilles and who, under the circumstances, is more likely to ask, "Are you mugs also seeing this?" There's also the subtle confusion introduced with "that one's steps displace." But Pinsky is forgiven since the alternative is to add another *that* to give us a heads-up that, whoops, a relative clause is coming. Zappulla, just to round this off, spends four lines that make the same point but surrender the seamlessness and elegance of the original:

. . . Look at him! You see?

It's obvious that anything he treads
On moves. I mean that one standing behind
His guide. The feet of dead men can't do that.

Why Chiron, caught by surprise at what he sees, would pause between *tread* and *on* and unnaturally split the verb from the preposition is beyond me, and that "It's obvious" seems more at home coming from the translator than from Chiron. Irritations such as these may not sink a competent and entertaining translation like Zappulla's; but Mandelbaum's is just barely that, and rarely entertaining. Such snafus neither rise to the level of inspired mistakes nor constitute radical interpretive pivoting to surprising innovations. You have to wonder about the editorial wisdom or marketing savvy that would elect to jettison a classic of the translator's art—Binyon's for Mark Musa, Ciardi's for Mandelbaum's—for a more workshop-friendly translation that's also dead-on-arrival.* Mandelbaum's may be workmanlike, but that's hardly argument for inclusion in a major anthology that will for some students be (outside of YouTube videos and video games) their *only* exposure to the poem.

Effective translation should always be accountable to the source without being obligated to it, though often accountability is achieved, or only possible as time goes by and the canon expands, by the addition of hefty scholarship. The recent bilingual *Inferno* from Robert Hollander and Jean Hollander is a deeply learned—and by its looks, totally accountable—version of Dante's poem included in the batch that began appearing over the past two decades; the Hollanders' combined CVs alone demand they be given special and deserved recognition. Theirs comes with a scholarly apparatus that balloons the text out to more than six hundred pages. Comprehensiveness comes at the cost of the intense readability and enjoyment of, say, Ciardi's version, yet it is still stirring to see two experts picking their way over the old ground and summarizing a good deal the amateurs overlooked or for whatever reason have left out. It's the Hollanders' notes alone to the poem—only Singleton's are more authoritative—rather than their translation that makes this an indispensable companion to Dante.

For instance, their note on the presence of the three metaphysical beasts that appear in Canto 1, which is the Dante homework nobody ever pays atten-

---

* Having mentioned him above, here is Laurence Binyon's now generally forgotten translation of *Inferno*, completed in 1933:

> Midway the journey of this life I was 'ware
>   That I had strayed into a dark forest,
> And the right path appeared not anywhere.
>   Ah, tongue cannot describe how it oppressed,
> This wood, so harsh, dismal and wild, that fear
>   At thought of it strikes now into my breast.
> So bitter it is, death is scarce bitterer.
>   But, for the good it was my hap to find,
> I speak of the other things that I saw there.

Binyon sustains this for the entirety of the poem, so it's clear that it can be done.

tion to and that most of us skip, is characteristically exhaustive. All you probably really need to know is that these three beasts—a she-wolf, a lion, a leopard—are figures traditionally supposed to represent, in the most respected and earliest accredited ancient sources, three of the seven deadly sins: lust, pride, and avarice. But the number seven is also significant in Dante's poem, and the Hollanders, not content with a nod toward the much longer scholarly conversation, describe at length a tradition of long-standing "disagreements" among commentators "as to which beast represents which Aristotelian/Ciceronian category of sin: Is the leopard fraud or incontinence? Is the she-wolf incontinence or fraud?" The Mother of all Footnotes to *Inferno* is theirs to 1:32–54, which runs for two full pages.

At another point, in Canto 4, Dante includes himself in the company of the greatest poets in history and leaves the reader wondering at this breathtaking act of sheer moxie. Again, the Hollanders come to the rescue:

> For a review of the various sorts of discomfort among the commentators occasioned by Dante's promotion of his own poetic career in this verse (some going so far as to insist that he displays humility here rather than pride) see Mazzoni. . . . It is clear that Dante is putting himself in very good company on the basis of very little accomplishment: a series of lyrics, the *Vita Nuova,* two unfinished treatises, and three cantos of the *Comedy*. His daring is amazing.

In fact, "daring" vastly understates the case. Here we are catching Dante in the act of acting as his own seminar or, to change the figure, betting on the inside straight. The fact that he pulls it off has made us forget, to continue the metaphor, how little he had to ante up—a fact that only the Hollanders seem either alert to or capable of reporting at length (the note goes on for an additional two paragraphs). The point, of course, is not mere donnish fussiness or squeamishness since they are neither donnish nor squeamish; what I love is the confidence they place in readers' abilities to make up their own minds, in perhaps their curiosity to learn more, as well as an example of the serious yet good-natured character of real scholarship when it's done by real pros with a sense of humor and who seem to love what they do. It's also a reminder that few things are ever written or read in isolation, and that the experience of reading Dante is too often a lonely one.

Of course, the price of fidelity to the original is often occasionally high, even unnecessarily so. In *Inferno* 2:52–54, Dante reveals his fear to Virgil about making the trip to Hell, and Virgil's response is to explain that his own intercession in Dante's moral crisis could not have occurred without the philanthropic concern of others. Dante has,

> Io era tra color che son sospesi
> e donna mí chiamò beata e bella,
> tal che di comandare io la richiesi.

In the Hollanders' translation, line 52 is perfectly literal, but perfectly unnatural:

> I was among the ones who are suspended
> when a lady called me, so blesséd and so fair
> that I implored her to command me.

Compare Ciardi:

> ... I was a soul
>
> among the souls of Limbo, when a Lady
> so blessed and so beautiful, I prayed her
> to order and command my will, called to me.

Ciardi is instantly clear, but you need the Hollanders' note, a model of scholarly economy and pointed rigor, to get out of the muddle over their use of *suspended* in line 52: "The verbal adjective *sospesi*," meaning the participle *suspended*, "that is, in a position between the presence of God and actual punishment, is a technical term for the virtuous heathens who dwell in Limbo." Which explains much: Limbo, partly the product of Dante's imagination, is a place of perfect inbetweenness, which will, like Hell of which it is the annex, disappear at the end of time. Such is the price of raw, literal rendition. The note then directs you to still additional commentary. Zappulla follows Ciardi in demystifying these lines' strangeness and gives, "While I was with the other souls in Limbo, / A lady came to me, she was so sweet, / So fair, I asked her to command my will." Pinsky takes the same intelligent shortcut: "it was / A Lady's voice that called me where I dwelled / in Limbo." Ciardi's note simply reads, "See Canto IV, lines 31–45, where Virgil explains his state in Hell." And that's that—why futz around over the importance to medieval theologians of a single Italian verb since we're not commenting on Aquinas but translating a poem that *is,* for the most part, all the commentary we need? In every context except the Hollanders', who invite it, it would be pure pedantry.

It seems to me incontestable that Ciardi's is the best choice if only from the standpoint of reader-friendliness. His decisions are directed by a familiarity with and fidelity to Dante's prosodic designs and may have led him to take liberties. Dante, for instance, never mentions the word *Limbo* or calls the place by that name in the example above. Yet when no *crux* is involved, you have to pause and wonder what might be the advantage of a translation that achieves scholarly comprehensiveness at the cost of another page or five of extended bibliographic apparatus. Part of this poem's pioneering importance, Ciardi seems to be saying, is that it *broke* from tradition by being written in the vernacular and not in Latin. It was meant to be read by dog-and-cat humanity as well as donnish monks in dusty hoods and by their living progeny, by members of the American Academy of Arts and Sciences and the various American institutions of higher learning. On the other hand, when their notes are not means of breaching the obstacle the translation has become—to paraphrase Eliot, a greater obstacle than the original itself—the Hollanders' version is both a recognition of the canonical realities and a thoroughly reliable backstop (along with Zappulla and, I would add, Binyon) to Ciardi's translation, which is still the champion.

—2009

Euripides's *The Children of Herakles*

A PREFACE

When I undertook a version of *The Children of Herakles,* of the extant translations, some (A. S. Way's) were out of print and available only through libraries; others, like David Kovacs's new Loeb Classical Library edition, were too expensive or difficult to obtain. Strictly speaking, moreover, these were translations and not, like my attempt, something between translation and homage. But in general these editions were competing only in the sense that somewhere in America they fought for shelf space. None I came across, with the possible exception of the new Kovacs (itself not available until early in the fall of 1996, after I began) and the Oxford edition of the mid-1970s, is capable of being performed:

> I hold it truth, and long have held:—the just
> Lives for his brother men; but he whose soul
> Uncurbed hunts gain alone, unto the state
> Useless, in dealings hard, is but to himself
> A friend—nor know this by report alone;

This is Way's handling of the play's opening; it is from the 1909 Loeb edition, in a language infinitely more unspeakable and dense than whatever conceivable discursive model Way was hearing. What, I kept asking myself, went through this translator's mind? Did anyone in 1909 still *use* the expression "to hold it truth," already on its way out when Jefferson used it? Metrically, and except for the choruses, Way's translation attempts to gain and hold the Miltonic high ground but in a plodding paint-by-numbers fashion. The third line scans stiffly, is given no help by the succession of long *u*'s (*unto, useless*), and surrenders what dignity it may have in line 4, when the unspeakable yields to the affected ("is but to himself / A friend"), nearly a parody of the fractured English I heard at the Italian Market growing up. At what price the pentameter? No matter the lexical accuracy of his rendering, the cost of such precision is unintentional farce and an impenetrable flat-footedness.

Relieved of the primary role of the translator, I worked here toward a text that was readable, if not actually performable, and if not on Broadway then in the sort of venues where I have heard or had my own plays read. Where several dependable Classicists had sought for absolute lexical accuracy, I took as my goal the exposition of character, and building on the dependable literacy of those translations—Professor Way's included—I tried for the direct ring of spoken English:

> If a lifetime of trouble has taught me a thing
> It's this, this alone: just men have just offspring.
> And those whose wills are unrestrained
> are worthless to their communities,
> and their own worst enemies. Life's taught me this.

If not commensurate with the accuracy of the versions whose unspeakability makes them useless as scripts, this one is founded on an acknowledgment of good scholarship, a certain humility before strugglers against different odds— and seekers of different goals—as well as a congruent admiration for the plays of Euripides and a life growing up among war- or life-weary immigrants like old Iolaus, the one speaking here.

I began with Liddell and Scott and A. Garzya's (1972) edition of the text and sweated over the first two hundred lines, often word by word. It had been decades since I translated the *Antigone* in high school and, later, the *Medea;* I had lost the feel of the Greek and especially the tensile strength, the give-and-take of the tighter dramatic meters. At one point I taped Iolaus's opening fifty-some lines and played the cassette while driving. From the outset it seemed that the play's meaning was kernelled in line 2: μεν δικαιοσ τοισ πελασ πεφυκ᾽ ανηρ, the just man has just offspring, an apparent corollary to the belief in the inheritance of what we call sin. Iolaus, an old family attendant, enters dispensing an old man's wisdom. He believes that some people are *by their very nature* "just," and therefore beget justice as naturally as they beget children. This play, in other words, will be about not only justice but, like all tragedy, about consequences.

Only after I had been through nearly a quarter of the text did it begin to rhyme itself out for me, at first in those places where the language seemed most naturally to hook toward parataxis. The result is a version rhymed (perfect-, slant-, and all variants in between) almost completely in couplets, yet still consistently and more or less confidently speakable. The rhythms come from a variety of sources—from my own declaiming of the Greek to my reading of and in environing translations (Way, Kovacs, Ralph Gladstone, Louis Méridier). Finally, though, my line owes as much to the range of tetrameters one grows up hearing—Pound, Browning, Gilbert and Sullivan, Housman and Hardy, and that canny outlier Theodor Seuss Geisel—as it does to whatever my own ear knows of rhythm.

The fates of Herakles and Eurystheus of Argos were tangled from the outset. Theirs is a cautionary fable of how the gods can do us nothing but harm or, if we're already in trouble, still worse harm. In *Iliad* 19, where Agamemnon welcomes Achilles back to battle and apologizes for his past behavior, in order to excuse himself he refers to the story of Herakles's birth and how it was complicated by Zeus's usual boastfulness and Hera's usual reactive jealousy. Zeus, who had conceived Herakles on the mortal Alcmene, on the day of the child's arrival announced:

> Today the goddess of birth pangs and labor
> will bring to light a human child, a man-child
> born of the stock of men who spring from my blood,
> one who will lord it over all who dwell around him (Fagles's translation)

Zeus, of course, means Herakles. Hera, meanwhile, muttering "You will prove a liar" under her breath, tricks her husband into swearing an oath on his boast, and naturally, henpecked but hardly uxorious, Zeus complies. Hera then races to Argos, the home of King Sthenelus, and induces labor in his wife, Nicippe, who is two months shy of term. The result is the boy Eurystheus, who, as the grandson of Perseus, is also of immortal stock. So the vow is fulfilled, but destiny takes hold of the wrong child. It's a perfect comedy of errors except that there is little comedy to come, only one more demonstration of the gods' ability to harm humankind even when they think they're doing it a favor. Eurystheus succeeds his father as ruler of Mycenae and becomes Herakles's taskmaster; it is for Eurystheus that Herakles undertakes his twelve labors.

Heracleidae, as the play is titled in scholarly literature, is listed officially as a tragedy. But it comes down to us damaged and fragmented, and if "a drama of displacement," from the outset I had difficulty naturalizing the description with what the play actually does. In many ways it seems to occupy the wrong category, or at least straddle another—certainly in the form we have it. Surmise has it that Euripides composed the play early in the Peloponnesian War, as a tribute to the liberality of Athenian political culture and cultural memory. Yet it seems far from tragic. In fact, it struck me as comedy, at least in the sense that Dante understood his own *Comedy*—as a story with a foul beginning and a prosperous conclusion, though here with a bizarre climax—as well as comic in less elusive modern senses.

Iolaus's opening speech lays out the issues. Iolaus and the children of his master, Herakles, have since the death of the children's father been in flight from Eurystheus—this, like *Medea,* will be another play about a foreigner painfully forced to emigrate to a land not entirely welcoming. On Herakles's death, Eurystheus had begun to fear the vengeance of the hero's male offspring and, following the long-standing tradition of all powerful bosses and of the vendetta, sought to kill them. But they escape with Iolaus, the family's surviving consigliere (there is really no other word for the familial and professional roles Iolaus fills) and their grandmother, Alcmene, and they wander throughout Greece seeking sanctuary. Only Trachis has thus far welcomed them, for which Trachis was cruelly punished—an event alluded to in Iolaus's opening speech. The play finds the exiles in their final stop, outside Athens, which is prepared to take them in and protect them. Then suddenly an oracle is produced that raises the play's central complication. The Athenian king, Demophon, announces the bad news: a virgin must be sacrificed before the Athenians can take the field against Eurystheus.

Iolaus's reaction is noble but muddleheaded: "Let me die instead. Give me to the Argives." Demophon correctly reminds him, neither female nor a virgin, that his offer is "high-minded but pointless" because Eurystheus is interested only in the children, who will grow up knowing that their duty is to avenge their father. The complication is apparently insoluble until Herakles's daughter

Makaria appears near mid-play ("Strangers, impute not for my coming forth / Boldness to me," as Way would have it) and offers herself up as the demanded sacrifice. And from this moment on, the dramatic arc subtends and seems to reverse itself. Given the lowdown by a semihysterical Iolaus, whose yelling actually stirs her out of her sanctuary and drives her into the open, Makaria's thinking is both clearheaded and frankly chilling. She resolves Demophon's dilemma by stepping up to confront her fate directly: "I'm ready to bear / the part of the victim. Let them slay me / or else accuse us of abusing this city." So remarkably lucid in fact is her argument that it lends the play a nobility and a logic so unforced that she seems to belong to another play, mainly because she is the only character who has actually understood the full import of Iolaus's opening lines: "If a lifetime of trouble has taught me a thing / it's this, this alone: just men have just offspring." Iolaus could hardly have imagined on whose shoulders this judgment would ultimately come to rest. The high-born are *fatally*—we might say *naturally*—responsible for the moral upkeep of the rest of us by their very example. For the first of two instances in the play, a woman, and here a young one, representing a class that had virtually no social power, recognizes and resolves the problem.

But with her entrance, the absurdities accumulate. She makes only one request—that Iolaus stand by her as she dies. But witnessing her death, he whines, "would kill me too." From here, Iolaus's character quickly shrinks to the proportions of farce and predicts the preposterous fairy-tale fate the gods spring on him (and us) late in the play, when his youth is miraculously if momentarily restored. Simultaneously, Alcmene's stature grows by grim contrast. She enters nearly on the heels of Makaria's exit, and from her opening lines she stands out as exactly the foil Iolaus's character demanded. He is all high rhetoric and bombast; she is thrill, earthy, shrewd, a pragmatic powerhouse, a fifth-century version of Shakespeare's Volumnia. She has only one goal—to protect her grandchildren—yet she is still a Mediterranean grandmother, and when one of them, Hyllus, arrives but fails to visit her, her reaction is refreshingly familiar, open, even a bit vulgar ("As for my grandson, he sets foot in this land / and he doesn't stop by?"). When she learns that Iolaus has plans to join the battle against Eurystheus, she comes right to the point: "You can't be serious. Leave the children with me / to go off and get killed? Have you gone crazy?" Alcmene seems perfectly suited, therefore, to uncover the solution to the play's second dilemma, when diplomatic protocol and the power of a vendetta coalesce in the capture of Eurystheus. What should they do with him?

Her recommendation is ruthless, and, for reasons Euripides avoids going into, the Athenians are perfectly fine with leaving it to Alcmene. Euripides's maturing interest in the old woman is of a piece with his departure from tradition in making her Eurystheus's killer; there is a more ancient version of the story in which Eurystheus is slain by Hyllus, who carries his head to his grandmother for her to mutilate. Thus, when Eurystheus is brought onstage in restraints near the end, he, like Agamemnon, uses Hera's baleful influence to excuse his awful behavior to a great warrior—Herakles, of course—but it is clear that the only person he actually fears is the truly terrifying Alcmene. The text is too incontestably lacunose to be reliable, but for the final time a woman bails out the generally hapless men with a timely suggestion.

What is the play then about? We can hardly imagine it written by that great religious apologist Aeschylus, or by Sophocles, the grand finesser of moral and philosophical differences who wrote characters of such moral ambivalence. In Aeschylus's hands this could have been, like *Seven Against Thebes,* another pious documentary on divine wisdom. One wonders how Sophocles's terrible insight into fate's undoing of human designs would have reshaped Makaria's sacrifice and this play; for she is no hard-barked Antigone, whose primary obligation is to her family and not social order. As always, Euripides stands apart in his fascination not only with how fate shapes character but by how character occasionally misleads Fate into the production of monstrosity. Fate, in Euripides, and far more than in his older contemporaries, is irreligious, famously nihilistic, and never to be denied. The result here is a bleak and slightly wacky outcome in which the principals are shaped by situations. An old man returns to battle, prays for rejuvenation, and is rejuvenated. A young girl offers herself as a sacrifice and is led offstage and never heard of again. When the bad guys get their due, the moralizing chorus limits itself to a four-line advertisement about neither morality nor politics but spiritual expediency: a swift mopping of the brow and a "Thank god that's over with." It all seems to amount to a statement, if it can be called that, that life in all its raw inexplicability is reflected in but never really clarified by our behavior, no matter what well-meaning fools like old Iolaus may say.

A Euripidean Polonius, Iolaus fails to see consequences, and his opening words make a sentimental point but miss the story's scariest but thoroughly Euripidean possibility. Just or unjust, human beings are inconsequential until fate forces them to act, and in action to affect another's life, which means usually to ruin it. From the drama of Sophocles Euripides learned only the implicit despair and the muted nihilism that Sophocles transforms into a heroic humanism. He comes to the material itself with a cool disregard for anything touched with benign supernatural influences. His gods are big, empty disasters, cartoons that our dreams color in, and his incurable obsession is with monstrosity. Thus the difference between the world's self-regarding geniuses and its fatuous time-servers, between a two-timing Jason, say, and a faithful Iolaus, is certainly not personality, that Elizabethan discovery, or even Classical hubris, but something like raw personal luck. This makes both the genius and the fool monstrosities, and one no more wants a visit from a Jason and Medea than from an Iolaus and Copreus, who are and who bring nothing but trouble.

If there is such a thing as canonical Greek tragedy, and if a nonspecialist is allowed to say so, in *Heracleidae* Euripides made a play as anticanonical, or, better, as anomalous as can be imagined—at least, that is, as it comes down to us, holes and all. And in that spirit I approached the text, which admittedly is neither the most polished nor most textually dependable in the corpus of Greek drama. Were it not for the death of Makaria, *Heracleidae* would be nearly a fifth-century *Twelfth Night,* with Copreus and Eurystheus coming off as a composite Malvolio. The comic elements impressed me at first as the most palpable in our age of the triumphant romcom, then pointed me toward a prosody of rhymed tetrameter couplets for the main dialogue and rhymed crisscrossed dimeters for the chorus. The persistent lightness of the whole (including the interpolated pun on Demophon's name) is in other words interpretive and not an attempt at parody. Finally, I've where possible avoided—essentially ignored— the play's problematic textual condition in these remarks out of candid and rational self-interest. My first encounter with the bare Greek left me with a clear and anxious recollection of variant-crowded footnotes and phalanxes of lines of poetry in editorial brackets. For obvious reasons I take no useful position on any of the texts' many cruxes, and at just about every fork have taken the road more traveled by better and better-informed scholars.

—1999

Prévert Now

Along with the fascist drift of its masters' politics, of Yeats, Eliot, and Pound, one of the more dismaying aspects of Modernism is how completely it not only ignored neighboring aesthetic movements—Surrealism, Futurism, Dadaism, for instance—but rarely bothered to treat contemporary history directly, at its most visceral, political level. The canonical Anglo-American poetry of the twentieth century took shape between the two bloodiest wars in human history, yet the response to it by some—excluding the novelists—was modest, even offhand. America especially, and at least until the arrival of the Beats, seems to have skipped what was fundamental to contemporaneous European poetry, its intense sociopolitical engagement, along with any real embrace of the vernacular, of the common experience of common people, or of what went on elsewhere in the world.

Take the major players. Eliot, the most influential of the Modernists, was dead set against any engagement except with a morose, aestheticized Anglicanism that gradually took the shape of the crypto-Christianity of the New Criticism. When asked to describe the sources of *The Waste Land,* probably by those who wondered if the title had something to do with the ravaged spaces separating the Allied from the German front lines in World War I, he replied that it was "a bit of rhythmic grumbling," his way of telling you to mind your own business; nor does he register the reality of WWII until, caught in the London Blitz, events compel him to. The word *war* occurs only twice in the *Four Quartets,* modified by "long-forgotten" and the second time by "constellated." Pound emphatically believed that history was a legitimate source of poetry, but the outcome of that belief—outside of section 5 of *Hugh Selwyn Mauberley,* his bitter response to WWI—is *The Cantos,* which with notable exceptions are all but unreadable except to experts and earnest students. He ends up a prisoner of a war, nearly no detail of which is recorded in the *Cantos* themselves until he writes of his own experience in the Pisan group.

This withdrawal from engagement wasn't merely an ex-pat phenomenon. The suspicion clinging to Wallace Stevens (who never left the country) is and has been more along the lines that he is guilty of an ethical violation: he barely mentions either of the two major wars that bookend his career. Evidence of a lack of a social conscience or a deep ambivalence? Marianne Moore's connection to global history seems to have exhausted itself in one early poem, "The Fish," which may or may not be about a warship torpedoed by a U-boat during World War I. Hart Crane, one of the joys of one's youth, seemed to lack interest in politics in general, local or global: "Crane," Blackmur noted, "was interested in persons rather than the class struggle." Too young to participate in World War I, which he seems barely aware of, he mentions domestic politics ("Black Tambourine") and a contemporary cultural figure ("Chaplinesque") once each in *White Buildings*.* And then there is Yeats. The greatest poet to write in English in the twentieth century was obsessed with politics, but mostly Irish politics, and even then, only those that threatened the Irish ascendancy. His obsession with aristocracy matured into the antihumanist fascism of his late plays and the truly ugly late pamphlet *On the Boiler,* published on the eve of World War II: "The danger," he wrote in 1938, "is that there will be no war, that the skilled will attempt nothing, that the European civilisation, like those older civilisations that saw the triumph of their gangrel stocks, will accept decay."

My list is hardly comprehensive, but comprehensiveness is a nuisance when you face the obvious: Modernism finally withered into what it always was, a resurrected Neoclassicism that championed the rational against unreason in any form; where it engaged living history, it was Pilate washing his hands before the multitude—it wanted nothing to do with history studied from the bottom up. Confronted with the role played by the "unconscious" in poetry, Eliot had reverted to vatic wisecracks ("the bad poet is usually unconscious where he ought

---

* An exception among the major voices was Williams, both of whose sons served in the U.S. Navy in the Pacific and were at sea during the bombings of Hiroshima and Nagasaki: "The War," he writes in 1944 in his preface to *The Wedge,* "is the first and only thing in the world today. The arts generally are not, nor is this writing a diversion from that for relief, a turning away. It is the war or part of it, merely a different sector of the field." He was openly hostile to his old friend Pound after World War II, his outrage is explicitly directed at *The Pisan Cantos'* winning the Bollingen.

to be conscious, and conscious where he ought to be unconscious"). "Unreason" meant the Freudian subconscious, or implied Romanticism and Coleridge's Primary Imagination, or Whitman's dismissals of history's "creeds and schools." In their places were the Imagist manifesto and the elevation of abstractions like *tradition, depersonalization,* and *technique.* In some too obvious ways, this need to make an end run around the Romantic aesthetic and the revolutionary politics of the Shelleys and Byrons explains not only the frank hedonism of Crane (another kind of isolationism) but to some extent the reactionary politics of the major figures—Pound's and Yeats's fascism, Eliot's royalism, even Stevens's quietism—and even the positions of poets on the margin, like the perpetual outsider Robinson Jeffers. But clearly, Modernism's go-to method of capturing the past—Pound's definition of an epic was "a poem that includes history"— was to reconstitute it as myth, Classical, occult, or religious, or as the outcome of a specific theory. When Pound finally is forced to dispense with myth and economics in *The Pisan Cantos* and to confront events directly, as a participant, it's only after he had been incarcerated for nearly a month in a six-by-six steel mesh cage, in Pisa.

One result is that Modernism's arrogation of the word *modern* is at best an imposture and at worst something of a bad joke. Robert Graves, who gave the movement its name in the mid-1920s, did so not only ironically but resentfully, and with real dismay. His specific gripe was against Eliot: *The Waste Land* had little or nothing directly to say about the wider historical context of its composition, which Graves couched in bitchy musings over what Eliot was up to while he himself was busy being wounded at the Battle of the Somme. Sour grapes, maybe, but Graves had a point, and Modernism's deadpan formalist aesthetic and alienation from the experience of dog-and-cat humanity would dominate poetry in America into the 1950s. The country had to wait for the Beats and a generation that included not only the confessional Plath and Lowell but Dugan, Baraka, Sexton, and Bly to read poems about domestic life, about hanging drywall, diapering babies, abortion, and waking up after a series of electroshock treatments. Between 1920 and 1950, there were some luminous exceptions— Gwendolyn Brooks's *Annie Allen* (1949), the controversial Jeffers, Williams's earnest experiment with spontaneity, *Paterson*—but homegrown American poetry seemed a tourist of its own contemporaneity. Between the wars only the novelists—Steinbeck, Dos Passos, Hemingway, Fitzgerald, Wright, Ellison, and

Hurston—seemed engaged with politics, global or local, and some directly; Hemingway, for instance, as a Red Cross ambulance driver and the first American wounded in WWI, and Dos Passos, as a participant in the Spanish Civil War. Except for outliers like the Harlem Renaissance group and writers on the socialist or communist fringe, like Ellison and Wright, no American seemed to be paying attention to what was going on in the wider American world or on its foreign battlefields.

Prévert's *Paroles,* published at midcentury, embraced everything that our partly homegrown, partly cosmopolitan poetics missed, or dismissed. Still gaining its due share of cisatlantic readers, who are learning late what French schoolkids grow up with and grow up memorizing, its importance is probably more pressing now than at any time since its publication over seventy years ago. These poems are first to last politically alert, culturally engaged, and, in contrast to any of the examples just produced, stripped of appeals to mythic orders or to a supposititious "Tradition" that, for Eliot and the New Critics who promoted him, was Pauline Christianity in late Edwardian drag. Prévert's poems were agnostic; they break rules; they insist that we pay attention to the men behind the curtain—the exploiters, bullies, grifters, liars, and cheats—as well as to those they exploit, like the homeless vagrants sleeping on park benches ("Le désespoir est assis sur un banc"). His poetry has no patience with abstractions or those infatuated with them. They're filled with puns—*puns,* and not sophisticated bilingual ones like those of Pound in *Mauberley*—and they play fast and loose not only with words but with the reputations of the powerful. The powerful also routinely engage in sophisticated wordplay—from inaugurals to state of the union addresses—but their wordplays are rarely enjoyable and often lethal.

So perhaps the strongest summary of the difference of Prévert's work from American verse is this: of the major extended works by Americans during or between the wars, the *Four Quartets, The Cantos,* and *The Bridge,* not one successfully "reads" the past, narrates current events, or finds an audience wider than the critical establishment or members of the American academy with a stake in their work. (Williams was the exception, but *Paterson,* which came out after the war, arose from his lingering disgust over *The Waste Land* and is at heart an aggressive re-embrace of American culture.) The responses recorded by Pound, Eliot, and Crane were either redirected through and dominated by refined Classical mannerisms, or, in the later case of *Paterson,* overwhelmed by the sheer wealth of unassimilated information. The actual present was either not treated as legit-imate history or as clutter, excrescence, something always in the way, so novel and "reportable" that it had to be celebrated in overwrought, dated idiolects.

For an American reader raised in the crypto-religion of the New Criticism, my own first encounter with Prévert was confusing. Prévert came across as a come-dian, even a vulgarian, before he matured into a refreshing alternative to what one grew up with. In my teens I found him simply "too easy" compared to classy Valéry, dangerous Rimbaud, or the orphic and barely approachable Mallarmé. He was formally shapeless and far too casual a craftsman when held up against Baudelaire, Verlaine, or even Apollinaire. He came across as irreverent, angry, profane, and too easily seduced by facile or unsubtle wordplay—the dinner partner who can't resist a bad pun. Even though he is a committed ironist, his favored mode is sarcasm, which is usually regarded as the lowest form of irony because it is the ironic register we first learn as children and use to express pas-sive hostility rather than rapier wit. He seems never to have heard of myth or the "mythic method"; the closer he gets to the traditional or the Classical, the more he seems bored with it, or so amused he gently parodies it. His French is idiomatic, easy to "get"; he takes things personally, has political views; and cru-cially, like all strong lyric voices, he has an eye for what the Establishment over-looks. Frank O'Hara's cry, "It's my duty to be attentive, I am needed by things as the sky must be above the earth," is the job description of the lyric poet: you're here to notice the little things—from that homeless veteran to the runaway teenager shivering in the middle of Place de la Concorde on (of all dates!) 15 August, the Feast of the Assumption of the Blessed Virgin, and one of the Ro-man Catholic Church's Holy Days of Obligation.

Prévert is also a canny raconteur, somebody you would love to dine or drink with. He knows how and when to get out of the way of a good story and allow the reader to fill in the blanks ("Le Message"). Second only to Joyce's own pro-fane version in the "Cyclops" chapter of *Ulysses,* his "Pater Noster" is the con-summate send up of the prayer the faithful recite in the confessional on Satur-day or on Sunday before the Doxology. (In season five of *The Sopranos,* Meadow Soprano recites the poem's opening, in translation, to her father.) Modernism carried its avoidance of clichés so far that it nearly succeeds in avoiding the vernacular entirely; the result is often bracing and new, but when it is not, the results can be disastrous—the glib, slap-dash pedantry of *The Cantos,* for in-

stance, or the mysticism of the overpraised *Four Quartets.* Cliché is mass response mass-reproduced. It is the soul of the greeting card, the dilution of feeling, language massaged by commerce and weaponized by mass culture. Clichés
survive because, as Harry Frankfurt writes of bullshit, they resist correction and
because we are too busy or lazy to examine the premises of its phrasings—*moral
compass,* for instance, suggests that there exists a moral North Pole, which, if
you press too hard, you're testily reminded is the Old Testament. The cliché is
a penny stock, or a junk bond; its perfection is perfection of the lowest order;
the system would collapse without it; many of us and most of TV's newspersons
and hosts and all politicians would be rendered mute. Nothing can compete
with a cliché because the competition is fixed.

Prévert understood the inner workings of the cliché and despised how clichés are deployed and administered by dictatorships to control populations. Yet
he never seems to have met a cliché he could not turn inside out, or a wordplay
he didn't like. Prévert is so defiantly in love with freewheeling wordplay and verbal mugging that the result sometimes defeats translation. When he embraces a
pun, it's in order to expose and exploit the so-called transparency of language,
always and everywhere, and sometimes even in the same poem. "Presque," a
meditation on the concurrence of good and bad in the world, goes out of its
way to dramatize its point by using the antonyms *bonheur* and *malheur,* roughly
"goodness" and "badness," in the same poem:

Presque

A Fontainebleau
Devant l'hôtel de l'Aigle Noir
Il y a un taureau sculpté par Rosa Bonheur
Un peu plus loin tout autour
Il y a la forêt
Et un peu plus loin encore
Joli corps
Il y a encore la forêt
Et le malheur
Et tout à côté le bonheur
Le bonheur avec les yeux cernés
Le bonheur avec des aiguilles de pin dans le dos

Le bonheur qui ne pense à rien
Le bonheur comme le taureau
Sculpté par Rosa Bonheur
Et puis le malheur
Le malheur avec une montre en or
Avec un train à prendre
Le malheur qui pense à tout . . .
A tout
A tout . . . à tout . . . à tout . . .
Et à tout
Et qui gagne "presque" à tous les coups
Presque.

Rosa Bonheur was a nineteenth-century artist and sculptor renowned for her representations of animals. Her country estate in Fontainebleau, where she lived and worked, was turned into a museum dedicated to her work after her death. To Prévert, however, it is her surname as much as her art ("un taureau sculpté par Rosa Bonheur") that is essential to the poem's operations. The paired antonyms do double duty as they build the nucleus. The products of what is good, which include the works of Bonheur, exist side by side with what is bad. No matter how "good" a work of art is or how successfully it meets its aesthetic goals, "good" and "bad" carry on necessary and highly active lives in the real world. What's more, they live in close proximity, almost touching. The poem's title is expressive of both irony and frustration: good and evil not only coexist but cohabit almost (*presque*) the same spaces ("Et le malheur / Et tout à côté le bonheur"). His wordplay is nearly impossible to render literally; once rendered, it's a bit limp on the page:

Almost

At Fontainebleau
In front of a hotel named the Black Eagle
There's a bull sculpted by Rosa Bonheur
A little further on and all around it
Is a forest
And a bit further still

A beautiful body
Surrounded by forest
And the bad
So close to the good
The good with its searching eyes
Lying in pine needles
Thinking of nothing at all
Like the bull
Sculpted by Bonheur
Then bad
With its gold watch
And a train to catch
Badness that thinks
One size covers all
Totally everywhere
Almost.

At one point in his career, Prévert retired to the hotel to complete a screenplay; the poem is a reflection on that sabbatical, not only from Paris but from his mistress, who seems to be the "Joli corps" of line 7. Looking outward from a window in the hotel toward the woods beyond, Prévert imagines the girl he loves lying out there on the forest floor and looking back up at him. Whether she is there in the flesh or not is hardly the point; it's the proximity of the visionary to the actual, the fact that vision and reality *nearly* touch, that creates the pathos created by imagined goodness, the lover present only in thought, and the bad luck or "badness" of her absence. At one stage in my working at this poem I tried to reproduce in English the ironic doubling of proper name and abstract quality, of *Bonheur* / *malheur;* I substituted Wright, as in Frank Lloyd, for Bonheur, but the pairing of Wright/right and "wrong" was, well, all wrong. I even substituted Taliesin for Fontainebleau; I discovered a Wright sculpture, *Boulder,* that might stand in for Bonheur's sculpted bull. The result was not pretty.*

---

* In my defense, "Joli corps," literally "beautiful body," is stripped of a definite or indefinite article and therefore an unconventional noun-adjective dyad; you would normally expect an article to precede the adjective. My research also led me to discover a strain or family of French bulls apparently named Joli Corps. Just as (Rosa) Bonheur and *malheur,* or ill fortune, are coequal and coexistent op-

The poem is a Blakean lesson in seeing "not with but through the eye." The more alert and attentive we are, the more the world's symmetries seem apparent; this alertness extends to language at the molecular level of puns, double entendres, even homonyms and near synonyms (*bonheur* and *malheur*). Even at its most alert, the mind patiently and proudly peels ideas apart, but the world refuses to follow, and wherever we go we encounter one more example of language and its frustrated intellectual dominance of the sensuous realm. The result is lyric, which is the expression of how human nature lives with and lives out its ambiguities, where reciting each line of verse is how the living can gain some sense of the meaning of *duration,* or what endures.

If Prévert can be considered a late Modernist, he was a notable if unconscious dissenter from its elevation of art to the alienating position assumed by its English and American masterpieces. He was also cool to the idea of the intellect as an unambiguously positive cultural value or, in the words from Aristotle quoted by Eliot in part 3 of "Tradition and the Individual Talent," that the mind is "immortal and immune to suffering." As a college freshman, this made Prévert and his poems seem merely silly. Yeats was anti-intellectual, Pound a pseudo-intellectual, but Prévert struck me as sharp, though merely clever in a sort of Wildean way. Many decades later, I think it more accurate to say that his view of the intellectual life was a product of the worst war the world has ever seen, and understandably, witheringly skeptical of platitudes and critical of those who get away with them. Where the intelligence errs, as he argues in "On Ne Faut Pas" ("The 11th Commandment"), it's in how it habitually peels facts away from values, ideas from applications, concepts from actions, even people from their words. His most exacting revelations invite flat-footed wordplays, as if to be human is to be part Cumaean Sibyl and part Daffy Duck—ludic, confusing, teasing, silly, and if ambiguous, productively so. At times the wordplays look less like windows into revelation than traps for pretension. Puns amuse (even when we don't laugh at them) because they suggest a world so perforated

posites, so too are the bronze bull housed outside the hotel and perhaps some real bull perhaps pastured out near the forest, the one admirable form (*joli corps*) aligned in his mind with the other, and the latest to emerge from a famous lineage (Joli Corps). I had to admit defeat; it seems more sensible that the second *joli corps* is the imagined one of his lover, and not some actual living animal set to pasture. Since then I've been unable to find the source of that earlier "discovery."

with overwear and accident that tragicomedy is always waiting to happen, especially when the wisdom-spouters tend to be blind to the possibility that facts
can change, that they arrive on perforated pages, that truth and lie not only coexist, but as America's truest overlord, the advertising industry, has long known,
that truths and lies sometimes *sound* nearly the same.

Poems that embrace the vernacular and its hit-and-run energy may also
openly court vulgarity. What's impressive is that they do so, usually, without
celebrating vulgarity, or without shrillness and stridency. Like Picasso and Coc-
teau's cocktail-napkin masterpieces, a Prévert poem can represent the instantaneous with an attentive but anxious, jumpy vitality. "La Belle Saison" contains
a whole dossier of unpacked implications:

La Belle Saison

A jeun perdue glacée
Toute seule sans un sou
Une fille de seize ans
Immobile debout
Place de la Concorde
A midi le Quinze Août

Nice Weather

Hungry spaced-out shivering
Alone broke
She's sixteen a runaway
Upright immobile
Middle of the intersection at Place de la Concorde
Lunchtime 15 August

The implied detail—that she's probably panhandling and hungry, and that's it's
mid-August and she's cold—has to be teased out. The taut, freeze-frame immediacy is the visual signature of twentieth-century literary technique, what the
"show, don't tell" rule means when it actually works. And something more: in a
bare six lines, he catches a solitary sixteen-year-old's hapless fragility in the mid-

dle of one of Europe's most populous and wealthy capitals. She is the homeless kid on a vent on Broadway cadging change, or the Black mother nursing a child in the back of Starbucks under a ratty blanket. The poem's cinematic concision reminds you that Prévert wrote screenplays. He may also be betraying the influence of Apollinaire—Apollinaire's "L'Adieu" is the same length—another spokesman for the surly but necessary untidiness of human language, which is most messy when it is most true. The difference is that Apollinaire was a die-hard formalist, or at least never far from the traditional formalism French poets have always respected, and he never seems at ease with details that demand a flat rendering; they must be surrounded in metaphor, charmed (as it were) into submission ("Bergère ô tour Eiffel le troupeau des ponts bêle ce matin," or "Les souvenirs sont cors de chasse"). Prévert's formal engagements, on the other hand, seem in contrast one-night stands, welcomed when successful, broken off when not. The essence of a Prévert lyric is that any moment contains *only* itself, and the poem's work is to make you experience our own hapless duration—the time it takes to speak the words that take us to the end of his line is how we experience that illusory sense of our permanence. It is the quality of wild and unwilled spontaneity that Americans value in Whitman and Dickinson, and in the twentieth century, in poets as different as Dugan and Ammons. It is exactly not, on the other hand, what we tend to value in quick-takes like Pound's "In a Station of the Metro," where the human element is absorbed first into a human "crowd" and then translated into natural "petals." People are seen from a train platform, then from twenty thousand feet. But who are they? Are we in that crowd?

Prévert's work places huge value on intimacy to the point where it may track into sentiment. It was "Confessional" two decades before confessionalism became a term of abuse for poetic oversharing, in the late 1960s, and so obviously "performative" the Beats found it irresistible (yet it survives on the page, as *text*). He wrote about everything: drunken plumbers, career losers, snails, an emperor, florists, gorgeous women, Napoleon's gut, runaway kids, Hitler, and the Blessed Trinity. He was never squeamish when it came to adopting testy or cumbersome personae, and excepting those poems where his rage overcomes him ("L'Effort humain"), his sense of humor is vigilant and refuses the empty specifications of ideology. In "Il ne faut pas," he carries on his debate with abstraction and its consequences by exploiting how the French words for the verb *lie* and the adjective *intellectual* (*mentir* and *mental*, respectively) appear to be cognate, though they are not. It's no wonder he was constantly "speaking truth to power": he had survived the German Occupation, that earlier post-truth epoch, as well as a Catholic school education. When the powerful act in ways that exceed our ability to satirize them, the satirist's last resort is to use the language of exploitation against itself. It is the way adolescents learn resistance, a poet's version of reaction formation: you mirror the authoritarian and his habitual distortions of common, everyday terms by inverting and turning those distortions inside out and mirroring them back. Published so soon after World War II, *Paroles* (1946) denounced all gloriously worded and empty abstractions. It is the book that established his reputation as a partisan of truth informed by experience—of everything, including politics. It is what used to be called, unhelpfully, and as if all poetry is *not* in some way political, "protest poetry."

The importance of Prévert's work was at first circumscribed here not only because of its socialist politics but also by its rhetorical looseness and a finger-pointing style more aligned with what the Beats were up to. It got to these shores a bit late, and at a moment when our poetry had surrendered to Eliot's overwhelming technical influence and his conservative aesthetic. Through the 1950s, though, Prévert's reputation grew, in part because the Beats, and particularly one of his best translators, Lawrence Ferlinghetti, seem to have learned something important from him. Seventy years on, his work has recovered much of the immediacy it had when it first appeared, reappearing in an era of growing authoritarianism, rampant demagoguery, and political decay dressed up as fake populism. It is *populist,* but in the most authentic sense, not associated with demagoguery or the bogus, Hydra-headed religious oligarchism that now surrounds us and defrauds us. Prévert's politics were always of the Left, and his poetry is vaguely "socialist-inspired," but it is never simply or haphazardly that. At its core it has the character of all important lyric—speech that reaches down and unflattens the world, speech felt "along the pulse," as Keats said. It is language that holds the world close and keeps it there for as long it takes for you to realize how briefly we embrace it.

—2018

Works Cited

Altieri, Charles. *Wallace Stevens and the Demands of Modernity: Toward a Phenomenology of Value.* Ithaca, NY: Cornell University Press, 2013.

———. "Wordsworth and the Options for Contemporary American Poetry." In *The Romantics and Us: Essays on Literature and Culture,* edited by Gene Ruoff, 184–212. New Brunswick, NJ: Rutgers University Press, 1990.

Ammons, A. R. "Bridge." In *The Contemporary American Poets: American Poetry since 1940,* edited by Mark Strand. New York: Mentor, 1971.

———. "Parting." In *The Selected Poems: Expanded Edition.* New York: Norton, 1986.

———. *A Tape for the Turn of the Year.* New York: Norton, 1965.

Arnold, Matthew. "The Function of Criticism at the Present Time." In *The Complete Works of Matthew Arnold: Lectures and Essays in Criticism,* edited by R. H. Super, 10 vols., 3:258–85. Ann Arbor: University of Michigan Press, 1960.

———. "Shelley." *Essays in Criticism: Second Series.* New York: Macmillan, 1896.

Arrowsmith, William. "The Lively Conventions of Translation." In *The Craft and Context of Translation,* edited by Arrowsmith. New York: Doubleday/Anchor, 1964.

Babbitt, Irving. *Rousseau and Romanticism.* Introduced by Claes G. Ryn. New Brunswick, NJ: Transaction, 1991.

Bate, Jonathan. *Romantic Ecology: Wordsworth and the Environmental Tradition.* London: Routledge, 1991.

Blackmur, R. P. "Lord Tennyson's Scissors." In *Form and Value in Modern Poetry.* New York: Doubleday/Anchor, 1957.

———. *Selected Essays of R. P. Blackmur.* Edited by Denis Donohue. New York: Ecco, 1986.

Bloom, Harold. *Poetry and Repression: Revisionism from Blake to Stevens.* New Haven, CT: Yale University Press, 1976.

———. *Wallace Stevens: The Poems of Our Climate.* Ithaca, NY: Cornell University Press, 1977.

Brodsky, Joseph. "Sextus Propertius." *Wilson Quarterly* 17, no. 4 (Autumn 1993): 86.

Coleridge, Samuel Taylor. *On Politics and Society.* Edited by John Morrow. Vol. 1 of *Coleridge's Writings.* Princeton, NJ: Princeton University Press, 1991.

Cowley, Abraham. "Pindarique Odes" (1656). In *Poetry and Prose,* 75. Folcroft Library Editions. New York: Oxford University Press, 1974.

Crane, Hart. "General Aims and Theories." In *The Complete Poems and Selected Letters of Hart Crane,* edited by Brom Weber, 217–23. New York: Doubleday-Anchor, 1966.

———. *The Letters of Hart Crane.* Edited by Brom Weber. Berkeley: University of California Press, 1965.

———. *The Poems of Hart Crane.* Edited by Marc Simon. New York: Liveright, 1986.

Dante. *Dante's Inferno.* Adapted by Sandow Birk and Marcus Sanders. Illustrated by Sandow Birk. San Francisco: Chronicle Books, 2004.

———. *Dante's Inferno.* Translated and annotated by Elio Zappulla. Illustrated by Gregory Gillespie. New York: Pantheon, 1998.

———. *The Divine Comedy.* Translated by Allen Mandelbaum. New York: Everyman's Library, 1995.

———. *The Inferno.* A verse rendering by John Ciardi with an historical introduction by Archibald T. MacAllister. 1954. New York: Mentor, 1982.

———. *Inferno.* Translated by Robert and Jean Hollander. Introduction and notes by Robert Hollander. New York: Doubleday, 2000.

———. *The Inferno of Dante: A New Verse Translation.* Bilingual edition. Translated by Robert Pinsky. Foreword by John Freccero. New York: FSG, 1996.

Davie, Donald. *Ezra Pound.* Modern Masters Series. New York: Viking, 1976.

———. *Ezra Pound: The Poet as Sculptor.* New York: Oxford University Press, 1968.

Dryden, John. "Preface to Ovid's *Epistles:* Translated by Several Hands (1680)." In *John Dryden, Of Dramatic Poesy and Other Critical Essays,* edited by George Watson, vol. 1, 268–73. London: J. M. Dent and Sons, 1962.

Eilenberg, Susan. *Strange Power of Speech: Wordsworth, Coleridge and Literary Possession.* New York: Oxford University Press, 1992.

Eliot, T. S. "Arnold and Pater." In *Selected Essays: New Edition.* New York: Harcourt, Brace, & World, 1960.

———. *The Waste Land. Collected Poems, 1909–1962.* New York: Faber and Faber, 1963.

Euripides, 4: Ion, Children of Heracles, The Madness of Heracles, Iphigenia in Tauris, Orestes. Edited by David R. Slavitt and Palmer Bovie. Philadelphia: University of Pennsylvania Press, 1999.

Finlay, John Martin. "John Finlay's *Hermetic Light* and the Seductions of Truth." In *In Light Apart: The Achievement of John Finlay,* edited by David Middleton, 23–62. Glenside, PA: Aldine, 1999.

———. "The Night of Alcibiades." *Hudson Review* 48, no. 1 (1994): 57–79.

Homer. *The Odyssey.* Translated by Robert Fagles, with an introduction and notes by Bernard Knox. New York: Viking, 1996.

———. *The Odyssey.* Translated by Robert Fitzgerald. New York: FSG, 1998.

———. *The Odyssey*. Translated by Stephen Mitchell. New York: Astria, 2013.

———. *The Odyssey*. Translated by Emily Wilson, with an introduction and notes by the translator. New York: Norton, 2018.

Howard, Richard. "A. R. Ammons." In *Alone with America: Essays on the Art of Poetry in the United States since 1950,* [1]–17. New York: Atheneum, 1971.

Hughes, Ted. *The Oresteia of Aeschylus: A New Translation*. New York: Farrar, Straus and Giroux, 2000.

Kenner, Hugh. *A Homemade World: The American Modernist Writers*. New York: Morrow-Knopf, 1975.

———. *The Pound Era*. Berkeley: University of California Press, 1971.

Levi, Primo. *Survival in Auschwitz*. New York: Scribner, 1961.

Lewis, Wyndham. "T. S. Eliot: The Pseudo-Believer." In *Men Without Art*, edited and afterword by Seamus Cooney, 57. Santa Rosa, CA: Black Sparrow, 1987.

MacFarland, Thomas. *Romanticism and the Forms of Ruin: Wordsworth, Coleridge, and Modalities of Fragmentation*. Princeton, NJ: Princeton University Press, 1981.

Moody, David. *The Epic Years 1921–1939*. Vol. 2 of *Ezra Pound: Poet*. Oxford: Oxford University Press, 2014.

Poe, Edgar Allan. *The Complete Works of Edgar Allan Poe*. Edited by James A. Harrison. New York: AMS, 1965.

Poggioli, Renato. *The Theory of the Avant-Garde*. Translated by Gerald Fitzgerald. 1968. New York: Harper & Row–Icon, 1971.

Pound, Ezra. "Binyon." Reprinted in *Make It New* 2, no. 2. https://www.makeitnew.ezrapound society.org/en/volume-ii/volume-2-no-1/conference-mla-2015?view=category&id=15.

———. *The Cantos of Ezra Pound*. New York: New Directions, 1970.

———. *Ezra Pound: Selected Prose 1909–1965*. Edited and introduced by William Cookson. New York: New Directions, 1973.

———. *Gaudier-Brzeska: A Memoir*. Rev. ed. New York: New Directions, 1970.

———. *The Letters of Ezra Pound: 1907–1941*. Edited by D. D. Paige. New York: Harcourt, Brace and World, 1950.

———. *Literary Essays of Ezra Pound*. Edited and introduced by T. S. Eliot. New York: New Directions, 1968.

———. *Personae: The Shorter Poems of Ezra Pound*. Rev. ed. Edited and annotated by Lea Baechler and A. Walton Litz. New York: New Directions, 1990.

———. "Translator's Postscript." In *Remy de Gourment: The Natural Philosophy of Love*, translated by Ezra Pound, introduction by Ashley Montagu, preface by Burton Rascoe, 149–58. 1922. Reprint, New York: Collier, 1972.

Pratt, William, ed. *The Imagist Poem: Modern Poetry in Miniature*. New York: Dutton, 1963.

Prévert, Jacques. *Paroles*. Paris: Gallimard, 1992.

———. *Paroles: Selected Poems.* Translated by Lawrence Ferlinghetti. Pocket Poems Series No. 9. 1958. Reprint, San Francisco: City Lights, 1990.

Prine, John. "Angel from Montgomery." *John Prine.* LP, 1971.

Rexroth, Kenneth. "The Poet as Translator." In *The Craft and Context of Translation,* edited by William Arrowsmith, 48. New York: Doubleday/Anchor, 1964.

Ruoff, Gene W. Introduction to *The Romantics and Us: Essays on Literature and Culture,* edited by Ruoff, [1]–12. New Brunswick, NJ: Rutgers University Press, 1990.

Stern, Gerald. "Behaving Like a Jew." In *This Time,* 31. New York: Norton, 1998.

———. "Bio I–V." Unpublished manuscript.

———. "Winter Thirst." In *American Sonnets.* New York: Norton, 2002.

Stevens, Wallace. *The Collected Poems of Wallace Stevens.* New York: Knopf, 1955.

Unterecker, John. *Voyager: A Life of Hart Crane.* New York: Farrar, Straus and Giroux, 1969.

Whalley, George. *Poetic Process.* Cleveland, OH: 1967.

Wheelwright, Philip. *Metaphor and Reality.* Bloomington: Indiana University Press, 1962.

Whitman, Walt. *Whitman: Complete Poetry and Selected Prose.* Edited by Justin Kaplan. New York: Library of America, 1982.

Williams, William Carlos. *Paterson.* New York: Penguin, 1983.

Wills, Garry. *Saint Augustine: A Life.* New York: Penguin, 1999.

Winters, Yvor. "The Progress of Hart Crane." *Poetry* 36, no. 3 (June 1930): 153–65. https://www.jstor.org/stable/20577597.

———. "The Significance of *The Bridge* of Hart Crane, or What Are We to Think of Professor X?" In *In Defense of Reason.* Denver, CO: Alan Swallow, n.d.

Wordsworth, William. "Preface to the *Lyrical Ballads.*" In *English Romantic Poetry and Prose,* edited and annotated by Russell Noyes. New York: Oxford University Press, 1967.

———. *Wordsworth's Poetry and Prose.* Edited by Nicholas Halm. New York: Norton, 2013.

Yeats, William Butler. *Autobiographies.* Edited by William H. O'Donnell and Douglas N. Archibald. Vol. 1 of *The Collected Works of W. B. Yeats.* New York: Scribner/Simon and Schuster, 1993.

———. *On the Boiler,* selections. In *Explorations: Selected by Mrs. W. B. Yeats.* New York: Collier/Macmillan, 1962.

———. "The Sorrows of Love." In *The Variorum Edition of the Poems of W. B Yeats,* edited by Peter Allt and Russel K. Alspach, 119–22. New York: Macmillan, 1957.

Index